Niagara *of* Capital

How global capital has transformed housing and real estate markets

ANTHONY DOWNS

ULI–the Urban Land Institute
1025 Thomas Jefferson Street, N.W.
Suite 500 West
Washington, D.C. 20007-5201

Library of Congress Cataloging-in-Publication Data

Downs, Anthony.
  Niagara of capital : how global capital has transformed housing and real estate markets / by Anthony Downs.
      p. cm.
    Includes index.
  1. Real estate investment. 2. Housing—Finance. 3. Real property—Finance.
  4. Housing—United States—Finance.
  5. Real estate investment—United States. 6. Real property—United States—Finance. I. Title.
    HD1382.55.D69 2007
    332.7'2—dc22

2007033399

ISBN: 978-0-87420-999-0

10 9 8 7 6 5 4 3 2 1
Printed in the United States of America.

The views expressed in this book are solely those of the author and not necessarily those of the Urban Land Institute or the Brookings Institution, their trustees, or other staff members.

ABOUT ULI–THE URBAN LAND INSTITUTE

The mission of the Urban Land Institute is to provide leadership in the responsible use of land and in creating and sustaining thriving communities worldwide. ULI is committed to:

▶ Bringing together leaders from across the fields of real estate and land use policy to exchange best practices and serve community needs;

▶ Fostering collaboration within and beyond ULI's membership through mentoring, dialogue, and problem solving;

▶ Exploring issues of urbanization, conservation, regeneration, land use, capital formation, and sustainable development;

▶ Advancing land use policies and design practices that respect the uniqueness of both built and natural environments;

▶ Sharing knowledge through education, applied research, publishing, and electronic media; and

▶ Sustaining a diverse global network of local practice and advisory efforts that address current and future challenges.

Established in 1936, the Institute today has more than 38,000 members in over 90 countries, representing the entire spectrum of the land use and development disciplines. Professionals represented include developers, builders, property owners, investors, architects, public officials, planners, real estate brokers, appraisers, attorneys, engineers, financiers, academics, students, and librarians. ULI relies heavily on the experience of its members. It is through member involvement and information resources that ULI has been able to set standards of excellence in development practice.

The Institute has long been recognized as one of the world's most respected and widely quoted sources of objective information on urban planning, growth, and development.

About the Author

Anthony Downs is a senior fellow at the Brookings Institution in Washington, D.C., where he has been since 1977. He also was a visiting fellow at the Public Policy Institute of California in San Francisco from July 2005 until February 2006. Brookings is a private, nonprofit research organization specializing in public policy studies. The Public Policy Institute of California is a similar organization specializing in such studies about California. Before 1977, Downs for 18 years was a member and then chairman of Real Estate Research Corporation, a nationwide consulting firm advising private and public decision makers on real estate investment, housing policies, and urban affairs.

He has served as a consultant to many of the nation's largest corporations, to major developers, to dozens of government agencies at local, state, and national levels (including the Department of Housing and Urban Development and the White House), and to many private foundations. President Lyndon Johnson appointed him to the National Commission on Urban Problems in 1967, and HUD Secretary Jack Kemp appointed him to the Advisory Commission on Regulatory Barriers to Affordable Housing in 1989. He is a director or trustee of General Growth Properties and the NAACP Legal and Educational Defense Fund. He was also a past director of the MassMutual Financial Group, Bedford Property Investors, the Urban Land Institute, Essex Property Trust, the National Housing Partnership Foundation, Penton Media Inc., and the Counselors of Real Estate.

Downs received a Ph.D. in economics from Stanford University. He is the author or coauthor of 24 books and over 500 articles. His most famous books are *An Economic Theory of Democracy* (1957), translated into several languages, and *Inside Bureaucracy* (1967). Both are still in print. His most recent books are *Still Stuck in Traffic* (2004) and *Growth Management and Affordable Housing: Do They Conflict?* (editor, 2004) from Brookings; *Costs of Sprawl 2000* (coauthor, 2002) from the Transit Cooperative Research Board; and *New Visions for Metropolitan America* (1994) from Brookings and the Lincoln Institute.

Downs is a frequent speaker on real estate economics, housing, transportation, smart growth, urban policies, and other topics. He has made over 1,000 speeches to hundreds of organizations of all types, and is well known for using humor to enliven his subjects.

Dedication

This book is dedicated to my many friends and colleagues in the real estate industry. Your knowledge, energy, skill, persistence, and generous willingness to share ideas and bring projects to life have inspired me for more than 50 years. I want to express my gratitude and admiration for your friendship and assistance, starting with my father Jim Downs, my best friend and first mentor. Also, I salute present and past members of Real Estate Research Corporation and the Urban Land Institute. Without all of you, this book could not have been written. Thanks.

Preface

The Niagara of capital described in this book is in my opinion one of the most important phenomena to occur in real estate markets in the past 50 years—one that will have lasting consequences for the global economy. The inspiration for the title came from Alice Connell, former head of mortgage investing for TIAA-CREF, who claimed she and her colleagues were "drowning in a Niagara of financial capital." For me, that remark sparked the image for what had been happening in real estate markets in the United States and elsewhere ever since the stock market crash in 2000, and even before.

When I started exploring what the *Economist* called the worldwide explosion of housing prices, I realized that the massive inflows of capital into real estate were not only driving property prices upward, but also having many other effects upon housing and commercial property—not to mention the global economy—that many people had not fully grasped.

For years, I have participated in conferences bringing together the brightest minds in the real estate finance and investment business. Those meetings provided me a basis for many of the ideas in this book as well as a sounding board. Most significant are the Urban Land Institute's annual seminar in New York City convened by Bowen "Buzz" McCoy, the Marshall Bennett Classic sponsored annually by Sam Zell and Peter Linneman, and Ken Rosen's semiannual Real Estate Advisory Committee meetings at Pebble Beach Lodge sponsored by the University of California, Berkeley's Fisher Center. Beyond the stimulation of the high-caliber people attending, I am blessed to be among an invaluable collection of friends and critics who shape and challenge my thinking.

When I asked Rachelle Levitt at the Urban Land Institute if ULI would be interested in a book called the Niagara of Capital, she immediately said, "Yes!" and sent me a signed contract. When I finished the initial draft in six months, Rachelle decided to get the book published in time for ULI's annual meeting in fall 2007. Speedy publication also keeps the topic timely and accurate, considering the vagaries of the stock market and the volatile nature of investors and analysts.

The book was greatly improved by excellent and comprehensive comments made by Peter Linneman of the Wharton School. Other colleagues who gave useful suggestions were my fellow board members at General Growth Properties: Alan

Cohen, Bernie Friebaum, Bob Michels, Tom Nolan, and John Riordan. ULI's expert reviewers were Stephen Blank, John McIlwain, and Dean Schwanke. My gratitude also to Buzz McCoy, formerly managing partner of Morgan Stanley, whose own book influenced me and who made wise observations on my draft; Ken Rosen of the University of California, Berkeley; Steve Weschler of the National Association of Real Estate Investment Trusts; Bob Gorham at the real estate law firm Holland & Knight; Ray Mikulich of Lehman Brothers; and Jack Rice with whom I worked for years doing a real estate seminar in Minneapolis. Laura Glassman and Jim Mulligan handled the editorial details with great patience and skill, and designer Betsy VanBuskirk and layout artist Susan Teachey are responsible for the book's appealing presentation. Without all their insights, experience, and thorough evaluation, this book would not have been completed successfully.

Anthony Downs
McLean, Virginia
August 2007

Contents

LIST OF FIGURES AND TABLES

CHAPTER ONE

A Niagara of Capital into Real Estate

Since 1997, an unprecedented inflow of financial capital has revolutionized American real estate, transforming long-dominant market relationships. This massive flood of money—called "a Niagara of capital" by one of the nation's largest mortgage lenders—has not affected America only. It is a global phenomenon felt in all developed nations.[1] It has stimulated a worldwide explosion in housing production and prices in all developed nations except Germany and Japan, thus changing the basic structure of household wealth in most of those nations—including the United States. Lower interest rates, coupled with the flood of capital into residential markets that led to a dramatic easing of credit terms to potential homeowners, encouraged millions of households to buy homes, thereby driving up home prices. That, in turn, made most homeowning households wealthier and made home values more important than corporate equities in overall household balance sheets. Moreover, the traditional skepticism of institutional investors toward commercial real estate has changed. Most such investors have experienced a paradigm shift in their view of the relative importance of stocks, bonds, and real properties—favoring more emphasis on real estate than ever before.

Two radical shifts in the financing of commercial real properties have occurred since the global crash in property values in the late 1980s and early 1990s.[2] The first shift was away from financing real estate mainly through debt borrowed from banks, insurance companies, and savings and loans. Those debts were usually held for the lifetime of the loans by each original lender. Instead, in the 1990s, commercial real estate became financed increasingly by floating stock issues in equity markets and creating debt through commercial, mortgage-backed securities sold in bond markets.

Acronyms and Abbreviations

CDO   collateralized debt obligation

CMBS   commercial mortgage–backed securities

CPI   Consumer Price Index

DJIA   Dow Jones Industrial Average

GDP   gross domestic product

HUD   U.S. Department of Housing and Urban Development

IMF   International Monetary Fund

NAR   National Association of Realtors

NAREIT   National Association of Real Estate Investment Trusts

NCREIF   National Council of Real Estate Investment Fiduciaries

Q   quarter

REIT   real estate investment trust

S&P   Standard & Poor's

ULI   Urban Land Institute

Thus, both the debt and the equity underlying real estate properties were split into many parts and spread among many investors. Such securitization gave rise to a huge increase in the role of real estate investment trusts (REITs) in owning and developing commercial properties. This substitution of equity for debt became necessary when U.S. federal government regulators pressured banks, insurance companies, and savings and loans to reduce their exposures to commercial real estate loans, in effect stopping them from originating more such loans. Federal regulators were reacting to massive overbuilding in the 1980s and subsequent losses in capital values in the real estate crash of the early 1990s. Developers and property owners needing capital to cope with falling rents and occupancy had no place to go for money but into equity markets. Hence, many put the properties they already owned into REITs and issued stock in those entities on Wall Street.

Gradually, commercial real property markets recovered as the overall U.S. economy expanded in the 1990s. This recovery enabled REITs to operate their pools of property both effectively and profitably. Yet REIT stock multiples (relationships between earnings and stock prices) lagged far behind those of high-tech or Internet companies, even though REITs were doing well financially on an operating basis. But then the Internet stock bubble burst in 2000. Prices of all types of stocks the world over plummeted—except for REITs and a few other firms with large and continuing cash flows. To avoid a major recession, central banks in developed nations cut interest rates and stimulated huge increases in general liquidity. Those expansionary monetary policies were augmented by central bank responses to the terrorist attacks of September 11, 2001. Investors had phenomenal amounts of money, but stock prices were collapsing and bond yields were plunging along with interest rates. So investors poured funds into real estate of all types and into other nonstock assets. This strategy led to striking increases in REIT share prices and real property prices generally. At the same time, most other stock values were still far below their year 2000 highs.

The resulting huge flow of money away from stocks and bonds into real estate properties of all types—and other forms of assets, such as commodities, high-risk bonds, and timber—drove real property market prices upward. This investment occurred even though U.S. commercial space market conditions were deteriorating from late 2000 through 2002 because of the weakened general economy. The result was an unprecedented disconnect between conditions in commercial space markets, where rents and occupancy were falling, and conditions in commercial property markets, where prices on well-occupied buildings with good cash flows soared. Keen competition among property investors loaded with money drove prices up and capitalization rates down, especially in the United States. An income property's capitalization rate, or cap rate, is the percentage of a property's value formed by its annual net income. It is computed by dividing a property's net income, usually unleveraged by debt, by its market value. The higher is the property's value in relation to its net income, the lower the cap rate. If the property is initially highly profitable to operate, it will produce a net income that is a relatively high percentage of its initial market value.[3] Thus, a property worth $1 million that produces a net income of $100,000 has a cap rate of 10 percent ($100,000 ÷ $1,000,000 = 0.10). But investors soon bid up the prices of such profitable properties, driving their cap rates downward.

The continuing flood of financial capital away from stocks and bonds into real estate and certain other types of assets has more recently led to the beginning of a second major shift in the financing of real properties. The huge supply of available capital in world financial markets has kept interest rates so low that debt capital has become far cheaper than equity capital. As a result, private equity funds have sprung up to take advantage of positive leverage possibilities. They raise private capital from investors and then borrow money at interest rates much lower than the rates of return they can get from investing that capital in operating properties. The traditional strategy of leveraged buyouts—purchasing equity control of existing companies and then burdening the assets of those companies with enormous amounts of debt— has begun causing private equity firms to buy out some REITs. Private equity funds are pools of investor equity capital aimed at (a) borrowing much larger amounts of money than their own equity at low interest costs, (b) investing that borrowed money and a small amount of equity in buying control of operating companies by purchasing their stock, (c) hoping to improve the operation of those companies and reduce the taxes they pay, and (d) holding those companies for relatively short periods before disposing of them for sizable profits. They make such profits by either (a) refinancing the debt they gathered to buy out the stockholders at even lower interest rates or (b) selling the properties at higher prices to buyers who are also using cheap debt to buy them, arbitraging tax rates between public and private forms of ownership, or taking those companies public again after raking off massive profits through debt finance. Thus, the substitution of equity capital for debt capital that fueled the rapid expansion of REITs in the 1990s and early 2000s shows some signs of being reversed by a substitution of very-low-cost debt capital for the costlier equity capital underlying many real estate properties, especially those in REITs. This second shift has just begun, however, so how fully it will reverse the earlier equitization of commercial property ownership is not clear. Moreover, recent increases in debt repayment problems in high-risk subprime home-lending markets have caused many lenders to reconsider their willingness to keep supplying debt of all types at low returns to themselves.

Another major trait of the huge flow of capital into real estate has been its global character. Although the United States remains the largest single real estate market in the world by a wide margin, a rising fraction of the capital invested here to buy American residential and commercial properties has come from investors located all over the world. Similarly, a rising fraction of the capital American investors are spending to buy real estate is directed at properties in other nations in Europe, Asia, and elsewhere. This foreign investment is in part a flight from the depreciating international value of the U.S. dollar. In 2006, investment conditions became quite similar in nearly all world markets—including improving space market conditions, rising property prices caused by intense competition among buyers, and continued massive inflows and outflows of capital between domestic economies and foreign ones. This aspect of the Niagara of capital is discussed in detail in the next chapter.

The Niagara of capital caused a virtual explosion of market prices in U.S. housing markets because low interest rates and easy credit terms generated by the huge supply of available funds opened the way for millions of formerly renter households to become homeowners and for millions of existing homeowners to refinance their homes and use the proceeds to buy better ones. So the demand for housing soared. In the ten years from 1990 to 2000, the median price in current dollars of existing single-family homes sold in the United States rose by 51 percent, comparable to the 47.9 percent that price had risen in the 1980s. But from 2000 to 2005, that price soared another 48.1 percent in only five years.[4] In real terms, U.S. median home prices rose 14.5 percent from 1990 to 2000, but 31.3 percent in half the time from 2000 to 2005. This super-speed escalation affected the welfare of American households in two opposite ways.

For households who initially owned their own homes, rising housing prices generated huge increases in the equities they held in those homes. Those households could—and did—borrow against those equities and use the wealth so monetized to fund all types of other consumption. That spending helped stimulate the prosperity of the entire U.S. economy. Moreover, low interest rates and easy credit terms encouraged millions of households who formerly rented to become homeowners. From 2000 to 2005, the number of households in the United States rose by 10.5 million, but the number of homeowning households increased by 10.2 million. Thus, additional homeowners equaled 97.1 percent of added households, although most new homeowning households had formerly been renters. The usual increase in demand for rental apartments generated by rising population disappeared as tenants flocked out of renting into owning.

The second major effect of the Niagara of capital on housing markets concerns the affordability of housing to millions of households in America and elsewhere. Whereas the market prices of housing throughout much of America, and in many other nations, have risen over 100 percent since the early 1990s, the incomes of most people living in that housing have not kept pace. True, many households who owned their own housing throughout this huge run-up in prices made great paper profits on the equity in their homes. In many cases, those enriched households were parents of younger households who aided their children with substantial loans financed by the parents' larger home equities. But many other households who did not own their own homes were having more and more difficulty paying for adequate shelter. This economic squeeze was partly offset by the development of ever easier means of borrowing money to buy a home, even for "subprime" borrowers without good credit records. Those means included low-interest mortgages, almost invisible downpayment requirements, interest-only mortgages for the first five to ten years, and so-called option mortgages in which monthly payments were initially less than interest and therefore the amount owed in the long run constantly grew larger. In addition, many lenders increased the fraction of a borrower's income that the borrower could use for paying off debt and still qualify for a loan. These devices helped expand the share of all households who were homeowners in spite of rising home prices. That share rose from 64.2 percent in 1990 to 66.2 percent in 2000 to 69 percent in 2006.

Nevertheless, in many areas, home prices rose so high they were out of reach of many moderate-to-middle-income households, even if they used the most ingenious financial gimmicks. Millions of households whose incomes were too low to qualify for such easy-credit treatments were forced to continue renting. Moreover, they did not gain rising equities from escalating home prices with which they could aid their children. For a while after 2000, apartment rents stagnated or declined because so many renter households were lured by new financial borrowing devices into becoming homebuyers and because many existing rental units were being converted into condominiums. But by 2006, with U.S. markets for selling both existing and new homes slowing down or declining, rents began to pick up again because fewer people were shifting from renting to homeownership. Even so, rents were at higher levels in relation to household incomes than they had been before the huge inflow of capital to real estate. One reason is that so many former apartment units had been withdrawn from renting for conversion to condominiums. Another is that rising costs of both utilities and land pressed landlords to keep rents as high as they could.

In sum, the Niagara of capital that flooded real estate markets after 2000 had immense effects on all aspects of such markets in the United States and elsewhere around the world. Those effects were continuing in 2007, when this book was written. Just how and why this happened, and what its long-run effects will probably be, are the subjects of this book. Chapter 2 describes the sources of all the capital that flowed into real estate. Chapter 3 discusses the effects of the Niagara of capital on housing markets. Chapter 4 analyzes how those impacts affected the traditional housing filtering process through which most American low-income households had traditionally obtained their housing. Chapter 5 discusses what "affordable housing problems" really mean and how recent capital flows have affected housing afford-ability. Chapter 6 analyzes what might be done to improve housing affordability. Chapter 7 examines the effects of the Niagara of capital on commercial property markets. Chapter 8 discusses what events or changes in conditions might stem the flow of the Niagara of capital into real estate. The final chapter speculates upon the long-term effects of this massive capital inflow into U.S. real estate.

Notes

1. I first heard the term "Niagara of capital" from Alice Connell, who was then in charge of real estate mortgage lending for TIAA-CREF. She used the term at the Bowen McCoy Real Estate Finance Symposium sponsored by the Urban Land Institute in New York City in December 2005. I am grateful for her generosity in allowing me to borrow this colorful metaphor.

2. This observation was made by Steve Wechsler of the National Association of Real Estate Investment Trusts at the Urban Land Institute Real Estate Finance Seminar in New York City in December 2006.

3. Properties that are not profitable will be shunned by investors, thereby driving their original prices downward in relation to their net incomes. This will make their net incomes higher percentages of their market values; that is, they will have higher cap rates after they are exposed to the market for a while. Thus, a highly profitable property that produces a net income that is a high share of its initial market value will soon have its market price driven upward by competition, so its equilibrium cap rate is much lower than its initial one.

4. Data from the National Association of Realtors, *Real Estate Insights*, various issues.

CHAPTER TWO

Where Has All the Money Come From?

The essence of the Niagara of capital is a massive flow of money into real estate and other markets—such as those for junk bonds, venture capital funds, and leveraged buyout funds—from a wide variety of sources. This chapter analyzes how much capital has flowed into U.S. real estate markets in the past few years and identifies some of its major sources.

HOW MUCH FINANCIAL CAPITAL HAS RECENTLY FLOWED INTO U.S. REAL ESTATE MARKETS?

In practice, U.S. real estate markets are divided into *residential markets* for single-family homes, condominiums, and small rental apartments, and *commercial markets* for office buildings, industrial buildings, shopping centers, other retail outlets, hotels, resorts, motels, large rental apartments, and other types of properties used for commercial purposes. Capital usually flows into these two broadly defined types of markets in somewhat different channels; so those two types of markets will be discussed separately in this part of the chapter.

Capital Flowing into Residential Property Markets

U.S. housing markets absorbed huge increases in financial capital in order to accommodate very strong demands for homeownership and housing refinance among American households, especially after 2000 (see Figure 2-1). The figure is based on a specific study of such originations sponsored by the Federal Reserve Board and conducted by Chairman Alan S. Greenspan and James Kennedy in 2005. From 1991 through 2000, total mortgages originated for such homes annually fluctuated in

FIGURE 2-1. **MORTGAGE ORIGINATIONS ON ONE-TO-FOUR-FAMILY HOMES, 1991–2004**

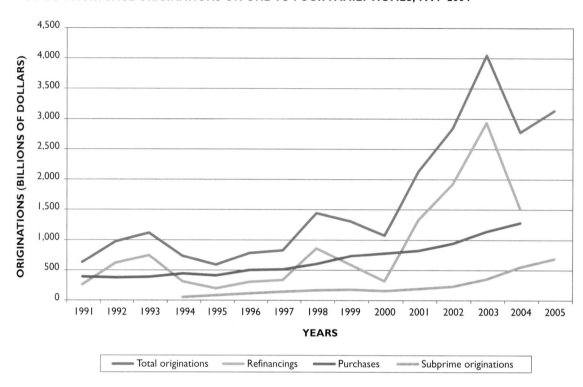

Source: Data from A. Greenspan and J. Kennedy, "Estimates of Home Mortgage Originations, Repayments, and Debt on One-to-Four-Family Residences," Federal Reserve Board, Finance and Economics Discussion Series Paper 2005-41.

value between $571 billion (in 1995) and $1.428 trillion (in 1998). But after 2000, such originations soared dramatically, almost quadrupling to a peak of $4.033 trillion in 2003 before dropping somewhat in 2004 and 2005. This surge was caused mainly by greater volumes of home refinancing as owners took advantage of lower interest rates to tap into the home equities created by rising home prices. As a result, the total amount of money owed by households (plus a minor amount by nonprofits) on home mortgages rose from $4.8 trillion in 2000 to $9.8 trillion in 2007, or by 104.2 percent.[1] Also, the total value of real estate owned by households alone rose from $11.450 trillion in 2000 to $20.5 trillion in the third quarter of 2006, or by 79 percent. Because the total number of households also rose in that period, the value of real estate owned per household increased from $122,600 in 2000 to $179,177 (in current dollars), or by 46.2 percent.

These data illustrate the immense amount of additional capital that American households required to fuel their purchases and refinancing of homes during a peri-

TABLE 2-1. **VOLUME OF EXISTING SINGLE-FAMILY HOME SALES**

Year	Number of Homes Sold	Average Price	Total Sales Volume
1990	3,211,000	$118,600	$380,824,600,000
1995	3,802,000	$139,000	$528,478,000,000
2000	5,152,000	$176,200	$907,782,400,000
2005	7,075,000	$233,300	$1,650,597,500,000
Percentage change, 1990–2005	120.33%	96.7%	333.4%

Source: Based on data from the National Association of Realtors.

od of rapidly increasing home prices. Further confirmation of this conclusion can be seen in Table 2-1, which shows the total amount of money involved in just *sales* of existing single-family homes in each of four years from 1990 to 2005, which is calculated by multiplying the number of homes sold by the average price per sale. (This table excludes refinancings of existing homes.)

Thus, the total sales volume of all single-family homes sold throughout the United States each year increased by over 330 percent from 1990 to 2005. This increase required an immense inflow of capital into residential markets. That capital was initially tapped by mortgage originators. They underwrote each home sale and then sold the mortgages they had created to secondary-market operators, such as Fannie Mae, Freddie Mac, and Ginnie Mae, or Wall Street firms. Those operators packaged the mortgages into bundles, securitized them, and sold them to a variety of investors in the forms of mortgage–backed securities, bonds, collateralized debt obligations (discussed later), or other instruments. In this manner, individual household buyers of housing were able to tap into the general investment market to finance their desires for homeownership or refinancing. As Table 2-1 shows, the total amount of capital flowing from investors of all types (and from all nations) into U.S. housing markets each year expanded greatly as part of the Niagara of capital into real estate.

Capital Flowing into Commercial Property Markets

Money flowing into commercial real estate markets from elsewhere can take several different forms:

▶ Equity capital entering real estate investment trusts (REITs) in public equity markets, either as initial public offerings, secondary stock offerings, or limited private placements.

▶ Private equity raised by funds from individual and institutional investors and used to purchase properties directly or to buy shares in REITs or other listed firms that

FIGURE 2-2. **CAPITAL FLOWS INTO U.S. COMMERCIAL REAL ESTATE MARKETS, 1988–2006**

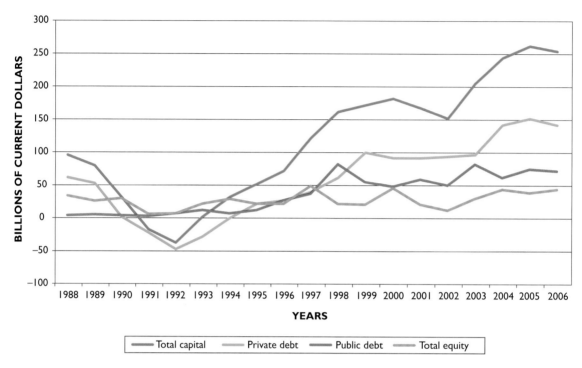

Source: Compiled by Linneman Associates, Philadelphia, Pennsylvania, from various sources.

own real estate. Such equity is normally heavily leveraged with debt to increase net returns to the equity owners.

▶ Public debt in the form of commercial mortgage–backed securities issued by various conduits and purchased by financial institutions or private investors.

▶ Private debt raised by private equity funds and used as leverage to augment their equity in their purchase of properties or stock in REITs and other real estate corporations, plus private debt raised directly by REITs borrowing from banks or investors, plus private debt raised by property owners to finance their projects or existing properties.

All four forms of capital flows are depicted in Figure 2-2. (Public and private debts other than public commercial mortgage–backed securities are combined in the figure.) The "total capital" line shows the remarkable surge of capital into U.S. real estate markets beginning after 1996 and exploding after 2002. Total capital flows fell sharply at the end of the 1980s when real estate property prices collapsed and federal authorities pressed banks, insurance companies, and savings and loans to reduce their holdings of real estate loans, which caused those institutions to stop making more such loans. Private debt declined as total capital flowing into real estate became negative from 1991 through 1993, when many private mortgage loans defaulted or were restructured. In that same period, public equity issues—which had been almost zero from 1988 through 1991—became a low positive figure. That occurred because many private developers switched their properties from private corporations to publicly traded REITs, which was the only way they could raise additional funds to cope with deteriorating market conditions.

The most striking aspects of this figure are (a) the net withdrawal of capital from real estate in the early 1990s, (b) the huge increase in total capital flows into U.S. real estate after 1996, and (c) the unequal relationship between equity and debt capital. Investors withdrew massive amounts of debt from real estate between 1990 and 1994, partly because of huge losses and defaults. Equity capital inflows—public and private combined—remained below $48 billion per year from 1988 through 2006, averaging $25.6 billion in that period.[2] Yet total debt capital started soaring in 1997 from $73 billion, almost doubled in 1998 to $140 billion, and exceeded that amount in six of the next eight years. Total debt capital averaged $12.6 billion per year from 1988 to 1996 and $159.5 billion per year from 1997 to 2006. Thus, the huge inflow of capital into U.S. real estate has been largely debt capital—including mortgage loans—aided by some increases in equity capital, including unrealized capital appreciation in the late 1990s. From 1997 through 2006, total capital entering real estate markets equaled $1.903 trillion dollars—but 83.8 percent of that amount consisted of debt capital.

WHY DEBT FINANCING SO GREATLY EXCEEDED EQUITY FINANCING IN REAL ESTATE MARKETS

This predominance of debt capital in financial flows into real estate undoubtedly results from five factors: (a) low interest rates after 2000; (b) the absence of debt capital entering real estate from 1990 through 1994; (c) large increases in net equities caused by rising property prices, against which the owners could borrow to monetize those unrealized capital gains; (d) a decline in both the actual and the perceived risk of lending because of the securitization of debt; and (e) massive mortgage borrowing by households pursuing home ownership. These factors are discussed below.

Relevant interest rates are shown in Figure 2-3. The Federal Reserve's desire to reduce interest rates is clearly shown by the line that tracks the federal funds rate. This rate is what the Fed uses to signal banks and other private lenders whether they should charge more or less for their funds than they have been doing. The Fed was promoting both low rates and greater liquidity in the early 1990s, in response to weakness in real property markets, and after 2000, in response to weakness in stock mar-

FIGURE 2-3. **KEY INTEREST RATES, 1987–2006**

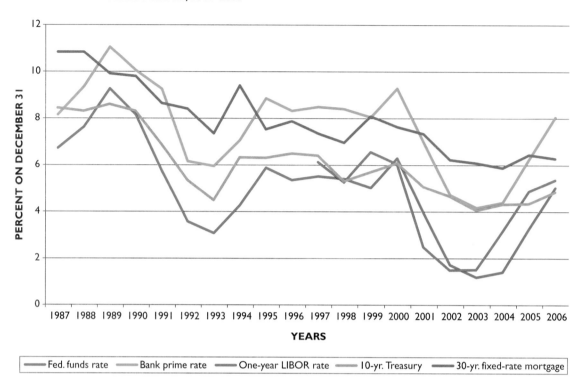

PERCENT ON DECEMBER 31

YEARS

—— Fed. funds rate   —— Bank prime rate   —— One-year LIBOR rate   —— 10-yr. Treasury   —— 30-yr. fixed-rate mortgage

Source: Federal Reserve Board, selected interest rates.

kets. Fixed-rate mortgages followed the general lead of the federal funds rate, but with average spreads over that rate of 261 basis points for a 15-year fixed mortgage and 300 basis points for a 30-year fixed mortgage.

The second cause of the high ratio of debt capital to equity capital entering real estate markets in recent years was the almost complete absence of debt capital entering those markets from 1990 through about 1993. Before 1989, most capital in real estate transactions was debt capital. Most developers and property buyers typically financed their transactions by borrowing, which they used to leverage the moderate to small amounts of equity they supplied themselves. Such high leverage provided them with relatively high rates of return on their equity, because debt interest rates were typically lower than the yields equity investors demanded. But in 1990, the federal government in effect stopped banks, insurance companies, and savings and loan associations from issuing additional debt based on commercial real estate because of the collapse in property earnings and prices caused by massive overbuilding in the late 1980s. Those institutions had been supplying almost all the debt capital used in

NIAGARA OF CAPITAL

commercial real estate transactions, as illustrated in Figure 2-2 by the negative flows of private and public debt capital from 1990 through 1994. The need to obtain additional capital from somewhere is what drove developers and property owners into forming REITs and floating stock issues in public equity markets. After 1994, when property markets had recovered from their worst conditions, the operators of REITs and traditional developers and property buyers began using debt capital again to leverage their own equity with about 40 percent to 50 percent borrowed money—both new equity and equity generated by rising property prices. Hence, both public and private debt entering real estate began to soar, rising especially rapidly after 2003.

The third factor encouraging more issuance of debt by lenders has been a huge increase in the securitization of debt. It especially involved commercial mortgage–backed securities (CMBSs) but also occurred concerning almost all forms of debt. Securitization reduces the degree of risk associated with any large loan in the eyes of those funding it. The principal lender divides the basic loan into many much smaller pieces, each of which that lender sells to a different funder. These pieces are also divided into different categories, or tranches, each associated with different terms and yields. They range from low-yield, low-risk tranches (considered AAA by rating agencies like Moody's) to high-yield, high-risk tranches (considered BBB because lower-rated debt is viewed as "junk"). The AAA tranche receives all of the interest and principal payments made by the borrower until holders of AAA securities have achieved the rate of return they were promised. Then interest payments go to holders of the next-riskier tranche. This process is repeated down to the lowest-ranking tranche, which is therefore the riskiest one, because its holders are last in line. Each secondary lender can regard the relatively small piece it funds as much less risky to its own financial welfare than if it were funding the entire loan, because it has much less at stake. This device also allows each lender to choose the degree of risk he or she is willing to accept, because low-risk lenders get first access to any loan repayments. Moreover, lenders can easily diversify their risks by buying relatively small pieces of loans on many different properties, rather than holding each loan entirely through its lifetime, as in the past. Hence, the rapid expansion of CMBSs in real estate markets since 1996 has reduced both the perceived and the actual degree of risk associated with real estate lending. This expansion is shown on Figure 2-4.

A more recent form of securitization consists of collateralized debt obligations (CDOs). In CDOs, many different pieces of securitized loans on different types of assets, including real estate and other types, are placed together into a single pool. Then this pool is securitized by dividing it into separate tranches with different repayment schedules from the underlying pieces of securitized debt (and therefore with different levels of risk) and by selling the pieces in each tranche to other in-

FIGURE 2-4. **U.S. ANNUAL CMBS ISSUANCE, 1992–2006**

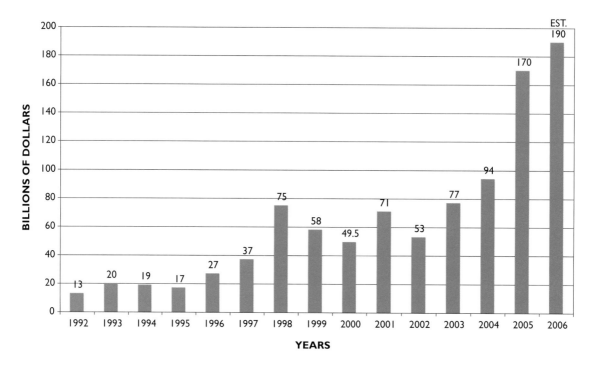

Source: *Commercial Mortgage Alert*, U.S. CMBS Insurance, http//:www.cmalert.com/data/cmalertdata/ABSData/cusbas.xls#Data!A1:D1 (accessed August 24, 2007).

vestors. Such "securitization squared" spreads the risk of lending to an even greater degree, presumably reducing the final risk to the ultimate holders of these CDOs. These instruments illustrate just how far the ingenuity of Wall Street's financial engineers can go to reduce the perceived risk of lending. CDOs also reduce actual risks when accompanied by more transparency and increased liquidity. But CDOs—like CMBSs—also reduce the possibility of creating viable workouts for owners of the properties concerned in case anything goes wrong in their markets, as typically occurs during recessions.

Today, a big part of the actual underwriting that every real estate lender does in relation to funding any particular real estate transaction is answering the question: "How much of this loan can I sell off to other funders, thereby reducing my own risk in this deal?" Such handoff underwriting has become almost more important than examining the particular characteristics of the real properties involved in the loan concerned. This is a significant change from past lending practices. Formerly, a Wall Street broker took as long as a whole year to analyze and sell a real estate portfolio, which involved reading every individual lease![3] The pressure to make decisions fast is surely responsible for much of the apparent decline in underwriting standards that real estate lenders have noticed over the past few years. At two real estate finance seminars I attended in December 2005 and December 2006, sponsored by the Urban Land Institute, representatives of major financial institutions responsible for billions of dollars in real estate loans declared that current underwriting standards have either "plummeted" or "disappeared altogether," compared to traditional standards. Their comments strongly reflect the effect on funder behavior of both securitized lending and intense competition among lenders caused by the large amount of capital that must be invested somewhere. Yet in spite of their complaints about lower standards, these lenders kept right on making more and more loans under those low or nonexistent standards. One major CMBS lender stated at a recent Urban Land Institute meeting that the typical real estate loan he makes stays on his books only 42 days on average. By then, he has divided it into smaller pieces and sold all of them to other investors at a profit. Not surprisingly, he considers that what happens to the underlying real property after those six weeks is no longer his problem—but theirs. Such financial legerdemain has caused the basic concept of real estate as a long-term investment to disappear from the thinking of many of the very investors financing real estate deals.

One of the elements of risk that securitization has not affected is that of assuming that the property owner's exit capitalization rate will be the same (or lower) than the one at which the owner bought the property. In other words, the owner can sell the property for more than the price paid for it. Many investors almost automatically make this assumption without carefully considering less-favorable possibilities— namely, that capitalization rates will rise and the property will sell for less than what the owner paid for it.

Another important result of securitization has been drawing many lenders who never paid much attention to real estate securities in the past into lending on real estate transactions. The reduced risk of such lending and the scarcity of competitive investments persuaded many sources of capital that had previously avoided real estate to start making real estate loans. That influx of capital has greatly broadened the available universe of real estate lending sources compared to its former restriction to banks, mortgage originators, savings and loans, and insurance companies. As a result, the total supply of money willing to enter real estate debt markets has grown much larger than before securitization became widespread. This expansion of the universe of real estate capital sources has been a major cause of the added money entering real estate markets.

A fourth reason that debt capital has been more available for investment in real estate than equity capital is that investors burned by their equity losses in the stock market from 2000 to 2002 increased their equity return requirements, mainly by shifting their equity investments to "opportunity funds" promising unusually high yields. Equity funds therefore became more costly to investment banking firms, though enough equity investing still occurred to make up for lower debt–to–value ratios in this period than later. Moreover, pension funds were better able to engage in liability-directed investing—that is, matching the timing of their future pension payment liabilities with the expiration dates on their investments—by using debts with specific expiration dates rather than by using equity. Therefore, they were more willing to put their capital into various forms of debt than to take equity positions— except in REITs. REITs had the advantage of maintaining low levels of debt in relation to equity, which shielded REIT equity owners from the kind of highly leveraged debt defaults that had occurred in real estate in 1990 and shortly thereafter.

This investor preference for the perceived lower risk of debt is somewhat ironic because of the subsequent behavior of private equity firms that sprang up in response to the immense availability of cheap debt. Those firms have recently based their equity profitability on increasing the amount of leverage with debt they use to buy up existing firms and properties, restructure them, and sell them, compared to the lower amounts of leverage they used in the 1990s. Such additional leveraging really replaces equity capital with debt capital in the financial structure of the bought-out firms. This replacement eliminates the cushion of equity that protected many of those firms from encountering financial difficulties because of high debt services from heavy borrowing. So by making borrowing easier, investors who lent money to avoid the risks of equity investment have encouraged private equity firms to use debt to replace equity. But that replacement shifts much of the previous equity risk onto lenders instead of equity investors. This behavior is not unique to real estate; private equity firms have long used leveraged buyouts that follow the same strategy. How this situation will play out in the future depends greatly on whether any severe economic downturn occurs in real estate markets. If such a downturn occurs, equity investors will not be the only ones who get hurt. The high fraction of cheap debt used in private equity buyouts would shift some of the pain onto lenders as well as equity investors.

THE GLOBAL NATURE OF THE CAPITAL FLOWS IN THE NIAGARA OF CAPITAL

One of the most striking aspects of the Niagara of capital is its worldwide nature. It is not just something happening in the United States. This fact is well documented by Jones Lang LaSalle in *Global Real Estate Capital: Moving Further and Faster*, published in early 2007.[4] According to Jones Lang LaSalle, total worldwide direct investment in commercial properties alone—including both equities and debts—reached $682 billion in 2006, up 38 percent from its highest level of $495 billion in 2005, and 93 percent above its level of $354 billion in 2003. Moreover, the share of all that direct commercial real estate investment consisting of capital moving across international borders rose from 24 percent in 2003 to 42 percent in 2006. Thus, cross-border capital flows increased from $85 billion in 2003 to $286 billion in 2006—a rise of 236 percent in just three years. Jones Lang LaSalle also estimated that total real estate investment in all types of properties (except single-family homes) reached $900 billion in 2006. The U.S. share of total direct commercial real estate investment in 2006 was 40 percent, compared with the United Kingdom's 15 percent, Germany's 9 percent, and Japan's 8 percent. One reason for the large flow of capital into the United States has been the declining value of the U.S. dollar in international trade, making U.S. properties cheaper in foreign currencies. Even more important has been the belief among foreign investors that the United States is still the safest and most secure place in which to invest. After all, the United States has the great protection of a legal system that can be relied upon and a political system not likely to collapse in revolution or an internal civil war. However, the relative shares of the United States and the United Kingdom have been declining because investment in other markets has grown faster recently. The largest single cause of the increasing financial volume of global real estate investment has been the rising prices of the properties involved, resulting mainly from competition by so many investors seeking to buy desirable real properties. That competition led to major compression of capitalization rates, which accounted for 50 percent of the rise in total dollar investment volume from 2005 to 2006, according to Jones Lang LaSalle's estimate. That firm also declared in 2006 that a global average of $5 in investor funds was looking for good projects for every $1 dollar of such products available. The resulting intense competition is what has kept real property prices rising so smartly. An additional reason for such strong competition for nonresidential properties is that increasing rents and occupancies after about 2003 promised investors better future economic results.

WHERE DID ALL THIS FINANCIAL CAPITAL COME FROM?

The recent and continuing inflow of financial capital into real estate markets has originated from several very disparate sources, which are briefly described in the following sections.

Effect of an Expanding Low-Wage Labor Force in China and India

Surprisingly, a major cause of large amounts of money flowing into U.S. and other real estate markets has been a huge increase in the low-wage industrial labor force in Asia. This factor has operated through a long chain of related events that are not obviously related to rising real estate prices in the markets of developed nations. The growth of well-trained, low-wage industrial workers in China, India, and a few other Asian nations has expanded the world's industrial labor force enormously since about 1985. The International Monetary Fund (IMF) has estimated that the world labor force engaged in international trade roughly tripled in size from 1985 to 2005, mainly through the addition of more very-low-wage workers.[5] Brookings Institution economists have estimated a more conservative 20 to 30 percent growth in the world's industrial labor force over the past two decades. Thus, huge increase in labor supply—at very low costs—effectively increased competition among industrial workers worldwide, thereby driving down product costs in globalized markets. Firms throughout the developed world were faced with low-cost competition that prevented them from raising the prices of the goods they produced or even from maintaining their previous prices. Many such firms responded by establishing their own production facilities in China, India, and other Asian nations, replacing jobs in their homelands with less costly workers. Wal-Mart is an example of a U.S. firm that cut its goods costs by procuring large amounts of its merchandise in China.

This process created a deflationary pressure on the prices of many manufactured goods throughout the world, thereby checking inflation in general. In fact, some central banks thought Asian workers would have so strong an effect that they decided to expand monetary liquidity in their nations to prevent deflation and slow the decline in real wages that many of their workers were facing. That increase in liquidity contributed to downward pressure on U.S. interest rates in the early 1990s and to level interest rates in the mid-1990s, as shown in Figure 2-3. Moreover, this anti-inflationary impact was greatly augmented by the next causal factor.

Some simplistic calculations can illustrate the effect of China's moving millions of workers into the world's industrial labor force (see Table 2-2). In its *World Factbook for 2006*, the Central Intelligence Agency estimates that the world's total labor force was 3.001 billion in 2005. Of that total, 21 percent were in industry, 42 percent in agriculture, and 37 percent in services.[6] That distribution implies the world's industrial labor force was about 630 million in 2005, or 9.7 percent of the world's total 2005 population of 6.450 billion. The same publication estimated that the Chinese labor force was 791.4 million, of whom 22 percent—or 174 million—were in industry. Thus, Chinese industrial workers constituted about 27.6 percent of the world's industrial labor force in 2005.

TABLE 2-2. **WORLD AND CHINESE INDUSTRIAL LABOR FORCE GROWTH, 1980–2005**

Items	1980	2005	Numerical Growth	Percentage Growth
World population	4,454,000,000	6,450,000,000	1,996,000,000	44.81
Percentage in labor force	44	46.53		
World labor force	1,959,760,000	3,001,000,000	1,041,240,000	53.13
Percentage of labor force in industry	19	21		
World industrial labor force	372,354,400	630,000,000	257,645,600	69.19
Industrial labor force as percentage of world population	8.36	9.7	1.34	16.03
Chinese total population	981,000,000	1,306,591,330	325,591,330	33.19
As percentage of world population	22.03	20.26		
Labor force as percentage of total population	60.5	60.57		
Chinese total labor force	593,505,000	791,400,000	197,895,000	33.34
Chinese industrial labor force as percentage of total labor force	15	22		
Chinese industrial labor force	89,025,750	174,000,000	84,974,250	95.45
As percentage of world industrial labor force	23.91	27.62		
Chinese industrial labor force growth 1980–2005 as percentage of world industrial labor force growth				32.98
Chinese industrial labor force growth as percentage of world industrial labor force in 1980				22.82

Sources: Central Intelligence Agency, *World Fact Book 2006*, and *Statistical Abstract of the United States, 2004–2005*, 841.

In 1980, the world's total population was 4.454 billion. If the industrial labor force was only 8.36 percent of the world's population at that time, it would have equaled 372.35 million persons. According to the World Bank, as reported by the Center for East Asian Studies at the University of California in Los Angeles, the population of China in 1980 was 981 million.[7] If the total Chinese labor force was the same percentage of China's total population in 1980 as in 2005 (60.5 percent), then the Chinese labor force was 593.505 million in 1980. I assume that the industrialized portion of the Chinese labor force was a somewhat smaller proportion in 1980 (15 percent) than in 2005 (22 percent). In that case, the Chinese industrial labor force was 89.025 million in 1980 compared with 174 million in 2005; so it had grown by 84.974 million, or 95.45 percent, in 25 years. The world's total industrial labor force had grown by 257.65 million in the same 25 years, or by 69.2 percent. Therefore, the growth of China's industrial labor force from 1980 to 2005 (84.97 million) constituted 32.98 percent of the growth of the entire world's industrial labor force (257.65 million) in that period. Moreover, the growth from 1980 to 2005 of the Chinese industrial labor force alone (84.97 million) was equal to 22.8 percent of the initial total world's industrial labor force in 1980 (372.35 million). Of course, these are rough estimates and can hardly be considered precise. Nevertheless, they indicate the order of magnitude of the effect of the growth of the Chinese industrial labor force on the world's industrial labor force in those 25 years.

Even in 2003, however, manufacturing wages in China were only about 16 percent of those paid in the United States.[8] That is far below industrial wages in many other developing nations, such as Mexico and Thailand.

By blocking any higher manufacturing prices throughout the world in the 1990s and later, this massive increase in the low-wage Chinese labor force—accompanied by a similar but smaller increase in the Indian labor force—restrained inflation worldwide and held down wages of manufacturing workers in most developed nations. It also generated large profits and higher incomes among Chinese and other Asian firms and workers. As discussed further below, Asian workers were motivated to save large shares of those profits and incomes. In China, most of those savings went into state-controlled banks because of a dearth of attractive alternatives. But the Chinese government realized its banks were incapable of efficiently investing those savings in China itself. Therefore, it caused the banks to use many of those savings to buy U.S. Treasury securities that helped finance more Chinese exports to the United States by sustaining America's balance of payments deficits.

In addition, when the stock market crash occurred in 2000 (as discussed below), the absence of inflationary pressures resulting from low-wage Asian workers permitted central banks in developed nations to slash interest rates to prevent a recession. That, in turn, was a major cause of the worldwide boom in housing prices analyzed in the next chapter.

A final effect of low-wage Chinese workers beneficial to many Americans was a flood of low-cost manufactured goods from China to the United States through such retailers as Wal-Mart, whose stores attract millions of American shoppers annually. These low-cost goods raised the living standards of many of those shoppers, including millions in the middle class.

Stock Market Crash of 2000–2002

World stock markets experienced an immense run-up in prices during most of the 1990s. It was stimulated by a boom in high-technology stocks, many related to the development of the Internet. Figure 2-5 shows what huge gains in values stocks experienced from 1991 through 1999. The two measures—the Dow Jones Industrial Average (DJIA) and Standard & Poor's (S&P) 500 Index—were 4.36 and 4.45 times as

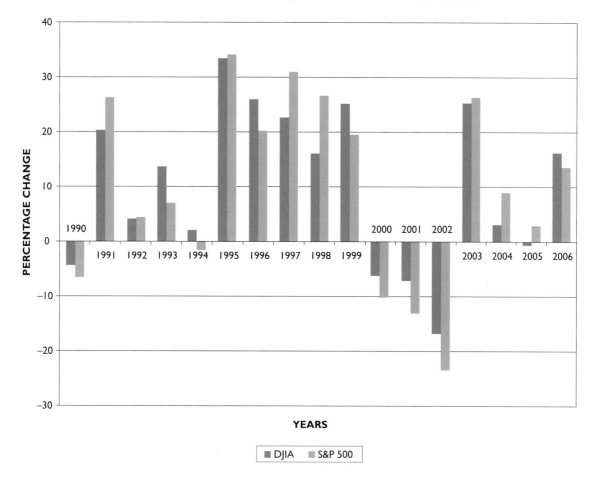

YEARS

■ DJIA   ■ S&P 500

Source: Standard & Poor's, Dow Jones.

high, respectively, on December 31, 1999, as they had been on December 31, 1990. The NASDAQ composite average nearly doubled in the single calendar year 1999, reaching a peak of 5,048 on March 10, 2000.

But then the Internet bubble burst and stocks came tumbling down. The DJIA dropped from its high of 11,310.64 on September 6, 2000, to a low of 7,462.84 on October 2, 2002—a decline of 34 percent. The NASDAQ composite average plummeted 72 percent from peak to trough, and the S&P 500 Index fell 36 percent from its high.

These huge declines in stock values affected the flows of funds into real estate in several ways. First, many investors reduced their holdings of stocks and bonds, and most investors stopped putting additional funds into them. Instead, investors shifted many of their available funds into real estate and other asset markets, which had not suffered any corresponding declines in property values since 1989–1990. Second, central banks throughout the developed world notably increased financial liquidity in their nations to forestall a major recession. Third, the same banks cut the interest rates they used to signal their commercial banks to cut rates. That signal plus increased monetary liquidity caused interest rates to decline across the board, especially from 2000 through 2003.

These three developments were a major cause of immense increases in the amount of capital flowing into real estate markets around the world, because real estate appeared to be the most attractive and readily available investment alternative. One of the biggest results was a worldwide boom in housing prices, strongly stimulated by falling interest rates and a greater focus of investment capital on real properties of all types. This boom (described in detail in the next chapter) helped drive up the values of homes owned by households in most developed nations except Germany and Japan. Rising home prices made millions of homeowning households in developed nations much richer than formerly. Many were able to borrow against the increased equity in their homes and expand their consumption. Thus, an ironic result of more low-wage workers in China and other parts of Asia, and of the stock market crash, was the enrichment of a majority of American households, because over 60 percent owned their own homes. The same factor that caused many politicians to rant against our loss of jobs to overseas firms—as well more consumption of low-cost merchandise—actually helped most American households become better-off financially. In contrast, competition from those same Asian low-wage workers also helped cause wages of American industrial workers to stagnate, reducing their economic welfare. This stagnation is apparent from Figure 2-6, which shows private real hourly wages declining steadily from 1972 through 1995.

Surplus Savings, Both Foreign and Domestic

The Federal Reserve Bank believes another major cause of this capital flood has been extraordinarily large savings by prosperous firms in developed nations and by both households and firms in emerging nations like China. As then Federal Reserve governor Ben S. Bernanke said in an April 2005 speech:

> A satisfying explanation of the recent upward climb of the U.S. current account deficit requires a global perspective that more fully takes into account events outside the United States. . . . I will argue that over the past decade a combination of diverse forces has created a significant increase in the global supply of saving—a global saving glut— which helps to explain both the increase in the U.S. current account deficit and the relatively low level of long-term real interest rates in the world today.[9]

FIGURE 2-6. **AVERAGE HOURLY WAGES IN THE PRIVATE SECTOR, 1950–2006**

Source: U.S. Bureau of Labor Statistics.

Because China has no national government safety-net system to protect its households, such as the United States' Social Security, Medicare, and other aids, Chinese households save high fractions of their incomes—probably over 30 percent—to protect themselves. As foreign investment capital poured into China to take advantage of low wage rates, incomes and savings by Chinese firms and households soared. But most Chinese savers have nowhere to put their funds except into Chinese national banks. Those banks are burdened with supporting remaining national-government-owned firms, most of which operate at losses. That fact, plus corruption among Chinese officials and opaque record keeping by Chinese private firms, means the banks are not very competent to make profitable domestic investments in China. The leaders of the Chinese government are aware of this fact. So those leaders have pressured the banks they control to invest overseas—especially in U.S. Treasury securities. This investment gives Chinese banks higher current yields than they can earn at home, although it risks future capital losses through devaluation of the U.S. dollar. Such purchases of U.S. Treasury securities also help finance continued trade deficits by America as U.S. residents buy more and more imports from China. The Chinese government needs to keep expanding such exports to employ the millions of workers looking for better jobs who continually stream into its cities from depressed rural areas.

Ironically, much of the savings of Chinese workers and firms invested in the United States and other developed nations underwrites capitalists and firms in those countries who invest in Chinese enterprises. In theory, the Chinese could invest in domestic enterprises directly, without first investing the money in the United States or other developed nations—if China had competent means of making profitable domestic investments. But the Chinese government's political need to keep expanding its modern industrial sector to employ its ambitious workers pressures that government to keep buying U.S. Treasury securities so America will keep on purchasing Chinese-made goods and investing in the plants that make them! In 2007, the Chinese government actually bought a 10 percent interest in the Blackstone private equity firm before its public offering. That purchase may be just one of many future attempts by foreign creditor governments to use funds from their export surpluses to the United States to purchase equity interests in American firms rather than risking future U.S. dollar devaluations by buying Treasury securities.

Nations, firms, and individuals outside the United States have increasingly lent money to Americans by using their surplus funds from exporting more to Americans than they imported from Americans to buy U.S. Treasury securities. That process has resulted in an enormous trade deficit for the United States as a whole. The overall trade deficit on a balance-of-payments basis, as calculated by the U.S. Census Bureau, is shown in Figure 2-7. The balance-of-payments deficit has exploded since 1999, rising from $107.9 billion (1.3 percent of American gross domestic product, or GDP) in that year to $856.6 billion in 2006 (6.5 percent of the 2006 GDP). This deficit has greatly increased the amount of Treasury securities held by foreigners. In 2000, $1.021 trillion of Treasury securities were owned by foreign governments, firms, and individuals, or about 32 percent of all such securities outstanding. In the third quarter of 2006, foreigners held $2.069 trillion in Treasury securities, or 45 percent of the total outstanding. Thus, foreign holdings of U.S. Treasuries more than doubled in five years. The U.S. balance-of-payments deficit has generated significant savings by foreigners that have swelled the overall supply of world savings looking for investment opportunities.

U.S. Corporate Profits

Another source of significant savings has been a rapid increase in corporate profits within the American economy. In 1986, during an oil price slump, corporate profits before taxes in the United States were just over 5 percent of GDP. But they gradually

FIGURE 2-7. **U.S. BALANCE-OF-PAYMENTS DEFICIT, 1970–2006**

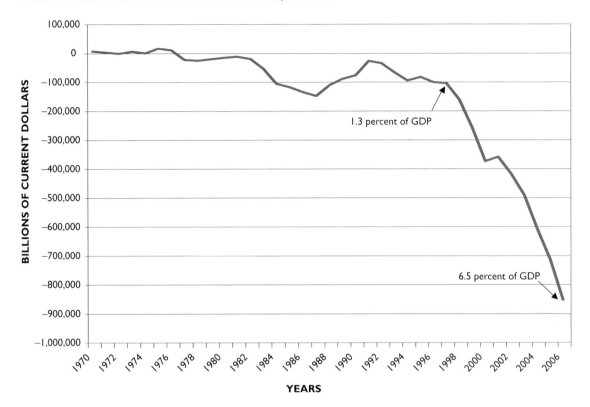

Source: U.S. Census Bureau, Foreign Trade, Statistics, U.S. Trade in Goods and Services – Balance of Payments Basis, 1960 through 2006, http://www.census.gov/foreign-trade/statistics/historical/gands.txt.

rose to almost 10 percent by 1997 and then slumped to 7.1 percent in 2001 (after the stock market crash and 9/11). But then savings began a rapid rise to 11.9 percent of GDP in 2005 and 13.4 percent in 2006. These changes are illustrated in Figure 2-8. Profits after taxes followed a very similar path, but undistributed profits—pure corporate savings—rose from almost nothing in 1986 to 5.24 percent of GDP in 2006.[10] As a result, many U.S. corporations have accumulated large stockpiles of cash. The most spectacular hoarder of cash was Microsoft. By July 2004, Microsoft had accumulated over $56 billion in profits being held as cash or other short-term assets. What has happened to U.S. corporate profits is very different from what has happened to U.S. workers' incomes, as noted earlier—partly because the low wages of Asian workers, along with changes in technology in U.S. manufacturing, keep strong downward pressure on American workers' wages. Those low wages have limited corporate labor costs, thereby helping corporations raise their profits to record proportions of GDP.

FIGURE 2-8. **TOTAL CORPORATE PROFITS AS PERCENTAGE OF GDP, 1980–2006**

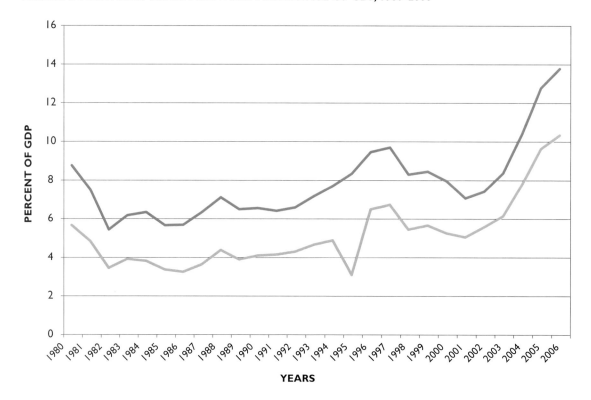

Source: Council of Economic Advisers, *Economic Indicators* (Washington, D.C.: Government Printing Office, January 1980 to March 2007).

Japanese Yen "Carry Trade"

During Japan's recent long period of deflationary pressure, the Bank of Japan kept interest rates close to zero to encourage more investment and borrowing. This policy motivated many hedge funds and other international investors to borrow money at rates of 1.5 percent or less and use it to buy foreign bonds, such as U.S. Treasuries yielding 4.5 percent. Such cheaply borrowed funds were also used to fund many other types of investments that promised higher yields than the cost of raising the money. However, no one really knows the overall size of this "carry trade" (the process of carrying yen elsewhere and investing them at a profit), although many informed observers believe it is quite large. True, such investors were risking the possibility that the Japanese yen would rise in value against the dollar if Japan's economy ever came to life again, which it has begun to do recently. Then those investors would have to repay their loans with more dollars than they were counting on when they made such investments. No doubt exists that up to now, however, the total amount of capital available for international investment has been notably expanded by the Bank of Japan's policy of maintaining very low interest rates. A substantial decline of the U.S. dollar against the yen might trigger a sudden flight for the exits by carry-trade investors, but the Bank of Japan does not seem anxious to encourage such a result because it wants to keep stimulating Japanese exports.

Rising Profits of Oil-Exporting Nations

Another cause of large-scale surplus savings around the world is the explosion in oil revenues received by nations with large oil deposits, especially Russia and several nations in the Middle East. These oil producers have enjoyed enormous profits from the world's rising demand for oil, thereby adding to the world's savings that must somehow be absorbed. The price of a barrel of crude oil has fluctuated wildly since 1973 when Arab producer states placed on oil embargo on exports during the Yom Kippur War between Egypt and Israel. Before that war, the world price was about $14.50 per barrel (in 2006 dollars), according to data from WRTG Economics, a specialist in energy prices.[11] The price then escalated to $40 per barrel in 2006 dollars, but then declined to about $33 per barrel until Iran's Islamic Revolution in 1979. The price then shot up to $68 per barrel until about 1981, but then plummeted to $20 per barrel by 1986. During the Gulf War in 1989, the price of oil rose again to $28 per barrel but then sank to about $18 per barrel in 1994 and to $13 per barrel in 1998. It then began a rapid ascent, stimulated by the amazing growth of the Chinese and other Asian economies, that was interrupted only briefly by the terrorist attack on the United States on September 11, 2001. The price reached $30 per barrel both just before and just after 9/11 and then shot upward to over $60 per barrel in 2006.

The recent surge in oil prices—beginning in 2002 from about $25 per barrel (in 2006 dollars) to $61 per barrel in 2006—saw a jump of 144 percent in real terms in just four years. Because total world oil production in 2005 was about 29.1 billion barrels per year, that price increase of $36 per barrel amounted to a windfall gain to all oil-producing nations of $1.046 trillion dollars (in 2006 dollars) in the year 2006 alone. The three largest oil-producing nations other than the United States are Saudi Arabia, Russia, and Iran—all major exporters of oil rather than consumers of most of what they produce. Together, those three nations accounted for about 28.4 percent of world oil production as of 2005.[12] So they received combined windfall gains of $297 billion dollars per year compared to what they had been receiving in 2002. Investing these huge sums and more from additional oil-exporting nations has been a large source of the world's excess savings. Most surplus Russian and Middle Eastern oil funds have not been invested directly in America or American real estate. But because money is fungible, those funds have contributed to the worldwide surplus of cash that indirectly pushed more money into American real estate.

Institutional Investors' Paradigm Shift to Capital Investment in Real Estate

The real estate property market collapse in 1990 and shortly thereafter reinforced a longstanding prejudice among financial institutions and their managements against putting significant amounts of money into real estate, as compared to other assets, such as stocks, bonds, and gold. Many pension funds had no real property holdings at all before 2000, even though real estate is one of the major asset classes in all modern developed nations. Many pension fund operators and managers of other financial institutions were not familiar with real properties. Also, they regarded such properties as unreliable. After all, real estate did not produce steady annual increases in earnings, such as they imagined "reliable firms" in other industries did. Real estate investments usually take years to create, especially if they are large; require long initial development periods with low earnings; must be fueled with large amounts of debt; are subject to periodic adverse cyclical movements in property markets and in interest rates; and need constant costly refurbishing and modernization. Also, real estate investments are burdened by complex taxation and accounting rules. Finally, for large corporations such as oil companies, most real estate properties are too small to be significant on their overall books and take up too much management time in relation to their contributions to annual earnings. For all those reasons, plus lack of easily available information about real properties and their markets, real estate was discounted by a large fraction of the financial institutions whose managers invest the world's major stocks of capital.

But all that changed almost overnight as a result of the stock market crash of 2000. After all, the relative attraction of any asset class depends as much on the attraction of its competitors in the investment world as it does on its own qualities. When stocks suddenly lost their allure after 2000 as a result of plunging market prices, and bond yields fell as central banks slashed interest rates to prevent a recession, real estate acquired a new glamour in the minds of the world's professional investors. A virtual paradigm shift occurred in their attitudes toward the desirability and advisability of putting capital into what was one of the largest asset classes in the world—and the source of immense amounts of private wealth in every nation. Consequently, such investors changed their willingness to put money into real properties of all types, given that nothing else was available with similar positive qualities. This attitudinal shift, plus the institutional changes created by securitization and increased transparency in real estate investment circles, vastly opened up the amounts of capital resources available to real estate markets. That change has been a major factor contributing to the Niagara of capital flooding into real property markets in the past decade.

Desire of Private Corporations to Shift Capital from Buildings to More-Productive Assets

Many private corporations around the world, especially in Europe, have begun following the American example of shifting assets from the real properties they owned and occupied to other forms of assets that might produce higher rates of return for their stockholders. Jones Lang LaSalle estimates that fewer than 25 percent of U.S. corporations own their own production buildings, but much higher percentages of European firms do. More and more of the latter have been shifting to leasebacks to free financial capital for other uses. Some of that capital once tied up in buildings is now looking for a place to get decent returns; ironically, it has often turned to real estate investing, frequently outside the originating nation. For firms to shift capital from their own buildings to real estate somewhere else may seem almost irrational, but doing so would make sense if some of the capital taken out of their own buildings was given to professional intermediaries to invest in more-profitable uses, and those intermediaries determined that foreign real estate was a sensible reuse at a given moment.

General Uncertainty about the Stability of World Economic and Political Conditions

Yet another cause of the financial flood into real estate has been general uncertainty about the future of the world's economic prosperity. With wars raging in Iraq, Afghanistan, Somalia, and Sudan; the threat of more terrorist attacks around the world; sluggish growth in Japan and slow growth in Europe until recently; political controversies in France and Denmark about the European Union's constitution and expansion; and soaring oil prices, many of the world's investors have been reluctant to plunge their capital back into non-real-estate-oriented stocks and bonds. They also regard American markets of all types as more immune to serious disruptions than those in emerging nations and even in Western Europe. Hence, worldwide investors are drawn to keep putting funds into American investment opportunities, especially real estate because it has recently outperformed most stocks and bonds.

Aging of Populations in Developed Nations

One further causal factor is the aging of the populations in the world's developed nations and in some emerging nations, such as China. With birthrates in parts of Europe and Japan falling below replacement levels, population growth getting close to or below zero, and more people living longer, a rising need exists for capital to support more retiring workers. Households and governments are under pressure to increase savings for this purpose and to invest those savings somewhere now. More-over, they are attracted to invest in real estate because both directly owned real prop-erties and REIT stocks tend to pay higher cash dividends in relation to their market prices than nearly all other stocks.

According to the Organization for Economic Cooperation and Development, assets held by pension funds in 30 member nations rose from $12.674 trillion in 2001 to $15.565 trillion in 2004, an increase of 22.8 percent in just three years.[13] Most pen-sion fund managers seek to invest their funds in the most-profitable ways consistent with the degrees of risk they are willing to take on. Hence, this rise in pension fund assets, plus the normal turnover involved in the reinvestment of previously existing pension assets that have matured, has supplied a significant share of the added capi-tal flowing into real estate. Pension funds have been especially important because their managers have generally increased the overall share of the total assets they have placed in real estate since the stock market crash of 2000–2002. Whereas many pension fund managers did not consider real estate a separate asset class until that crash occurred, most have now determined that they ought to maintain a significant fraction of their assets in real properties, REIT shares, or loans based on real estate.

Emergence of New Nations and Firms into World Markets

A significant share of the financial capital now looking for real estate investments is coming from nations or firms that were only recently able either to generate such capital or to control where it was invested. Some of those nations and firms are in Eastern Europe, where their international investment behavior was for a long time limited by their connections with the former Soviet bloc and then delayed by their struggles to develop firms that could compete in international markets. Other emer-ging nations in Asia, the Middle East, and Latin America now have private firms and investors with significant incomes but a great reluctance to keep their investments within their own fragile economies. So they have put large shares of their capital into the global search for sound real property investments. The number of such firms and individuals with rising earnings looking for somewhere secure to put them is rising constantly as world prosperity increases. Because the United States is still almost universally regarded as the safest and most secure place in which to invest—except for the risks of further U.S. dollar devaluation—much of that capital has flowed into American real estate markets or U.S. Treasury securities. This source of capital is like-ly to remain strong unless the dollar suddenly plunges in international trading value.

This analysis and the earlier discussion of the effects of low-wage Chinese work-ers were recently confirmed in Alan Greenspan's new book, *The Age of Turbulence*, published in September 2007. Greenspan described the effects of the end of the Soviet Union and the fall of the Berlin Wall as follows:

> Soon well over a billion workers, many well-educated, all low paid, began to gravitate to the world's competitive marketplace from economies that had been almost wholly or in part centrally planned and isolated from global competition. . . . The International Monetary Fund estimates that in 2005 more than 800 million members of the world's labor force were engaged in export-oriented and therefore competitive markets, an increase of 500 million since the fall of the Berlin Wall in 1989 and 600 million since 1980, with East Asia accounting for half the increase. . . . This movement of workers into the marketplace reduced world wages, inflation expectations and interest rates, and accordingly significantly contributed to rising world economic growth. . . . The competitive effect . . . suppressed the wages of workers not directly in the line of fire of low-price imports [and] competitively suppressed export prices of all economies. . . . China is by far the dominant contributor to the trend.[14]

Relatively Superior Economic Performance of Real Estate Compared to Its Major Alternatives

The final causal factor has been the superior financial performance over the past decade or longer of real properties around the world, and especially in the United States, compared to stocks and bonds, plus increased transparency and new investment vehicles in real estate itself—including REITs and commercial mortgage–backed securities.

The attraction of each asset class to investors is always a matter of its relative performance compared to the alternatives. Real estate's risk-adjusted return on investments has been better than those of most stocks and bonds over a considerable period, starting around 1990. A key reason is that the collapse of property prices in and after 1990 overshot the mark as investors avoided real estate like the plague. That reaction made many properties that still had significant potential earning power—at least in the future—egregiously underpriced. Therefore, over the next decade, such real estate properties provided much higher yields against the low prices paid for them than alternative investments in stocks and bonds. In addition, real estate returns had a low correlation with the returns of other types of stocks and with bonds. Therefore, adding real estate to a financial institution's portfolio reduced its volatility and added to its overall return.

Figure 2-9 shows the annual cap rates for four types of properties: apartments, industrial, office, and retail. These data were initially quarterly reports lagged by 18 months, but I have converted them into annual average capitalization rates, or cap rates, to smooth out otherwise jagged curves.[15] This graph shows that cap rates for all four major types of commercial properties moved very closely together. They all reflect a sharp increase from 1990 through 1995 and lasting until the early 2000s. The rising cap rates in that period indicate downward pressure on property prices,

FIGURE 2-9. **NCREIF CAP RATES BY PROPERTY TYPES, 1990–2006**

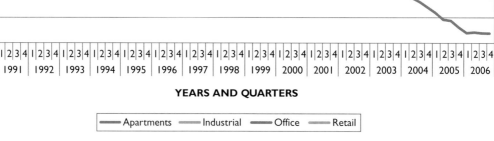

YEARS AND QUARTERS

Source: National Council of Real Estate Investment Fiduciaries.

though prices fell much more than these cap rates because net incomes from property also fell. Hence the basic income used to derive property values was much smaller than in the 1980s. The average cap rates for all four property types were between 7.29 and 8.09 percent.

How has the direct ownership of real estate properties measured by those cap rates compared to the performance of the stock market in general? Standard & Poor's 500 Index is the most comprehensive of the major stock indices, containing stocks of far more individual firms and a greater variety of types of firms than either the Dow Jones Industrial Index or the NASDAQ composite index. Figure 2-10 compares the annual returns of the S&P 500 Index stocks with the annual returns of the National Council of Real Estate Investment Fiduciaries (NCREIF) Index. The most striking thing about this chart is the tremendous volatility of the S&P 500 annual returns compared to the relatively stable movement of the NCREIF average. In reality, the NCREIF average's low volatility occurs because NCREIF's data are based on annual appraisals,

FIGURE 2-10. **NCREIF AND S&P 500 TOTAL ANNUAL RETURNS**

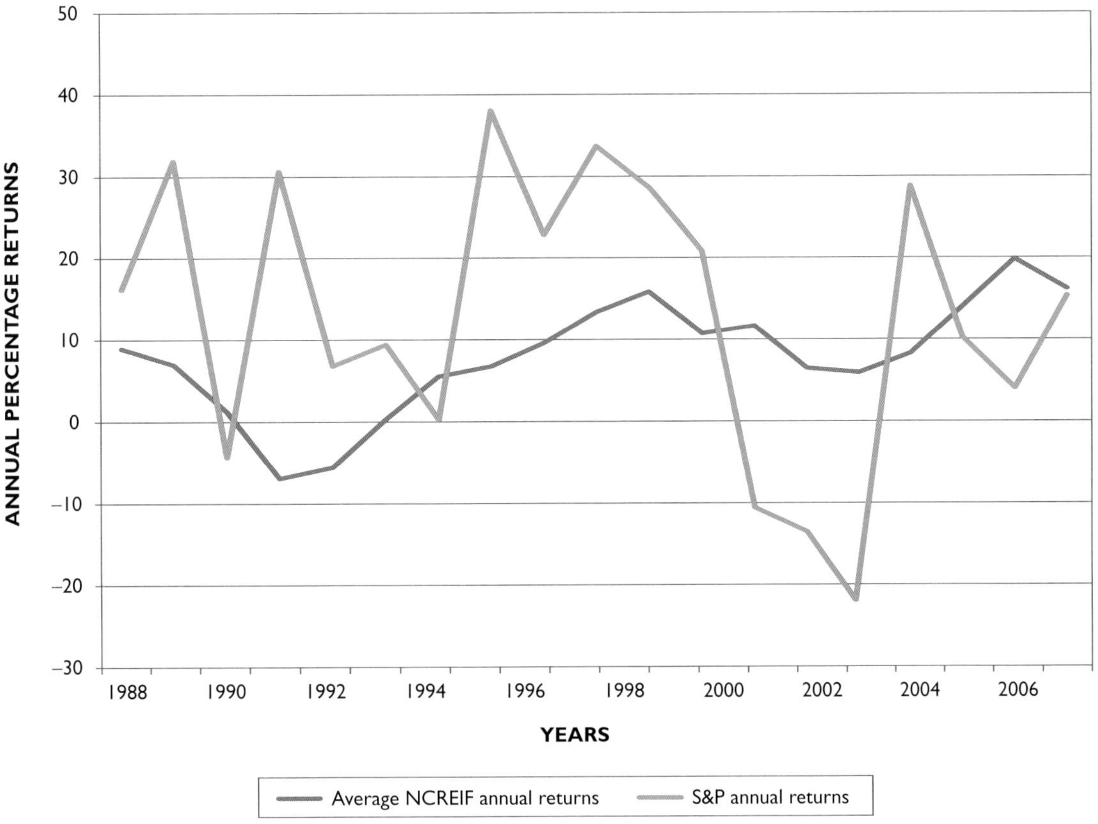

Sources: NCREIF Property Index, Standard & Poor's.

not daily changes in property market prices. Hence, their low volatility is a result of inadequate information rather than a real factor. For a better comparison, however, I have smoothed the quarterly cap rates for the four property types into annual average rates. Overall, S&P 500 annual returns ranged from –22.1 percent to +37.6 percent, averaging 13.44 percent. That was higher than the average return of 8.6 percent for the NCREIF Index.

Much more impressive has been the performance of the stocks of real estate investment trusts, especially since 1999. The National Association of Real Estate Investment Trusts (NAREIT) keeps an index of the stock prices of all equity REITs. If the base value of that index is set at 100 at the end of 1998, it was about 387 on May 22, 2007. In short, REIT stocks as a group almost quadrupled in value since the beginning of 1999. In sharp contrast, if the S&P 500 Index is also set at 100 at the end of

1998, it was about 124 on May 22, 2007. So the S&P index, after falling 36 percent in the stock market crash of 2000–2002, has recovered only to a net gain of 24 percent since early 1999, whereas REIT shares as a whole gained well over 300 percent in that same period—and a few REITs gained much more.

Repricing of Financial Risks Caused by Securitization of Loans

As explained in an earlier section, extensive securitization of loans by banks, CMBS conduits, insurance companies, mortgage originators, and everyone else lending or borrowing money has reduced both the actual and the perceived risk of lending as compared to what they were before securitization. The actual risk was reduced by greater transparency of information, more spreading of the risk of each loan among many lenders, greater liquidity in debt markets, and greater diversification of the debt holdings of individual lenders. Securitization also broadened the set of lending institutions willing to put money into real estate. But another effect of securitization has been what the Federal Reserve calls mispricing the risks involved in real estate loans.

Many lenders unfamiliar with real estate markets and what can go wrong in them have underestimated potential problems that could arise from such loans, especially in a serious economic downturn. As a result, they have not charged sufficient interest on their loans, or insisted on restrictive enough lending terms, to offset those risks appropriately. This miscalculation has reduced the cost of borrowing funds to complete real estate transactions below what it would be if adequate charges were made to compensate lenders for the inherent risks in their loans, especially risks of default. True, default rates on real estate loans have remained quite low by historical standards—except for subprime loans made in housing markets. So the extent of such mispricing of risk may not be very great, especially because most REITs have significant percentages of their total worth in the form of equity rather than debt.

One especially widespread risk involves the difficulty of restructuring loans made on a commercial property that encounters financial troubles in an economic downturn as a result of falling rents or occupancy. The ownership of loans underwriting many such properties has become extremely fragmented among many unrelated lenders. None of them is either willing or able to work with the borrowers to restructure the underlying transaction if economic difficulties arise. In that case, the borrowers will have great difficulty determining which suppliers of funds need to be consulted and worked with to rearrange loan terms and avoid bankruptcy. Although CMBS deals often designate "special servicers" who are supposed to work out such restructuring if the need arises, their abilities to react through workouts are limited by their tax liabilities and other legal restraints. Moreover, these arrange-

FIGURE 2-11. **COMPARING NAREIT INDEX TO S&P 500 INDEX, 2007**

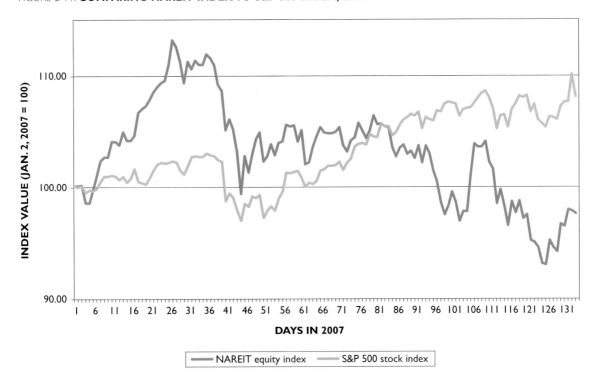

Sources: Data for NAREIT index: National Association of Real Estate Investment Trusts and Bloomberg.com; data for S&P 500 Index: finance.yahoo.com.

ments have never been tested in a really serious or widespread economic downturn that places heavy strains on many real properties. If that happens, as it has often occurred in the past, some lenders may find that they have not charged sufficient interest on their loans to make up for the delays and complexities that will hamper getting their money back entirely, if at all.

This result is caused by intense competition among capital suppliers to make deals so as to earn returns on the funds entrusted to them. Many lenders have complained that they do not have enough time to thoroughly investigate potential deals before having to decide whether they are willing to commit funds to those deals, because competitors are willing to do so. This competitive pressure helped weaken the underwriting standards involved in real estate transactions, especially at the height of the lending frenzy in 2004 and 2005. As a result, more money has been put into real estate than really should be there if risks were being adequately rewarded.

This situation may be one cause of the decline in REIT stocks relative to non–real estate stocks that has occurred since February 7, 2007, after REITs had hugely outgained the major stock indices for several years. From that date through mid-2007, the NAREIT equity index has fallen in value by 16 percent below its high point, whereas the S&P 500 stock index has risen 4.3 percent, as shown in Figure 2-11. This reversal of pricing direction by REITs has two likely causes. One is that some of the money that fled from most stocks into real estate en masse after 2000 may have started to pull back to at least some extent. The second is a fear that rising interest rates, such as the ten-year Treasury rate's exceeding 5.15 percent, may undercut the future profitability of commercial real estate in general.

AN ALTERNATIVE VIEW OF MISPRICING REAL ESTATE

Peter Linneman of the Wharton School at the University of Pennsylvania believes real estate markets have suffered from another form of mispricing caused by investor ignorance of the true nature of real estate.[16] To some observers, real estate is a hybrid investment combining two elements of return: (a) cash flows from operations and (b) possible appreciation in the market value of a long-lived asset. Linneman argues that real estate equity should be priced to yield returns somewhat below those of corporate equity stocks (which he estimates to be 6 percent per year plus inflation, or 8.5 percent recently) because those stocks produce more-volatile returns than the fixed-lease arrangements that underlie commercial real estate cash flows. In contrast, total real estate equity returns should be above the ten-year Treasury note yield "to the extent that beta (a measure of a stock's value volatility compared to the volatility of the whole stock market) exceeds zero," because Treasury yields are not volatile. This pricing would make the total expected yield on real estate equity—including cash flow yield and an allowance for inflation—about equal to the yield on BBB-rated corporate bonds. Those bonds have higher yields than ten-year Treasury bonds but lack the expected appreciation of stocks (which Linneman equates to the rate of inflation). According to Linneman, it further would imply that "the typical real estate cash flow cap rate should be 25 to 100 basis points below the ten-year Treasury yield." Therefore, "higher expected returns mean that real estate properties are underpriced" in relation to their true risk in relation to BBB corporate bonds and ten-year Treasuries, whereas "expected returns below this level indicate that real estate is overpriced" in relation to its true risk. (These conclusions follow because higher yields on real estate mean lower property prices, and lower yields mean higher property prices.)

Linneman also points out that yields on real estate equity were significantly higher than those on corporate equities or bonds in 1993, which means real properties were then underpriced by his measures. He attributes this condition to the need to attract capital into real estate from investors who were unfamiliar with real properties while the federal government had closed off traditional debt capital sources. Also, interest rates on CMBS debt securities were much higher than those on corporate bonds for the same reason.

> By the end of 1998 [however] . . . equity had tentatively entered real estate via real estate private funds and REITs, while CMBSs brought debt back into real estate with disciplined underwriting . . . Real estate cash flow cap rates varied between 8 and 10 percent from 1993 to the end of 2001. Since the end of 2001, they have steadily fallen to approximately 4.7 percent [in 2006]. In addition to this initial cash flow return, one anticipates receiving an appreciation return roughly equal to the expected rate of inflation. Over the past decade, this inflation has generally been 2 percent to 3 percent.

Linneman further contends that real estate properties (including REITs) were substantially underpriced (in relation to his view of their true risk compared to that of alternative investments) from 1990 through 2002. Just the cash flow cap rate for real estate (which does not take appreciation into account) then exceeded the total return from stocks. During the late 1990s, real estate was earning well, but investors continued to underprice it because technology stocks were producing much higher total returns in the stock market—until the crash in 2000. After that crash, real estate property prices rose, but prices of non-REIT stocks fell even further. However, "[n]ot until March 2006 did [the expected real estate cash return] approach the BBB bond yield. That is, until March 2006, real estate was underpriced in spite of four years of large and continuous declines in cap rates. . . . For the first time in 16 years, real estate is not massively underpriced."

Linneman's analysis assumes that there is one "correct" way to price real properties, which is based on its returns relative to those of BBB bonds, Treasuries, and other corporate equities. Thus, he claims he knows better than the market itself what the "true" price of real estate should be, toward which he believes the actual price will converge over the long run. I certainly agree with Linneman that the market can make huge mistakes in judgment, as its experience in the past 20 years clearly shows. I also believe his analysis of what the returns on real properties should be is reasonably accurate.

In fact, by Linneman's own analysis, real estate in the form of REITs appeared somewhat overpriced as of the date of this writing (June 21, 2007). He says that the yield on real estate should be similar to that on corporate BBB bonds, which was Treasuries (5.13 percent) plus 320 basis points, or 8.33 percent. But NAREIT says the actual yield on REITs thus far in 2007 was 3.79 percent. Linneman says the cash flow rate on real estate should be 25 to 100 basis points below the ten-year Treasury yield, which was 5.13 percent. So the real estate cash flow yield should be 4.13 to 4.88 percent, but the actual dividend yield on REITs so far in 2007 was 3.79 percent. Linneman says the appreciation rate of real estate should be about the rate of inflation, which he said was 2.5 to 3.5 percent. But according to NAREIT, REITs have been declining in price since February 7, 2007; so their price on June 21 was below what it started at in 2007. REITs did not appreciate in the first half of 2007 as a whole. All these data indicate that, by Linneman's rules, real estate in the form of REITs had too low a yield in June 2007, which means it was overpriced. Linneman agreed with this analysis and said perhaps that is why REIT prices have been falling since February 7. Thus, recent trends appear to support the plausibility of Linneman's method of estimating the "appropriate pricing" for real estate.

BASIC IMBALANCES IN WORLD COMMERCE AS A CAUSE OF THE NIAGARA OF CAPITAL

Another way to look at the origin of the Niagara of capital flowing into real estate markets is that it results from a fundamental imbalance in world trade flows during the past decade or so, plus the flight from stocks previously described. On one side of this trade imbalance is the U.S. economy, still by far the world's largest. American citizens have been importing much more than they have been exporting, thereby creating a large international trade deficit. On the other side of the imbalance are the producers of surplus capital looking for someplace where their capital can capture profitable returns. Their surpluses have resulted from exports to the United States based on low wages or oil production in their own nations, from high savings levels and low consumption growth in those nations, from the withdrawal of money from—or avoidance of—stock markets after the 2000 stock crash, from their uncertainty about world economic prospects, and from their belief that the United States is a relatively safe and secure place in which to invest. A large portion of those surpluses have been flowing into the United States and thereby helping pay for the huge trade deficits that Americans have generated.

But this imbalance cannot be sustained indefinitely because it generates certain changes in conditions that affect its continuance. In particular, continuous declines in the international trading value of the U.S. dollar—which have already been occurring for several years—will affect whether the United States can continue to import so much more than it exports when the dollar prices of its imports keep rising and those of its exports keep falling. Thus, even if the motivation for continuing huge U.S. trade deficits remains strong among Americans, on the one hand, and Chinese, Japanese, and other foreign holders of our currency, on the other hand, it is not clear that such deficits are sustainable. How they might be corrected would hugely affect the Niagara of capital. Two fundamentally different possible scenarios for ending this imbalance are discussed in detail in Chapter 8.

FIGURE 2-12. **ANNUAL PERCENTAGE CHANGE IN U.S. CPI, 1970–2006**

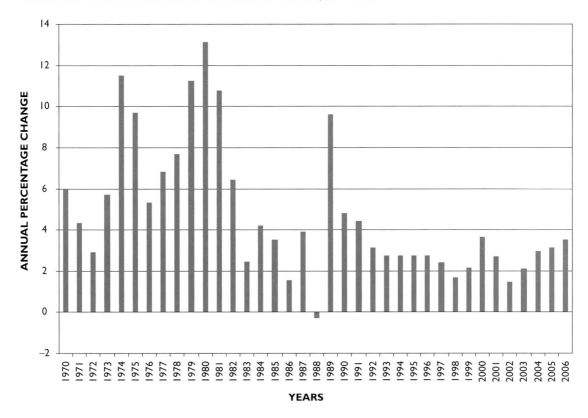

Source: Consumer price data from U.S. Bureau of Labor Statistics, Consumer Price Indexes.

WHY HASN'T ALL THAT MONEY CAUSED MORE INFLATION?

If U.S. real estate markets have been flooded by money in the past few years, why has more general inflation not occurred in the U.S. economy as a whole? After all, inflation is usually caused by rapid growth in the money supply in relation to the supply of goods that are available for purchase. Yet the largest increase in consumer prices as measured by the Bureau of Labor Statistics since 1991 was 4.23 percent, and the annualized average for 1992 through 2006 was 2.58 percent, as shown in Figure 2-12.

One reason for relatively low general inflation has been that the U.S. money supply has not grown rapidly in relation to the economy's gross domestic product. In fact, in relation to GDP, less money has been in circulation recently than earlier, as shown by Figure 2-13. In this figure, M1 consists of currency, travelers checks, demand deposits, and other checkable deposits. M2 consists of M1 plus money market mutual funds, savings deposits, small time deposits, and retail money funds.

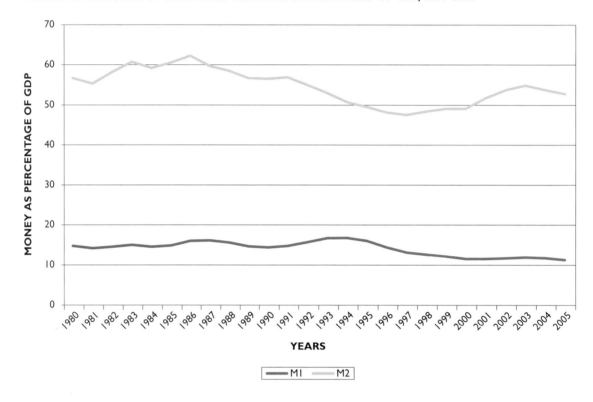

Sources: Money supply data: Federal Reserve Board, Money Stock Measures, Table 1; GDP data: Council of Economic Advisers, *Economic Indicators* (Washington, D.C.: Government Printing Office, various monthly issues).

This figure shows that M1 has remained between 10 percent and 20 percent of GDP throughout these 14 years and has actually been a lower percentage of GDP since 1994 than it was in that year. Similarly, M2 has been a lower percentage of GDP since 1991 than it was in that year, although it rose slightly from 1997 to 2003.

In contrast, the prices of real properties have experienced considerable inflation during the flood of funds into real estate. This can be shown by the decline in capitalization rates that has occurred regarding all types of commercial properties, plus the striking rise in home prices since 1990 and especially since 2000.[17] Unfortunately, no single standardized source of data is available for commercial property cap rates, which vary greatly across the country and among different property types. Therefore, I have averaged the estimated cap rates for four types of property for two years (1996 and 2005) as made by three skilled real estate experts: Real Estate Analytics, a consulting firm; the National Council of Real Estate Institutional Fiduciaries, a group of property owners who pool their operating data; and Rosen Con-

TABLE 2-3. **DECLINING CAPITALIZATION RATES FROM 1996 TO 2005**

Property Type	1996 Estimated Cap Rate	2005 Estimated Cap Rate	Derived 1996 Price	Derived 2005 Price	Percentage Change in Price
Retail	8.70	6.57	$1,149.43	$1,522.84	32.49
Apartments*	8.75	6.07	$1,142.86	$1,648.35	49.23
Industrial	8.97	7.20	$1,115.24	$1,388.89	24.54
Office	9.08	7.13	$1,101.93	$1,403.51	27.37

Source: Author's calculations using cap rate sources cited in accompanying text.

* Some observers believe that the 2005 cap rate for apartments should be as low as 4.5 percent. If that were true, the derived 2005 price would be $2,222.22, a gain in price of 94.4 percent over the 1996 price.

sulting Group, another consulting firm. The results are shown in Table 2-3. Each cap rate is used to calculate the market price of a fictional property with a net income flow (free and clear) of $100 for each of two years. Then the percentage increase in the price caused by a decline in cap rates is calculated, as shown in the table. Other estimates showing much lower cap rates in 2005 would produce greater price increases than those set forth in this table; so these are conservative estimates of price appreciation.

During the same ten years, the Consumer Price Index (CPI) for all urban households rose 24.5 percent. Thus, two of the four property types increased in price significantly more than the CPI, one increased slightly more, and one rose in price about the same. From mere cap rate compression alone, apartments rose in price much more than the other three types of property. Moreover, Table 2-3 underestimates the actual increases in commercial property prices that took place from 1996 to 2005 because it does not take into account higher income flows from such properties. If increases in net incomes from 1996 to 2005 were applied against the lower cap rates in the table, the resulting escalations in property prices would be much larger. For example, if the assumed net income of $100 per year in 1996 went up just 1 percent per year, it would have increased by 9 percent by 2005 to $109. For offices, the value of the property in 2005, using a 7.13 percent cap rate, would be $1,528.75, for a gain of 38.7 percent instead of the 27.37 percent shown in the table. Similar or even larger increases would apply to the other property types; however, I do not have accurate estimates of the amounts by which such net incomes rose during the indicated period.

In the same period, the median price of single-family homes sold in the United States soared 79 percent, according to the National Association of Realtors. And the median household income in the United States (in current dollars) rose about 27 percent. So real estate—especially residential properties—rose in price much more than consumer goods generally. This increase indicates that the increased money in the economy was more focused on real properties than on consumer products generally. That is surely one reason why overall inflation did not reflect any huge increase in the supply of money available to households and investors.[18]

CONCLUSIONS

This chapter's analysis makes clear that many different economic forces have recently operated to increase the flow of financial capital into American—and other—real estate markets, especially since 2000. Unfortunately, no reliable way exists to estimate just how much money each of the sources discussed has actually poured into real estate, partly because all those sources have also placed money in other uses and investments.

A second conclusion is that the forces influencing investors to put more money into real estate have included major shifts in the mental or psychological ways in which investors view real estate in relation to other potential uses of funds. In the 1970s, real estate was viewed as a hedge against the strong inflationary forces then affecting the U.S. economy. That view changed when the Federal Reserve attacked inflation with very high interest rates in 1981 and more-favorable tax laws were introduced. The deregulation of savings and loans plus those favorable tax laws created newly positive attitudes toward real estate investment in the 1980s up to 1986, when a new tax law took away most of those favorable aspects. Then foreign investment stimulated rising prices and more overbuilding through 1989. After the real property market crash in 1990 until about 1993, real estate was regarded as a relative pariah among types of assets by many managers of financial institutions. That hostility arose primarily because of the adverse effects upon real property values of severe property overbuilding in the late 1980s. Although real property market conditions improved greatly in the 1990s, this antipathy to real estate did not really disappear among many professional investors for pension funds and other financial institutions until the stock market experienced a similar crash of values in 2000. Then the role of pariah shifted from real estate to stocks in general, except for stocks in REITs. Many investors who saw their dot-com stocks go up in smoke without leaving any tangible assets behind decided that real estate's physically tangible nature made it seem a much more satisfactory asset class. How long this reversal of attitudes will last will be discussed in later chapters. If experience is any guide, it will take another crash in real estate markets, or a meteoric rise in the prices of non-real-estate-oriented stocks, to produce a new psychological alignment among asset classes in the minds of both amateur and professional investors.

A third conclusion is that at least five of the 13 major sources discussed in this chapter that contribute to the flood of capital into real estate are very likely to continue for some time into the future. Those five causes are the effect of low-wage Asian labor, the savings from oil sales by major oil-producing nations, a paradigm shift among investors favoring real estate, the aging populations in many developed nations, and the desire of new firms and nations to invest their earnings in the United States because of its relative political and economic security (except for the declining value of the dollar). Several other sources of the Niagara of capital are likely to diminish because of slowing U.S. growth and rising prosperity outside the United States. They include the stock market crash of 2000, the surplus savings in other nations, the Japanese yen carry trade, the superior performance of real estate, and U.S. corporate profits. In sum, the Niagara of capital into U.S. real estate is likely neither to disappear altogether nor to remain quite as strong as it has been recently.

Notes

1. Data from the Federal Reserve Board, Flow of Funds Accounts, Balance Sheets of Households and Non-Profit Organizations, June 2007 issue.

2. It is difficult to estimate how much equity capital went into "opportunity funds" created to buy distressed properties during this period. Hence, the total amount of equity capital may be underestimated somewhat. Kenneth Rosen of the University of California pointed this out to me.

3. Buzz McCoy pointed out this contrast to me, and I am thankful for his many helpful comments.

4. Jones Lang LaSalle, *Global Real Estate Capital: Moving Further and Faster* (Chicago: Jones Lang LaSalle, 2007).

5. International Monetary Fund, *World Economic Outlook: Spillovers and Cycles in the Global Economy* (Washington, D.C.: International Monetary Fund, 2007), 162. The IMF computed the international trade labor force by assigning a weight to each nation's total labor force according to the ratio of its total exports to its gross domestic product. This comparison gave rise to an increase in the international trade labor force from an index number of 125 in 1985 to an index number of 375 in 2005.

6. Central Intelligence Agency, "World, Economy," *World Factbook for 2006*, https://www.cia.gov/library/publications/the-world-factbook/index.html (accessed January 10, 2007).

7. UCLA Center for East Asian Studies Web site, http://www.isop.ucla.edu/eas/statistics/wb-population.htm (accessed May 6, 2007).

8. International Monetary Fund, *World Economic Outlook*, 172.

9. Ben S. Bernanke, "The Global Savings Glut and the U.S. Current Account Deficit" (Homer Jones Lecture, St. Louis, Missouri, April 14, 2005).

10. Data on corporate profits and gross domestic product from Council of Economic Advisers, *Economic Indicators* (Washington, D.C.: Government Printing Office), March 2007 and earlier issues of this monthly publication.

11. WRTG Economics, "Oil Price History and Analysis," http://www.wtrg.com/index.html (accessed January 8, 2007).

12. Data from Central Intelligence Agency, *World Factbook for 2006.*

13. Data from Organization for Economic Cooperation and Development, http://www.oecd.org/dataoecd/29/14/36208036.xls (accessed January 10, 2007).

14. Alan Greenspan, *The Age of Turbulence* (New York: Penguin Press: 2007), 382–84.

15. A capitalization rate, or cap rate, is computed by dividing the cash flow return on a property by its market value to find what percentage the cash flow forms of the market value. This calculation can be reversed by estimating the cap rate as a percentage, then dividing the actual cash return by the cap rate to estimate the property's market value. For example, if property X produces a net cash flow return of $1,000 per year, and the cap rate for that type of property is 6 percent, $1,000 divided by 0.06 produces a result of $16,666.67 as the estimated market value of the property. Thus, when cap rates fall, property prices rise, and vice versa.

16. Peter Linneman, "The Equitization of Real Estate," *Wharton Real Estate Review* 10, no. 2 (Fall 2006): 5–26. All quotations in this section are from this source.

17. See note 14 for an explanation of capitalization rates.

18. John McIlwain of the Urban Land Institute pointed out to me that because rents were relatively flat in this period because of so many renters switching to homeownership, the rent equivalent component of house values in the CPI calculations understated home price appreciation, thereby keeping official measures of inflation lower than they should have been.

CHAPTER THREE

Effects of the Capital Flood on Housing Markets

The capital that flooded real estate markets during the past decade had dramatic and powerful effects on housing markets. That capital generated an upward explosion of housing prices in nearly all developed nations and many emerging nations, and a boom in new housing construction and the sales of existing housing in many. This chapter explores the impacts of the capital flood on housing, especially in the United States.

HOUSING PRICE MOVEMENTS IN THE UNITED STATES

After the mid-1990s, the following five factors initially drove U.S. housing prices strongly upward:

▶ Monetary authorities pushed interest rates down and liquidity up to help avoid a recession after the stock market crash of 2000 and the terrorist acts of September 11, 2001.

▶ Housing lenders had developed efficient means of tapping into general credit markets to support home mortgages, mainly through securitization in secondary mortgage markets.

▶ General credit markets were flooded with funds because of the Niagara of capital.

▶ Competition among lenders because of their huge supplies of money pressured them to ease credit terms and make home mortgage borrowing easier, including expansion of subprime lending at high interest rates to households with poor credit records.

▶ Normal demographic changes, such as population growth and heavy immigration, generated a strong demand for housing.

When those factors began pushing housing prices upward faster than in the past, that rise generated three other factors that further accelerated home price increases:

▶ Many renter households realized they could use easier credit terms and low interest rates to buy homes formerly unavailable to them—even though the prices of housing were rising. Therefore, renters strongly pursued homeownership—a key element in the "American dream" of success.

▶ Renters' desires for homeownership were strengthened by the prospect of making financial gains from rising home prices.

▶ An unusually large number of speculators bought homes intending not to occupy them but to "flip" them for profits. This activity notably expanded the total demand for housing.

FIGURE 3-1. **U.S. MEDIAN SINGLE-FAMILY HOME PRICES IN CURRENT DOLLARS, 1968–2005**

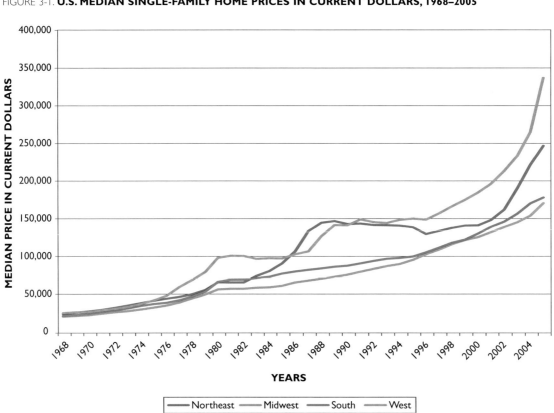

Source: National Association of Realtors data.

FIGURE 3-2. **ANNUAL PERCENTAGE CHANGES IN U.S. MEDIAN HOME PRICES, 1969–2005**

Source: National Association of Realtors data.

In Figure 3-1, data from the National Association of Realtors (NAR) show the resulting effects on housing prices for the four regions defined by the U.S. Census Bureau in all of its data: Northeast, Midwest, South, and West. Home prices rose sharply
in the West above those in other regions in the late 1970s and early 1980s and again
in the late 1980s, then flattened in the recession of the early 1990s. Prices in the
Northeast similarly rose well above those in other regions in the late 1980s but flattened in the 1990s. Prices in the Midwest and South rose at moderate rates until 1996.
After 1996, prices in all four regions accelerated, skyrocketing in the West and in the
Northeast after 2000. Figure 3-1 clearly shows the effect of the Niagara of capital on
U.S. home prices.

These regional shifts in rates of price increase are shown in more detail in
Figure 3-2. Annual percentage price increases were greatest in the inflationary period of the late 1970s, and then in the Northeast in the 1980s and the West in the late

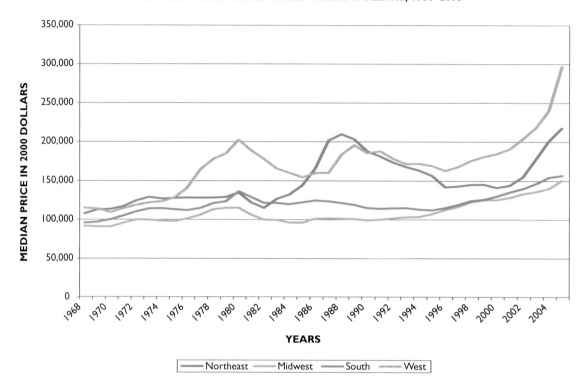

Source: National Association of Realtors data.

1980s. The big percentage price gains after 1996 in all four regions—though lower than earlier percentage gains—clearly reflect the massive inflow of financial capital into residential markets.

Figures 3-1 and 3-2 show median housing prices in current dollars; hence, they reflect the effects of inflation in general as well as specific effects from the Niagara of capital flowing into real estate. Figure 3-3, however, shows the same information in 2000 dollars, that is, corrected for inflation. In reality, almost all persons operating in U.S. housing markets—including buyers, sellers, brokers, homebuilders, lenders, and appraisers—normally deal in current dollars rather than inflation-corrected real dollars. But economists usually ignore what actual real estate practitioners do; instead, economists transform current property prices into real prices, as in Figure 3-3. In real terms, median home prices in the Midwest and South remained relatively flat from about 1973 to 1996, but then rose 50 percent by 2005. In contrast, real prices in the West soared in the late 1970s' inflation, declined in the early 1980s, rose from 1986 to 1989, declined from 1989 to 1996 in the California recession, and then skyrocketed 69 percent to 2005 under the effect of the Niagara of capital. Prices in the Northeast were flat from 1973 to 1982, then shot upward 89 percent to 1988, gradually declined by one-third to 1996, and then went up 38 percent to 2005.

Some experts prefer using home price measures based on same-unit resales (such as the Freddie Mac home price index) to avoid exaggerating price increases caused by the rising average sizes and qualities of new homes sold over time. But the NAR data based on median prices actually show lower price increases than same-unit-resale indices, so I prefer the NAR data, which are both more conservative and also available for more regions.

The data shown by the preceding figures do not reflect even higher price increases in certain major metropolitan areas across the nation, especially in California. Table 3-1 indicates median home price increases in current dollars in those metropolitan areas that had the highest median prices in 2005 (and for which data were available back to 1990). This table also shows that home prices in the nation as a whole rose twice as fast from 2000 to 2005 than they had from 1990 to 2000. National median prices increased about 50 percent in both periods, but the earlier period was twice as long as the later one. This difference clearly indicates the huge effect of the Niagara of capital into real estate after 2000—the year the stock market crashed.

THE HOUSING PRODUCTION BOOM IN THE UNITED STATES

Construction of new housing in the United States has featured great variations from one year to the next and especially from one cycle to the next, as evidenced by Figure 3-4, which is based on data from the monthly *Economic Indicators* published by the U.S. Department of Commerce. Total housing production from 1960 to 2005 fluctuated around the average of 1.809 million units (including manufactured or mobile homes) in a pattern of four definite housing cycles. All four cycles peaked in annual housing production of 2 million or more units over two to three years, including the cyclical peak in 2004 and 2005. Each of the first three high-volume peaks (1971–1973, 1977–1979, and 1984–1986) contained three years in which more than 2 million units were produced. The fourth peak (2004–2005) did not, because new production fell below 2 million in 2006. Also, after each of the three high-volume years in the first three peaks, new housing production declined sharply over the next two to five years. The total construction decline from the last 2 million–plus year averaged 40 percent, or more than 940,000 units. One reason for those declines is that all three earlier production slides were associated with economic recessions—that is, years in which U.S. real gross national product declined. That happened in 1974–1975, in 1980 and 1982,

TABLE 3-1. **MEDIAN HOME PRICE CHANGES IN METROPOLITAN AREAS AND REGIONS**

U.S. Metropolitan Areas and Census Regions	Median Price in 1990	Median Price in 2000	Median Price in 2005	% Gain 1990–2000	% Gain 2000–2005	% Gain 1990–2005
	(Current dollars, thousands)					
San Francisco–Oakland–Fremont, CA	262.2	517.1	715.7	97.22	38.41	172.96
Anaheim–Santa Ana, CA	243.6	316.2	691.9	29.80	118.82	184.03
San Diego–Carlsbad–San Marcos, CA	185.5	269.4	604.3	45.23	124.31	225.77
Honolulu, HI	325.0	295.0	590.0	(9.23)	100.00	81.54
Los Angeles–Long Beach–Santa Ana, CA	211.5	215.9	529.0	2.08	145.02	150.12
New York–Wayne–White Plains, NY-NJ	174.7	257.0	497.0	47.11	93.39	184.49
NY: Nassau-Suffolk, NY	164.9	214.0	465.2	29.78	117.38	182.11
Washington–Arlington–Alexandria, DC-VA-MD-WV	144.7	178.8	424.7	23.57	137.53	193.50
Boston–Cambridge–Quincy, MA-NH	182.3	276.1	414.0	51.45	49.95	127.10
Sacramento–Ardn–Arcade–Roseville, CA	127.7	145.2	375.9	13.70	158.88	194.36
Riverside–San Bernardino–Ontario, CA	130.4	138.6	374.2	6.29	169.99	186.96
Miami–Ft. Lauderdale–Miami Beach, FL	90.0	142.2	371.1	58.00	160.97	312.33
Reno-Sparks, NV	106.4	157.3	349.9	47.84	122.44	228.85
Seattle–Tacoma–Bellevue, WA	136.1	198.2	316.8	45.63	59.84	132.77
Las Vegas–Paradise, NV	88.6	137.4	304.7	55.08	121.76	243.91
Metropolitan Averages	**171.6**	**230.6**	**468.3**	**34.4**	**103.1**	**172.9**
Entire United States Average	**92.0**	**139.0**	**208.7**	**51.1**	**50.1**	**126.8**
Northeast Region	141.2	139.4	244.9	(1.27)	75.65	73.41
Midwest Region	74.0	123.6	168.9	67.03	36.65	128.24
South Region	85.9	128.3	176.3	49.36	37.41	105.24
West Region	139.6	183.0	300.2	31.09	64.02	115.02
Regional Average	**110.2**	**143.6**	**222.6**	**30.32**	**55.01**	**102.00**

Source: National Association of Realtors.

and in 1991. This historic record strongly implies that total U.S. housing starts will decline significantly in 2007 and 2008, and perhaps even into 2009.

After the third of these downward cyclical movements ended in 1991 with housing starts at only 1.185 million units, a long recovery began. It was stimulated in part by the Niagara of capital flowing into U.S. housing markets. From 1996 onward through 2006, new housing production was higher than the long-term average of 1.809 million units in every year, rising gradually to a peak of 2.205 million units in 2005. This housing construction boom was a major positive force in the overall recovery of the U.S. economy after the stock market crash of 2000 and the terrorist attacks of September 11, 2001.

FIGURE 3-4. **TOTAL U.S. HOUSING STARTS, 1960–2005**

FIGURE 3-4. **TOTAL U.S. HOUSING STARTS, 1960–2005**

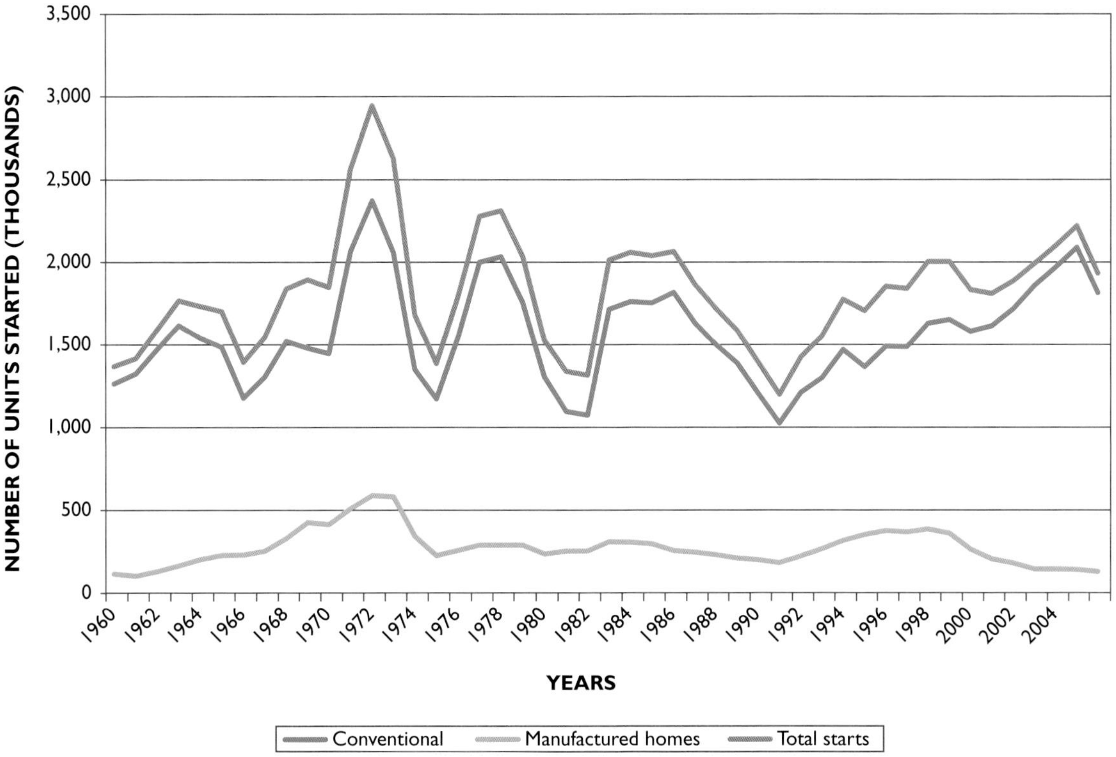

Source: U.S. Department of Commerce, *Economic Indicators.*

The flood of money available for lending to homebuyers and homebuilders was surely a major factor stimulating this production surge. Another effect of that flood was the easing of credit terms for homebuyers produced by lenders' ingenuity. Credit easing included the following arrangements:

▶ Reducing downpayment requirements to bare minimums so many homebuyers could get new homes with no more than 3 percent or even zero down. Such low downpayment requirements were initially set for veterans or other potential buyers with special qualifications, and then they were extended to more and more buyers without special qualifications.

▶ Increasing the share of total income that potential homebuyers could use to service the debt necessary to purchase a home.

▶ Using interest-only mortgages in which no amortization was charged for the first three to ten years. After that, amortization began, and monthly payments rose sharply.

▶ Using "option mortgages" under which initial payments were less than the amounts needed to cover interest alone, but the differences were added to the amount of debt owed. This arrangement allowed marginal households to buy homes more easily but required longer periods for them to pay off these loans and a sudden jump in monthly payments when full amortization began.

▶ Allowing homebuyers to self-certify their income information rather than checking that information with the employers concerned.

▶ Using floating-rate mortgages based on low, short-term interest rates for the first few years of the loan, after which the loan reverted to fixed-rate terms at higher interest rates.

As real estate economist Kenneth Rosen often observed, "Anyone breathing enough to fog a mirror could qualify to get a loan on a home." These devices also created higher risks of borrower default in case of any economic downturn or personal borrower difficulties. But lenders were so eager to put the funds they controlled to work that many did not seem worried by that possibility. After all, those funds were normally not their own money, and after they had securitized the loans they made, those funds were off their books. Taking high risks had long been typical of lenders during housing boom periods but was even more accentuated by the Niagara of capital.

Another aspect of the housing production boom of the early 2000s was the larger role in total production played by condominium units, especially those in new high-rise buildings or converted existing rental apartments. Condominiums could be smaller and therefore somewhat less costly than single-family detached units. Also, high-rise condominium units could be built on urban sites unsuitable or too small for many detached homes. Condominium units also appealed to two booming markets: households wanting to live near vibrant downtowns, and aging empty-nester baby boomers who wanted to move out of large homes they no longer needed or could no longer care for themselves. High-rise condominiums were also promoted by city governments eager to revitalize their sagging downtown business districts. Consequently, the share of condominiums in total multifamily construction rose notably after 2000, especially in a few markets like Miami and Las Vegas.

One more factor is that the percentage of homebuyers who were investors— that is, speculators seeking from the start to resell at a profit the homes they bought— rose to record levels in many markets in 2005 and 2006, approaching one-third of total sales, according to an estimate by David Seiders, chief economist for the National Association of Home Builders. This factor contributed to the immense increase in the number of single-family homes sold annually: from 3.2 million in 2000 to 7.1 million in 2005—a rise of 122 percent in five years. It also caused annual home sales to get ahead of true demographic demand, setting the stage for a large decline in new-home construction and significant increases in foreclosures after 2005, when the housing market peaked.

HOUSING PRICE MOVEMENTS OUTSIDE THE UNITED STATES

Similarly spectacular price increases occurred in other nations around the globe, especially after 2000. However, the flood of capital into real estate markets began to get underway on a global basis after 1980. Therefore, this discussion of the effects of that flood upon world housing markets will begin in 1980, before the real Niagara of capital.

The *Economist* began tracking global housing prices in 2002, but its reporters dug up data on 13 nations that went back to 1980. The magazine has returned to the subject of global housing prices many times since then and has updated its price measurements on a roughly annual basis. By reinterpreting data gathered by that magazine from 20 nations, I have drawn up three graphs that show how housing prices moved in 12 countries—plus the United States—for which data go back to 1980 (Figures 3-5, 3-6, and 3-7).

FIGURE 3-5. **PERCENTAGE INCREASES IN EUROPEAN, CANADIAN, AND U.S. HOUSING PRICES, 1980–2001**

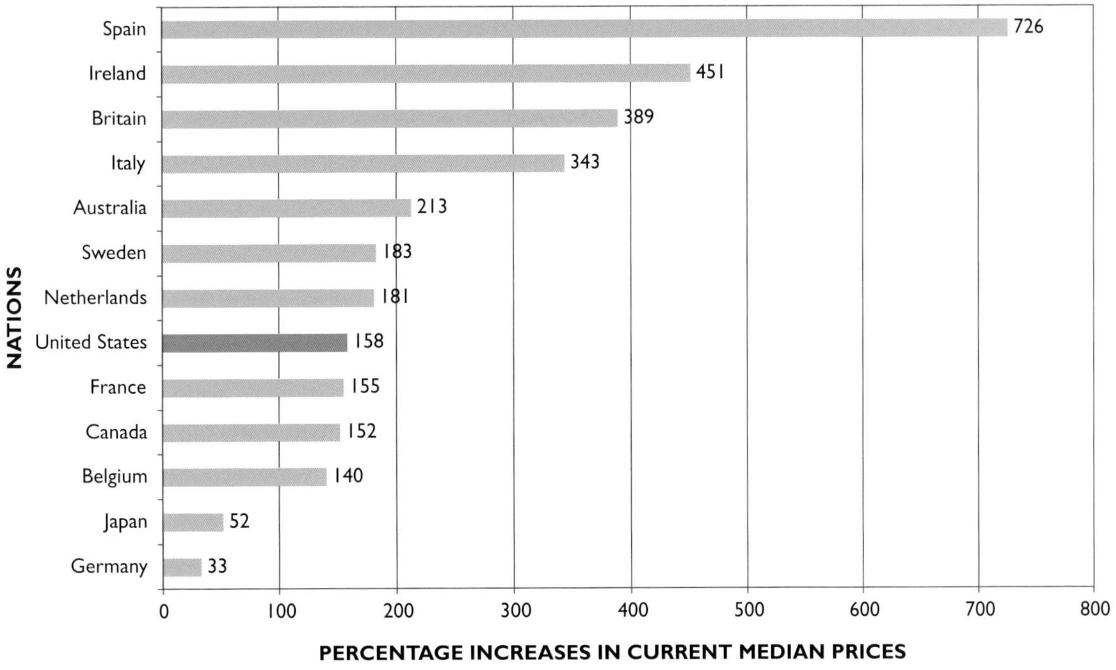

PERCENTAGE INCREASES IN CURRENT MEDIAN PRICES

Source: The *Economist* surveys.

FIGURE 3-6. **PERCENTAGE INCREASES IN EUROPEAN, CANADIAN, AND U.S. HOUSING PRICES, 2001–2006**

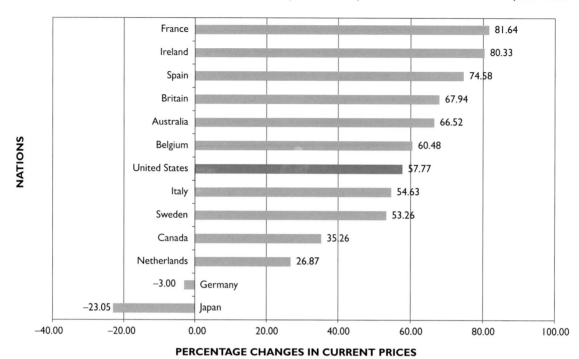

PERCENTAGE CHANGES IN CURRENT PRICES

Source: The *Economist* surveys.

Figure 3-5 covers the 21 years from 1980 to 2001. It shows that home prices rose most in Spain, Ireland, Britain, and Italy—far outpacing price changes in the other nine nations. Spanish prices rose 726 percent in just 21 years, which is a compound annual growth rate of 10.6 percent. In the United States during the same period, median home prices rose at a compound annual rate of 9.0 percent. The U.S. data supplied by the *Economist*, however, indicated faster American home price increases than data provided by the U.S. National Association of Realtors. The latter source showed a compound annual growth rate of only 4.2 percent in the same 21 years (during which national median home prices measured by NAR rose 137 percent).

Figure 3-6 shows percentage price increases in housing from 2001 to 2006 for the same nations. In this period, price increases were rapid in nine nations, including the United States. The compound annual growth rates for these nine nations ranged from a low of 8.5 percent in Sweden to a high of 12.7 percent in France, with the United States at 9.6 percent. (NAR data for the same period produced a U.S. compound annual growth rate of 6.97 percent.)

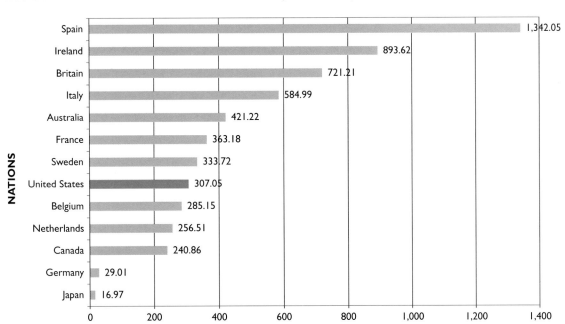

FIGURE 3-7. **PERCENTAGE INCREASES IN EUROPEAN, CANADIAN, AND U.S. HOUSING PRICES, 1980–2006**

PERCENTAGE INCREASES IN CURRENT MEDIAN PRICES

Source: The *Economist* surveys.

Figure 3-7 covers the entire period from 1980 to 2006 and indicates that housing prices in that overall period rose most in Spain, mainly because Spain had the biggest initial spurt from 1980 to 2001. From 2001 to 2006, Spain's home prices rose 60 percent, but Ireland's prices soared 80 percent and those in France rose 81 percent. Overall, housing prices in 7 of the 13 nations shown in Figure 3-7 increased more from 1980 to 2006 than those in the United States. In Spain, Ireland, and Britain, housing prices increased more than twice as much as those in the United States, according to the *Economist*'s data. (However, median housing prices in the United States as tracked by NAR rose 232 percent from 1980 to 2006, as compared with the 307 percent estimated by the *Economist*.) Even if the data on which this figure is based are somewhat inaccurate, housing prices in many nations around the world clearly zoomed upward from 1980 to 2006—especially from 2001 to 2006—even more than those in the United States.

In a separate analysis, I compared percentage increases in European housing prices from 1980 to 2001 with percentage increases in the populations of the same nations from 1980 to 2000. No statistically significant relationship existed between population growth rates and rates of housing price increases in 13 nations; the correlation between those two sets of data was –18.8. Italy had the slowest population growth rate in this period but the fourth-highest housing price increase rate; Canada had the second-highest population growth rate but the 11th-highest rate of housing price increases. So rising home prices were not caused by rising populations, although these data do not count transient and tourist visitors, who surely played a role in raising the seasonal demand for housing in Spain.

DID HOUSING CONSTRUCTION BOOMS OCCUR RECENTLY OUTSIDE THE UNITED STATES?

Whether foreign housing markets experienced a construction boom like that in the United States during the big housing price increases from 2000 to 2006 is difficult to determine from available statistics. I have been able to gather the following evidence:

▶ In Canada, new housing construction averaged 148,569 units from 1990 to 1999 but rose to an average of 199,460 from 2000 to 2005—an increase of 34.2 percent. This increase indicates some positive effect of the Niagara of capital in Canada.

▶ A tabulation of housing starts among 21 mainly European nations with 529 million residents and 227.5 million dwelling units in the years from 2000 to 2003 (different years for each nation) showed that 18.2 million units were constructed in 1993 and 18.9 million in 1997, but only 15.4 million in both 2001 and 2003.[1] These data do not reflect any housing construction boom in most of these mainly European nations.

▶ As shown in Figure 3-8, French housing starts in total declined gradually from a high of 419,000 units in 1980 to a low of 255,000 in 1993 (including both individual units and collective units, such as apartments, hotels, and nursing homes).[2] Annual starts then rose gradually to between 300,000 and 325,000 from 1998 and 2003, but shot upward in 2004 and 2005, reaching 410,000, evidencing a moderate production response to more financial capital in those two years.

▶ Specific data on housing units completed in the entire United Kingdom show that the number of units built each year remained relatively flat from 1990 through 2003, averaging 186,690. In the next three years, starts rose to an average of 203,618, a gain of 9 percent. That increase indicates a boomlet but is not clear evidence of a strong effect from money inflows to the United Kingdom's housing market.[3]

▶ Spain's population and housing stock rose. The estimates shown in Table 3-2 confirm that Spain had a big housing construction boom from 2001 to 2006—building more new units each year than France, Germany, and Italy combined. From 1998 through 2005, Spain added 3.5 million new dwelling units, culminating in a record 730,000 in 2005. Spain then added an estimated 815,000 more in 2006. This boom was

FIGURE 3-8. **HOUSING STARTS IN FRANCE, 1980–2005**

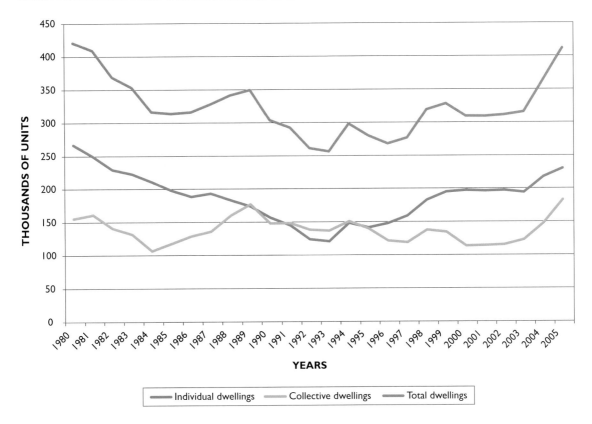

Source: French Ministry of Transportation, Infrastructure, Tourism, and the Sea, Office of Economics, Statistics, and Forward Planning, http://www.insee.fr/en/ffc/chifcle_fiche.asp?ref_id=NATTEF11401&tab_id=233 (accessed January 22, 2007).

greatly influenced by many foreign households buying second homes in Spain's sunny climate. Hence, it was surely not caused entirely by the flood of capital into real estate but was undoubtedly assisted by that flow of funds.[4]

▶ In Japan, the number of new housing units built in 1997 was 1.341 million. In every year from 1990 through 1996, more units than that were built, and in every year from 1998 through 2006, fewer units than that were built, according to the Ministry of Land, Infrastructure, and Transport—not evidencing a housing construction boom in Japan produced by large capital inflows after 2000.

▶ In Sweden, housing starts ranged from 12,050 units in 1997 to 19,100 in 2002, then rose rapidly to 22,060 in 2003, 27,500 in 2004, 32,000 in 2005, and 44,900 in 2006.

TABLE 3-2. **INCREASES IN SPANISH POPULATION AND HOUSING STOCK, 1981–2006**

Year	Population	Housing Unit Stock	Numeric Change in Housing Units	Average Annual Unit Change
1981	37,800,000 (est.)	14,742,000	—	—
1991	38,872,268	16,948,308	2,206,308	220,630
2001	40,847,341	20,823,369	3,875,061	387,506
2006	43,739,556	24,056,755 (est.)	3,233,386	646,677

Sources: Spain's populations in 2001 and 1991 and number of housing units in 2001: Instituto Nacional de Estadistica, *Censos de Poblacion y Viviendas 2001*, http://www.ine.es/revistas/cifraine/cifine_cen01.pdf; number of dwellings per 1,000 residents used to calculate the number of housing units in 1981 and 1991: Organization for Economic Cooperation and Development, "Economic Survey of Spain, 2005: Stabilizing the Housing Market," http://oecd.org/dataoecd/53/3/34586052.pdf (both sources accessed January 14, 2007); number of dwelling units per 1,000 residents for 2006 (550, compared with 510 in 2001) estimated by the author.

This surge is consistent with a significant effect from inflows of financial capital as part of the Niagara of capital.[5]

More-comprehensive housing production data going back to 1990 are not readily available for the other nations mentioned.

WHY DIDN'T MASSIVE CAPITAL INFLOWS INCREASE THE NUMBER OF HOUSING UNITS BUILT?

In pure economic theory, if the demand for a product rises enough to drive up its price, then the profitability of creating that product increases. Such higher profitability normally motivates manufacturers to create more of such a product. Sooner or later, the quantity created rises enough to drive the product's price back down close to the actual cost of building the product, thereby reducing profitability. Why did that not happen to housing? When the demand for housing rose because so many households wanted to invest capital in something other than the stock market, why did American homebuilders not just create enough new housing to meet that demand without the huge increase in prices we have experienced? As will be shown, that is what happened in all other major surges in housing demand after World War II.

The answer to that question involves several factors. First, building a dwelling unit is a very complicated process. It requires combining several quite different ingredients, all initially owned by different parties and subject to separate legal regulations and restrictions. The basic elements include land; infrastructures, such as streets, water systems, electric systems, and sewerage systems; building materials;

labor; financing; internal systems, such as plumbing, electricity, air conditioning, heating, and lighting; and the services of specialists, such as architects and interior designers. Every local government has its own regulations governing the conditions under which these elements can be put together, how they should be put together, how they ought to relate to each other, and who can occupy the resulting dwelling. The process is so complex that at least several months are normally required to build a dwelling unit even after all the legal permissions have been acquired and the financing arranged.

The second factor is that many local governments do not want large increases in the number of dwelling units built within their boundaries; thus, they actively create barriers to new construction. This factor is often the result of political pressure from homeowning residents. As noted earlier, they often do not want much or any new construction in their communities—especially new, lower-cost housing units. They typically fear such housing would cause possible declines in the prices of their existing homes, which are their principal financial assets. The barriers they support range from outright moratoria on new building to zoning requirements concerning minimum lot sizes, minimum setbacks of dwellings from the edges of lots, onerous requirements about what building materials can be used, restriction of wages to those paid to union workers, and rules against cutting down trees. Obtaining local government permission to build a dwelling may take many months even when the plans meet all local requirements. All of these barriers add to the cost of creating dwellings in such communities.

A striking example of such restrictions concerns land uses in the San Francisco Bay Area—which contains the United States' most expensive housing. The city of San Francisco has a population density of more than 16,900 persons per square mile within its 46.7 square miles; it is one of the most densely populated cities in America. Almost all of its hilly terrain is covered with closely packed dwelling units. In contrast, the other eight counties in the Bay Area are all developed at very low densities. In all but Sonoma and Solano counties, which are the farthest from downtown San Francisco and therefore just beginning to be developed, low density exists mainly because so much land has been legally set aside as open space or as terrain used to collect water for city uses. This situation can be seen in Table 3-3.

The city and county of San Francisco (which are identical) contain 11.4 percent of the Bay Area's total population in 0.7 percent of its area. Marin County, just north of San Francisco across the Golden Gate Bridge, has a population density lower than that of the entire state of Maryland, although Maryland contains 18.8 times as much land area. If all of the Bay Area outside San Francisco were settled at only one-fourth the density of San Francisco, or 4,228 persons per square mile (which is lower than

TABLE 3-3. **BAY AREA DEVELOPMENT**

Bay Area County	Land Area in Square Miles	Percentage of Total	Population in 2003	Percentage of Total	Persons per Square Mile
Alameda	737.6	10.7	1,495,400	21.4	2,027.4
Contra Costa	719.9	10.4	1,003,800	14.4	1,394.4
Marin	519.8	7.5	250,300	3.6	481.5
Napa	753.7	10.9	130,900	1.9	173.7
San Francisco	46.7	0.7	786,900	11.3	16,850.1
San Mateo	449.1	6.5	712,800	10.2	1,587.2
Santa Clara	1,290.7	18.6	1,723,900	24.6	1,335.6
Solano	829.2	12.0	416,500	6.0	502.3
Sonoma	1,575.9	22.8	473,300	6.8	300.3
Totals	**6,922.6**	**100.0**	**6,993,800**	**100.0**	**1,010.3**
Less San Francisco	6,875.9	99.3	6,206,900	88.7	902.7

Source: California Statistical Abstract for 2004, Table A-1, and Table B-3, http://www.dof.ca.gov/HTML/FS_DATA/STAT-ABS/documents/StatAbstrct04www.pdf (accessed August 19, 2007).

the density of all Los Angeles suburbs combined), it would have a population of 29.1 million persons, rather than 6.9 million. But Bay Area residents have assiduously prevented anything remotely approaching such development in the name of protecting open space—and, incidentally, making the prices of homes in that area the highest in the nation.

A third reason why housing production did not explode when prices rose so greatly is a shortage of available land lying close to existing centers of employment or to very highly valued amenities. Some housing sites are regarded as much more desirable than others because of their locations. When the demand for housing rises strongly, the prices of the most-favorable sites are bid up much higher than the prices of less-favorable sites. That is why housing sites along the Pacific Ocean in California or along the Atlantic Ocean in Florida are much more expensive than sites farther inland, other things being equal. It also helps explain why housing in metropolitan areas that can expand outward in all directions from an established downtown center (as in Atlanta, Dallas, or the Twin Cities) is generally less expensive than housing that is prevented from doing so by water or mountainous terrain or a national border (as in San Diego, Seattle, or Chicago).

A fourth reason why rising housing prices did not call forth immense increases in new construction is that the homebuilding industry focuses on building new units that provide the greatest profit margins. Hence homebuilders usually create new units that are larger, equipped with more amenities, and higher in price than most existing units. Their profit percentages are higher on such units than on smaller, less luxurious units. Yet the latter are precisely the type that most households suffering from housing affordability problems most need.

Moreover, when demand for the material used in building homes rises across the globe, the costs of constructing homes also rises. This happened after 2000, in spite of the stock market crash, because Chinese demand for steel and concrete and other building materials expanded rapidly as investors increased China's production facilities and the Chinese government made preparations for the forthcoming Olympics in Beijing. These developments, plus intense competition for skilled labor among workers employed by homebuilders, drove up the costs of building all types of real estate, including homes and especially apartments. That increased cost limited the ability of homebuilders to rapidly expand the supply of housing in response to increases in demand after 2000. The same development increased the tendency for homebuilders to raise their prices in the face of strong demand.

Another aspect of homebuilding that limited the supply response to rising prices is the tendency of large-scale builders to stop building when current prices start to decline. When prices had risen significantly after 2000, those builders reacted by getting hold of larger land supplies, but they tended not to construct actual units until they had received specific orders. A study by the Harvard Center for Textile and Apparel Research found that among builders who created 500 or more units in 2004, 73 percent of the units built were sold before construction began.[6] If the overall response of the market drove prices downward, these builders stopped construction to limit their potential losses. This tendency by large-scale builders, who account for about one-fourth of all new American homes, has prevented— and may continue to prevent—increases in total supply large enough to drive home prices downward significantly.

A final reason why housing supplies have not risen enough to prevent home prices from rising—as of 2007—is the behavior of investors who buy homes not to occupy them but to speculate on further increases in housing prices. Such investors also tend to withdraw from the market whenever home prices start downward. David Seiders, the chief economist for the National Association of Home Builders, estimated that about one-third of the housing market in 2005 and 2006 consisted of such investors. But they are now sitting on the sidelines because they do not expect prices to keep on rising as they have in the recent past.[7] In some areas, if these speculators are a high percentage of all homebuyers and they abandon their investments when they cannot resell them at a profit, then they may overload the local market with empty units foreclosed by lenders, putting downward pressure on housing prices. In all preceding housing-demand surges, investor demand played a much smaller role—almost all demand came from households wanting to occupy the homes they bought.

All the preceding factors worked together to translate the high demand for housing generated by both demographic forces and the Niagara of capital more into increased prices than expanded construction volumes. Although housing production did rise sharply from 1.185 million in 1991 to 2.205 million in 2005, an increase of 86 percent in 14 years, median home prices for the entire United States rose from $97,100 to $207,000—a gain of 113.2 percent—in the same period. This finding contrasts remarkably with the relationships between home construction volumes and home prices in previous housing-demand surges since World War II. From 1966 to 1972, housing starts (including mobile homes) shot upward from 1.382 million to 2.933 million, or by 112.2 percent in six years, while median home prices in current dollars rose from $17,414 to $26,700—a gain of 53.3 percent. Similarly, from 1975 to 1978, in the midst of severe general inflation, housing starts rose from 1.373 million to 2.246 million, or by 63.5 percent in three years; whereas median home prices escalated from $35,300 to $48,700, or by 37.9 percent. A third surge in housing production occurred from 1982 to1986, when starts soared 54.6 percent from 1.325 million to 2.049 million, but median prices rose only 18.4 percent from $67,800 to $80,300. Thus, in all previous major housing-construction surges after World War II, the number of units built rose much more in percentage terms than the prices of all housing units sold in current dollars. But the opposite happened from 1991 to 2005—thanks in large part to the Niagara of capital flows in that period and the easy credit terms it generated.

THE HOMEOWNER WEALTH ENRICHMENT EFFECTS OF RISING U.S. HOME PRICES

One of the most important effects of rising home prices in the United States has been the enrichment of homeowners through substantial growth in their home equities. This increase in homeowner equity can be estimated in two ways. One is by acquiring data on household balance sheets from the Federal Reserve Board's *Flow of Funds Accounts of the United States*. These data include the Fed's annual estimates of household real estate holdings and mortgage debts. Further information about the amount of secondary mortgage debt and home-equity lending can be derived from the Federal Deposit Insurance Corporation's Web site, which sets forth measures of those two types of borrowing against homeowners' total mortgage debt. By combining these two sources of data, I have estimated the total amount of homeowners' equity and borrowing for the years 1990, 1995, 2000, and the third quarter (Q3) of 2006 (see Table 3-4). The total value of real estate held by households rose from $6.608 trillion

TABLE 3-4. **HOME WEALTH ANALYSIS**

Billions of Current Dollars

Item	1990	1995	2000	2006 Q3	1990–1995	1995–2000	2000–2006
Value of household real estate	6,608.50	7,631.10	11,450.70	20,480.50	1,022.60	3,819.60	9,029.80
Percentage increase		15.47	50.05	78.86	204.52	763.92	1,504.97
Household mortgage debt	2,641.60	3,252.00	4,906.50	8,879.30	610.40	1,654.50	3,972.80
Percentage increase		23.11	50.88	11.11			
As percent of total real estate value	39.97	42.62	42.85	43.36	59.69	43.32	44.00
Net household real estate equity	3,966.90	4,379.10	6,544.20	11,601.20	412.20	2,165.10	5,057.00
Percentage increase		10.39	49.44	1.27			
Home-equity loans	234.31	288.45	496.05	1,804.27	54.14	207.59	1,308.23
Percentage increase		23.11	71.97	(4.61)			
As percent of household mortgages	8.87	8.87	10.11	20.32			
Other mortgage debt	158.23	194.79	374.37	712.12	36.56	179.57	337.75
Percentage increase		23.11	92.18	20.26			
As percent of household mortgages	5.99	5.99	7.63	8.02			
Net net equity after all debt removed	3,574.36	3,895.85	5,673.79	9,084.81	321.49	1,777.93	3,411.02
Percentage increase		8.99	45.64	1.26	64.30	355.59	568.50
Net equity as percent of real estate value	54.09	51.05	49.55	44.36	31.44	46.55	37.78
All debt as percent of real estate	45.91	48.95	50.45	55.64	68.56	53.45	62.22

Sources: Federal Reserve Board, *Flow of Funds Accounts of the United States*, various years, and Federal Deposit Insurance Corporation.

in 1990 to $7.631 trillion in 1995, a 15.5 percent increase in five years. In the next five years, however, that total rose to $11.451 trillion, a 50 percent increase. Then, in the six years from 2000 to 2006, the value of household real estate rose to $20.480 trillion—a gain of $9.029 trillion, or 78.9 percent. All these immense increases in gross wealth were caused by rising home prices. Because those prices rose much faster from 2000 to 2006 than formerly, homeowners' gross equity did also.

Much of this huge gain in home values was offset by owner borrowing against those same homes, both to buy them in the first place, and then to borrow against their remaining net equity to finance nonhousing consumption. Table 3-4 shows that total borrowing against home equity rose from 45.9 percent of household real estate in 1990 to 55.6 percent in the third quarter of 2006, which I assume also applies in the fourth quarter. That rise in debt coverage reflects (a) lower-downpayment purchases after 2000, thanks to easier credit terms—which necessitated bigger mortgages; (b) bigger mortgages required to buy more-expensive homes; and (c) more borrowing against home equities to finance other types of consumption. Even after all that greater borrowing, net free-and-clear homeowner equities increased by $3.411 trillion from 2000 to 2006, to a total of $9.085 trillion. That amount was larger than the total gross market value of all household real estate in 1990.

A second method of calculating increases in homeowner equity bases estimates of home values on NAR measures of home prices. If the median prices reported by NAR for each year are taken to be market prices of all the housing in the United States, new and old, including those millions that were not sold, then the total value of owner-occupied homes can be computed by multiplying those national median prices by the number of owner-occupied units in each year. I also estimated the mortgage debt against those values by using the same percentages of mortgage and home-equity debt against total lending as in the first analysis. This approach (see Table 3-5) results in lower estimates of homeowner equity buildup than did the estimates based on Federal Reserve Board data. The total market value of household real estate for 2005 (assuming it consists entirely of homes) is estimated as $18.1 trillion, compared with the $20.48 trillion from Federal Reserve data, or 12 percent lower. This disparity results in part because households own some real estate other than their homes—such as housing units they rent out, retail stores, or their places of business—a fact captured by the Federal Reserve data but not by my NAR estimation method. But the same basic idea emerges from both approaches: rising home values produced enormous increases in both gross and net wealth for American homeowners.

CORRECTING THE ANALYSIS FOR CHANGES IN HOUSEHOLD NUMBERS, INFLATION, AND BORROWING

Using the Federal Reserve data, the preceding analysis shows an increase in the market value of household real estate assets from $6.608 trillion in 1990 to $20.480 trillion in 2006—a gain of 210 percent in 16 years. But these figures exaggerate the net gain in homeowner wealth because (a) more homeowners existed in 2006 than in 1990; (b) homeowners borrowed against the market values of their homes, reducing their net equities; and (c) general inflation was responsible for some of the increase in home prices from 1990 to 2006. Corrections are necessary to account for these effects.

In 1990, according to the U.S. Census, America had 59.0 million homeowning households. By 2005, according to the American Housing Survey, homeowners reached 74.9 million, 2.7 million more than in the 2003 American Housing Survey. I estimated

TABLE 3-5. **HOME WEALTH ANALYSIS BASED ON NAR DATA**

Year	Total Housing Units	Owner Percentage	Owner-Occupied Homes	National Median NAR Home Value	Total Real Estate Gross Value	Percent All Debt on Homes	Debt Amount	Net Equity
1990	106,983,000	56.7	60,659,361	92,000	$5,580,661,212,000	45.90	$2,561,523,496,308	$3,019,137,715,692
1992	112,655,000	57.5	64,776,625	110,500	$7,157,817,062,500	48.95	$3,503,751,452,094	$3,654,065,610,406
2000	119,628,000	59.6	71,298,288	139,000	$9,910,462,032,000	50.45	$4,999,828,095,144	$4,910,633,936,856
2005	126,864,000	69.0	87,536,160	207,000	$18,119,985,120,000	55.64	$10,081,959,720,768	$8,038,025,399,232

Source: National Association of Realtors.

the number of 2006 homeowners by dividing that gain in half and adding it to the 2005 total. That calculation yields a total of approximately 76.4 million homeowners in 2006. If the $6.6 trillion total value of real estate held by homeowners in 1990 is divided by 59.0 million homeowners, the result shows the average homeowner in 1990 had a home valued at $111,864. That figure compares with the average home-owner's home value of $268,062 in 2006. In 1990, homeowners had borrowed an average of 45.9 percent against their home values, leaving them with an average net equity of $60,519 in that year. In 2006, homeowners had borrowed an average of 55.6 percent against their home, leaving them with an average net equity of $119,020 in that year.

All those numbers are in current dollars. The Consumer Price Index (using 1982–1984 prices as equal to 100) for all urban consumers was 130.7 in 1990 and 201.6 in 2006. So consumer prices (not home prices, but a measure of general infla-tion) rose 54.25 percent from 1990 to 2006. Therefore, the value of the average 1990 homeowner's net equity in 1990 should be increased to $93,350 in 2006 dollars. This adjustment indicates that the net equity value of homeowners, corrected for infla-tion, rose by $25,670, or 27.5 percent, from 1990 to 2006.

But 2006 homeowners had also borrowed more against their home equities than had 1990 homeowners. The 2006 owners borrowed 55.6 percent, or $149,042 in 2006 dollars. The 1990 owners had borrowed an average of 45.9 percent, or $51,381 in 1990 dollars. Converting that amount into 2006 dollars makes it $79,199. So 2006 homeowners had borrowed in 2006 dollars an average of $69,843 more against their home equities ($149,042 compared with $79,199) than 1990 homeowners had borrowed against their homes. If that benefit is added to the gain in net equity, the 2006 homeowners benefited by a total of $189,043 (their remaining net equity of $119,200 plus the extra borrowing of $69,843 they had made), compared with a corresponding benefit to 1990 homeowners of $93,350. Thus, when all the financial adjusting is done, the average 2006 homeowner had gained a net benefit in 2006—in 2006 dollars—from higher housing prices almost exactly double the benefit gained in 1990 by the average 1990 homeowner. These complicated calculations prove that rising home prices significantly benefited homeowners by increasing their true wealth, even after allowing for inflation and the increased number of homeowners.

The increased borrowing by homeowners in 2006 also created a corresponding increase in their debts, which they eventually would have to repay. Taking that increased debt into account greatly reduces the net advantage of homeownership in 2006 compared with that in 1990, at least in real terms. As I noted earlier, however, most homeowners do not think in real terms but in current dollars when calculating their profits from homeownership. Hence, in their own minds, they had profited sizably from homeownership, although they had to borrow more against their higher home values to realize that gain.

This homeownership benefit is even more significant when looked at in aggregate terms—that is, taking all homeowners and other households into account. In 2000, according to the U.S. Census Bureau, America had 69.816 million homeowning households, and their net equity in real estate (after subtracting their home mortgages and other borrowing against their homes) was $6.544 trillion, according to the Federal Reserve Board. By 2006, the net equity of households in real estate reported by the Federal Reserve Board had risen to $10.945 trillion. Correcting for inflation would increase the 2000 value of households' net equity to $7.663 trillion, resulting in a net gain from 2000 to 2006 of $3.282 trillion, or 42.8 percent. True, more homeowning households existed in 2006 than in 2000, but for the moment, I will focus on aggregate totals, not totals per homeowning household.

The Federal Reserve Board flow of funds analysis shows that the net worth of all households—their total assets minus their total liabilities—rose from $41.770 trillion in 2000 to $55.626 trillion in 2006, a gain of $13.86 trillion, or 33 percent. However, the 2000 net worth figure should be raised by 17.1 percent to correct for inflation and make it comparable to the 2006 figure. That adjustment makes the 2000 net worth $48.912 trillion and reduces the total gain in net households' worth in 2006 dollars to $6.71 trillion, or 13.7 percent. But, as noted, homeowners alone gained a net increase in equity in their homes of $3.282 trillion. That was equal to 48.9 percent of the total gain in net worth of all U.S. households—including both renters and homeowners—from 2000 to 2006 (in 2006 dollars). Thus, *increases in total homeowner wealth from 2000 to 2006—resulting directly from rising home prices—accounted for almost half of the total gain in all American households' net worth in that period.* Yet even in 2006, homeowners' net equity in their homes was only 19.7 percent of the total net worth of all households, including both owners and renters. The main reason for this seemingly inconsistent result is that households sustained significant losses in corporate equities and mutual fund shares from 2000 to 2002. They had not yet made up for those losses by the end of 2006. The total value of households' (and nonprofit organizations') holdings of such stocks fell from $10.491 trillion in 2000 to $6.657 trillion in 2002 and had recovered only to $10.445 trillion by the end of 2006.

Thus, increases in the net worth of homeowners' wealth in their homes from 2000 to 2006 saved the entire household sector from more serious losses in the stock market and cushioned their combined net worth from 2000 to 2006. This homeowner equity enabled households to continue relatively high levels of general consumption, supporting the overall growth of the American economy. Of course, those increases in net equity wealth generated by homes directly benefited homeowners only, leaving the 31 percent of all American households who were renters out in the cold, so to speak. Yet by preventing the entire household sector from suffering major economic losses, the enrichment of homeowners resulting from rising home prices sustained the prosperity of the whole American economy. This is certainly an important social benefit of rising home prices, although it accrued directly to only about two-thirds of all American households. For the other one-third, rising home prices reduced their economic welfare considerably.

OTHER SIGNIFICANT EFFECTS OF INCREASED HOMEOWNER WEALTH FROM RISING HOME PRICES

Other repercussions on the American economy and American housing markets of these big increases in wealth are discussed in the following sections.

Increasing the Desire for Homeownership

Rising home prices greatly intensified the already strong desire of American households who did not own their own homes to become homeowners. They were motivated by the desires both to acquire ownership before prices got any higher and to benefit subsequently from rising equities. As a result, the percentage of households who are homeowners rose notably from 64.0 in 1990 to 64.8 percent in 1995, 67.2 percent in 2000, and 69.0 percent in 2006.

Stimulating Personal Consumption Based on Borrowing Against Home Equities

The ability to borrow against net home equity and use the resulting funds to finance other consumption stimulated strong growth in retail sales in the American economy. Personal consumption in current dollars had been between 67 and 68 percent of gross domestic product in every year from 1990 through 1998. It then rose to 70.8 percent in 2003 and remained at 70.6 percent in 2004 and 2005. Personal consumption spending also rose faster than personal disposable income. In constant-value 2000 dollars, it was 92 percent of personal disposable income in 1992, rose to 94 percent from 2001 through 2004, and hit 98 percent in the third quarter of 2005. Thus, income increases alone were not responsible for the entire rise in personal consumption during this period; borrowing against home equity also played a part.[8] That helps explain why home-equity loans rose from $406 billion in 2000 to $1.804 trillion in 2006. This consumption-raising effect of the flood of capital into real estate undoubtedly stimulated the overall prosperity of the American economy from 2003 through 2006.

Increasing the Strength of Local Exclusionary Housing Policies

Rising home prices also created an increased sensitivity among homeowners—especially in the suburbs—toward protecting the increased economic values of their homes from anything that might lower those values. For most American homeowners, the money they had in their homes was their major financial asset. Benefiting from increases in the value of that asset was a key means of increasing homeowners' financial wealth. Hence, many homeowners became strongly opposed to any possible changes in their neighborhoods that they believed might cause the values of their homes to decline or even to stop rising.

A majority of American homeowners believe that permitting any new dwelling units in their neighborhoods that are either (a) single-family homes with much lower prices than their own homes or (b) multifamily dwellings, especially rentals, would tend to lower the market values of their own homes. Therefore, most of those homeowners are opposed to allowing additional lower-cost dwellings or apartments nearby. They readily communicate this view to the elected officials in the communities where they live. Naturally, those officials are receptive to homeowners' views because the officials owe their incumbency to continuing local political support. In most American suburbs, homeowners are a clear majority of all residents; so their views strongly affect the policies of local governments. Thus, rising home prices accentuated already existing exclusionary attitudes among suburban homeowners and many suburban local governments. In my opinion, that has been a key force supporting exclusionary zoning and other housing-related policies that restrict the housing choices of low-income Americans.

Taking Out Tax-Free Capital through Refinancing

When home prices rose especially rapidly from 2000 to 2005, and interest rates declined, many homeowners decided to refinance their homes and take out tax-free cash they could spend in any way, even if unrelated to housing. They could do so without raising their monthly mortgage payments because lower interest rates permitted them to borrow more money than they had borrowed when they originally bought their homes while making the same monthly payments.

For example, a homeowner who purchased a home in 1990 at the nationwide median price in that year paid $92,000. If the purchaser obtained an 80 percent, fixed-rate, 30-year mortgage at the then prevailing interest rate of 9.75 percent and made a 20 percent downpayment of $18,400, the homeowner's monthly payments would be $632.34, for a total of $7,558 per year. By 2000, the home had risen in value to $139,000, and interest rates had declined to 7.58 percent. If the homeowner refinanced his or her home with another 30-year, fixed-rate mortgage at that lower rate, he or she could borrow $89,754 and make the same monthly payments of $632.34. No downpayment would be needed because the borrower already owned the home. The homeowner still owed $78,178 on the initial mortgage, which would have to be paid off. After doing so, each homeowner would have $11,576 left over—tax free— to spend as he or she wished.

Of course, the homeowner would have to keep making monthly payments for another 30 years, but his or her income had probably risen in the 10 years since buying the home, making payments easier than formerly. If any such households could afford to make larger monthly payments without undue strain, they could extract even greater amounts of cash by refinancing with larger mortgages. In addition to the cash infusion from the new loan, larger mortgages with higher monthly payments would give them larger interest-payment deductions from their federally taxable incomes.

If the same household waited until 2005 to refinance, the homeowner could get a new loan for an even larger amount. In 2005, the mortgage interest rate was 6 percent and the home had risen in value to $307,000, so any lender would be quite happy to make a new loan for $105,496, which was only 34 percent of the home's market value. Yet the homeowner could support this loan with the same monthly payments of $632.34. Because the homeowner would then still owe $75,210 on the initial loan, he or she would have to pay that off, leaving the homeowner with $30,285 in cash as tax-free spending money. Yes, the homeowner would then have to keep paying off those second loans for another 30 years, but the monthly costs would not have risen at all.

Millions of American homeowners took advantage of such possibilities by refinancing their homes as interest rates declined after 2000. As a result, mortgage refinancings rose from $572.5 billion in 1999, or 44.4 percent of all home mortgage originations, to $2,914 billion in 2003, or 72.3 percent of all such originations, as shown earlier in Figure 2-1.

Reducing the Affordability of Homeownership

Despite the fact that many former renters became homeowners from 1995 to 2006 because of falling interest rates and easier credit terms—even though home prices were rising—those rising home prices put homeownership even further beyond the reach of millions of other American households than it had been before 1995. This result negatively affected American society in three ways. First, it increased the difficulty of many households in acquiring decent shelter at all, because rental costs also rose along with ownership costs, though not nearly as fast. From 1990 to 2000, the median rent in current dollars paid by American renters rose at a compound rate of 2.67 percent per year, but from 2000 to 2006, rents rose at a compound rate of 4.3 percent per year. Second, rising home prices created an increasing bifurcation of society into those who were or thought they could soon become homeowners and those who thought becoming homeowners was virtually impossible for them because of the high—and rising—costs of doing so compared to their relatively static incomes. Third, rising housing costs reduced the housing standards of living for households who were buying homes in areas with very high housing costs, such as the coastal areas of California. Because of high housing costs there, young households had to wait longer than those living elsewhere in the nation before acquiring enough funds to amass a downpayment or to support the mortgage payments necessary to buy a home. Moreover, when they did buy a home, it was much smaller in size than homes of similar prices in other parts of the nation and likely to be much farther away from local employment centers, thus requiring longer and costlier commuting trips. The issue of reduced affordability is discussed further in Chapter 5.

Reducing the Ability of Employers to Attract Workers from Other Regions

Housing is a major part of the cost of living in most parts of America, but housing costs vary immensely from one region to another. Thus, median housing prices in California are more than 2.5 times greater than those in the nation as a whole or in many other specific regions. Firms located in high-housing-cost areas like California have a harder time attracting workers to move there, in spite of the area's many non-housing amenities, than they would if housing costs were lower. Moreover, many California households have decided to sell their homes at California prices, take their sales profits and buy much better homes for lower prices elsewhere, and then move to those alternative locations. This possibility—plus a recession in California in the early 1990s—helped create net domestic out-migration in the 1990s from California to several other nearby states, namely Oregon, Washington, Arizona, Nevada, Colorado, Idaho, and Montana. Foreign immigration into California, however, especially from Latin America, continued apace, although California's net population growth rate was lower in the 1990s than in either the 1980s or the 2000s.

Changing the Asset Composition of the Balance Sheets of Millions of American Households

The percentages of total household assets formed by major asset classes at different dates are shown in Table 3-6. The top section sets forth various types of assets in billions of current dollars; the bottom section shows what percentage each asset class is of the total for that year. The value of real estate assets held by households consists mainly of their homes. That value tripled from 1990 to 2006, rising $13.872 trillion over 16 years. About $9.030 trillion of that increase, or 65 percent, occurred from 2000 to 2006 as a direct result of rising home prices, plus a notable increase in population. Total assets of households rose by $17.873 trillion in the same six years. Thus, increases in real estate assets from 2000 to 2006 were about half of households' total increase in asset values in that period, even though real estate was only 30.6 percent of all household assets in 2006. In the same period, the value of corporate equities and mutual fund shares combined fell by $514.8 billion. Those assets declined from 21.3 percent of all household assets in 2000 (and from 24.85 percent in 1999 when they peaked) to 14.9 percent in 2006. Thus, real estate became by far the single most important asset class in household balance sheets, thanks mainly to rising home prices. That fact helped reinforce the desire of homeowners to protect the market values of their homes by preventing any less-expensive homes from being built nearby.

Altering the Basic Relationship between Income and Cost of Shelter in America

Because home costs rose substantially from 1996 to 2006, but household incomes for the vast majority of Americans were relatively stable, the basic relationship between the cost of shelter and income was fundamentally changed for many American households. The median household income for the United States in constant 2005 dollars was $43,366 in 1990 but had risen only to $47,599 by 2000; it then declined to $46,326

TABLE 3-6. **BALANCE SHEETS OF HOUSEHOLDS**

Item	1990	1995	1999	2000	2006 Q3	Changes in Values 1990–1995	1995–2000	2000–2006 Q3
Billions of Current Dollars								
Real estate	6,608.5	7,631.1	10,403.0	11,450.7	20,480.8	1,022.6	3,819.6	9,030.1
Deposits	3,264.5	3,365.5	4,022.8	4,022.8	6,425.5	101.0	657.3	2,402.7
Corporate equities and mutual funds	2,274.6	5,386.6	12,193.1	10,492.5	9,977.7	3,112.0	5,105.9	(514.8)
Pension fund reserves	3,461.8	5,767.8	9,065.3	9,069.0	11,633.8	2,306.0	3,301.2	2,564.8
Equity in noncorporate businesses	3,229.6	3,640.4	4,510.0	4,748.4	7,140.9	410.8	1,108.0	2,392.5
Total	**24,290.1**	**32,616.4**	**49,074.7**	**49,177.2**	**67,050.2**	**8,326.3**	**16,560.8**	**17,873.0**
Percentages								
Real estate	27.21	23.40	21.20	23.28	30.55			
Deposits	13.44	10.32	8.20	8.18	9.58			
Corporate equities and mutual funds	9.36	16.52	24.85	21.34	14.88			
Pension fund reserves	14.25	17.68	18.47	18.44	17.35			
Equity in noncorporate businesses	13.30	11.16	9.19	9.66	10.65			
Total Percentages in These Categories	**77.56**	**79.07**	**81.90**	**80.90**	**83.01**			

Source: Federal Reserve Board, *Flow of Funds Accounts of the United States.*

in 2005. Over these 15 years, that income rose by only 9.7 percent to 2000, then fell to a point only 6.8 percent above its 1990 level, according to the U.S. Census Bureau, P-60 Reports. In the same 15 years, the median price of homes sold in the United States as a whole in constant dollars rose 14.6 percent from 1990 to 2000 and 31 percent from 2000 to 2005. Thus, especially after 2000, housing prices diverged sharply from household incomes in a manner that made paying the expenses of living in "decent" shelter increasingly difficult for millions of American households. This relationship is analyzed in detail in Chapter 5.

HAS HOMEOWNER WEALTH BEEN INCREASED BY RISING HOUSING PRICES IN OTHER NATIONS?

The immense increase in homeowner wealth generated in the United States by rising home prices in the past decade is probably not unique. However, adequate data to analyze whether similar wealth increases also occurred in other nations are not easy to obtain. One nation for which I have been able to gather such information is the United Kingdom. The Royal Institute of Chartered Surveyors in the United Kingdom has published on its Web site data concerning the size of the United Kingdom's housing stock from 1971 through 2006 and the numbers of new housing units built in each year from 1991 through 2006. Prices of housing units were available in the form of a price index at Nationwide.co.uk based on prices in the first quarter of 1993 set at 100.[9]

By dividing the fourth quarter 1993 average housing unit price for the entire United Kingdom (172,065 pounds) by the price index for that same period (345.1), I derived the average U.K. home price in the third quarter of 1993 (49,858 pounds). In the absence of specific data, I arbitrarily assumed that U.K. homeowners in 1993 had the same 47 percent of total debt against their gross equity as did U.S. owners in that year. Therefore, owners in 1993 had an average net equity in their homes of 26,425 pounds. Total net homeowner equity in the United Kingdom in that year was 418.8 billion pounds.

In the fourth quarter of 2006, U.K. homeowners were borrowing 55 percent against their total gross equities of 3.201 trillion pounds, based on the average 2006 price. That left them with a total net equity (having removed all debt) of 1.440 trillion pounds, or 77,499 pounds per homeowner.[10] Over this 12.75-year period from 1993 to 2006, U.K. homeowners who had owned homes throughout that period experienced a net increase in their home equities on the average of 51,004 pounds (in current prices)—a 65 percent gain over their net home equity in 1993. Rising home prices had increased the gross market values of their homes by 245 percent (a compound annual growth rate of 10.2 percent) and handed each of them an increase in net equity 2 percent larger than the total market value of their homes in 1993.

This analysis proves that rising home prices generated a huge increase in homeowner wealth in the United Kingdom from 1993 to 2006 similar to that which took place in the United States. Data to carry out similar analyses in other foreign nations are not easily available. However, home prices rose much faster in other nations outside the United States—such as Spain and Ireland—than in the United Kingdom. Therefore, comparable increases in homeowner net equities in their dwellings almost certainly occurred in those nations too. Thus, the huge effects of the Niagara of capital upon the economic welfare of homeowning households were undoubtedly a worldwide phenomenon wherever home prices increased rapidly.

HOW THE NIAGARA OF CAPITAL RAISED THE
INCOMES OF REAL ESTATE AGENTS

Homeowners were not the only group of Americans enriched by the Niagara of capital. Realtors and other real estate agents engaged in the sale of homes also profited mightily from this big inflow of capital into housing markets. The National Association of Realtors is the largest professional organization for real estate brokers. Figure 3-9 shows that the number of real estate agents joining that organization soared after 1998 and especially after 2000.[11] In 1998, NAR had 718,483 members, but that number shot up to 1,272,057 in 2005—a gain of 553,574, or 77 percent, by 2005. The only similar explosion of NAR membership occurred from 1974 to 1979 when that number zoomed from 134,362 to 755,650—or 462 percent—in just five years. That earlier rise in membership was also related to rapid increases in housing prices during the inflationary period of the 1970s. Then the median home price for the entire United States rose 74.0 percent from 1974 to 1979, comparable to its increase of 61.2 percent from 1998 to 2005. Also, the total number of people engaged in selling housing was much larger than the number of NAR members. NAR itself estimated 2.5 million persons were engaged in selling homes as of 2006, or double the NAR membership.

What was attracting so many people into selling homes was the possibility of gaining ever-larger commissions as the prices of homes soared. NAR members normally charge a 6 percent commission, regardless of the prices of homes involved. Hence, as home prices rose, so did commissions. This correlation held true even though NAR claims the level of commissions actually paid its members was between 5 and 6 percent, allowing for occasional discounts. NAR publishes surveys of the incomes received by its members with differing levels of experience in the business. Figure 3-10 shows their incomes by years of experience in selling homes in the years 1997, 2001, 2002, and 2004. The median incomes of Realtors with more than 25 years of experience rose from $53,200 in 1997 to $92,600 in 2004—an increase of 74.1 percent in seven years. In the same seven years, the national median household income in current dollars went from $37,005 to $44,000—a gain of 18.9 percent. Some, but not all, of the Realtors with less experience also had big increases in income from 1997 to 2004: only 4.7 percent for those with less than five years' experience, 31.6 percent for those with 6 to 10 years, an 8.9 percent drop for those with 11 to 16 years, and a 26.4 percent gain for those with 16 to 25 years.

Real estate agent income data for earlier periods are hard to obtain, but little doubt exists that incomes of most rose along with housing prices. Moreover, because housing prices are likely to remain much higher than they were in the past, the incomes of real estate agents will probably also remain much higher. This effect may be somewhat diluted, however, by the much larger number of agents competing for the

FIGURE 3-9. **NAR MEMBERSHIP, 1970–2005**

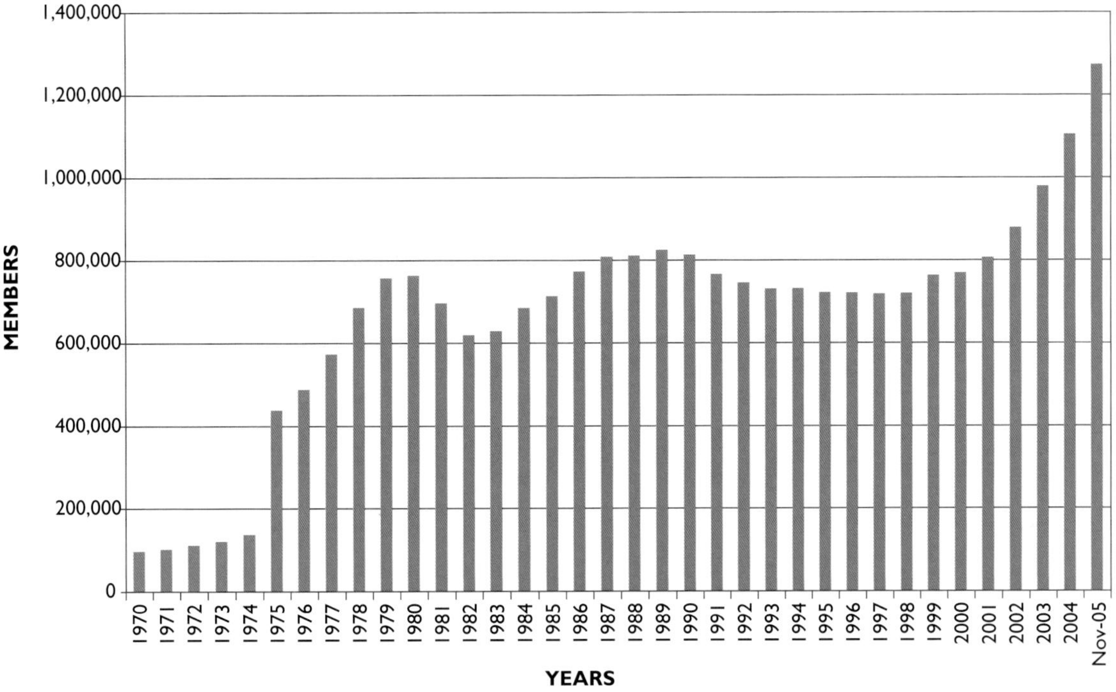

Source: Donna McCormick, "Field Guide to National Association of Realtors Membership Statistics, 1908 to Present"; http://www.realtor.org/libweb.nsf/pages/fg003 (accessed May 2007).

business of selling homes. Past experience shows that big increases in the number of real estate agents tend to slow down the rate of increase of their median incomes—especially among agents who are relatively new to the business. Even so, real estate agents as a group clearly have profited significantly from the Niagara of capital into residential markets.

WHY GOVERNMENT SAVINGS STATISTICS DO NOT COUNT HOMEOWNER EQUITY GAINS AS WEALTH

The U.S. government does not count increases in households' equities in their homes as true wealth as measured in the National Income and Product Accounts. Those accounts are designed to measure the nation's total production of goods and services. But increases in home equity caused by rising housing prices are capital gains—that is, increases in the prices of existing assets—not increases in the nation's total physi-

FIGURE 3-10. **MEDIAN INCOMES OF NAR RESIDENTIAL BROKERS, 1997–2004**

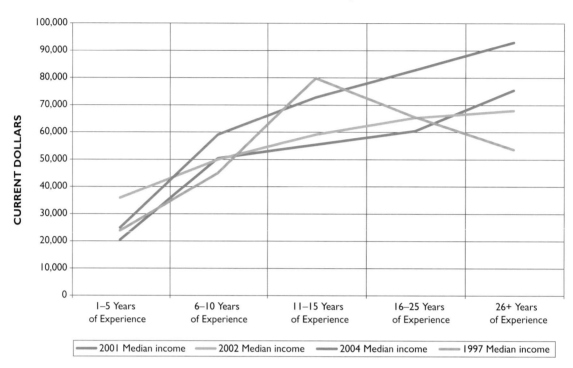

Sources: *Realtor,* compensation studies in 1997, 1998, and 2001.

cal assets. Because home-equity increases do not involve the production of actual goods and services, those increases are not counted as household savings either. In contrast, increases in homeowners' equity in their houses are counted in the Federal Reserve flow of funds accounts as gains in the financial assets of households, which are measures of financial wealth.

Gains to homeowners from rising equity in their homes can be converted into real assets from their point of view if the homeowners either (a) sell their homes and use the profits to purchase other goods and services or (b) borrow against their higher equities and spend the money buying other goods, such as automobiles, furniture, food, or vacations. But in the second case, those added assets are offset by increased homeowner debts against their homes—debts that reduce the amount of net equity remaining in those homes. Moreover, homeowners must repay those debts through higher mortgage or home-equity loan payments over time.

Nevertheless, homeowners themselves realize that if they sell their homes at much higher prices than they paid for them, without investing in improving those

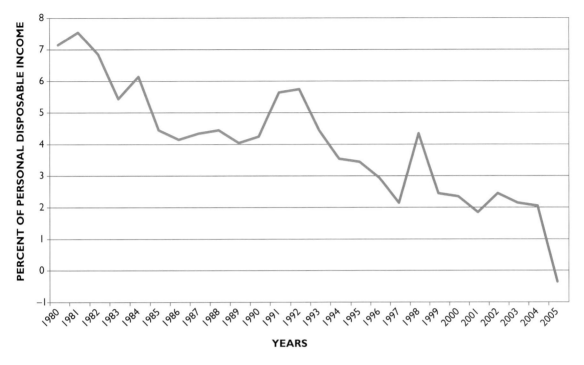

FIGURE 3-11. **SAVINGS AS A PERCENTAGE OF DISPOSABLE PERSONAL INCOME, 1980–2005**

Source: Council of Economic Advisers, *Economic Indicators* (Washington, D.C.: Government Printing Office), various months.

homes, they have gained true purchasing power and wealth from increases in home prices. They can use that greater purchasing power without any offsetting increases in their debts. So they regard increases in their home equities as real wealth, even though those increases remain only potential wealth until they sell their homes.

The esoteric reasoning by national income accountants focused on measuring total national production runs counter to the on-the-ground experience of American homeowners. They clearly regard increases in the net equities in their homes caused by rising home prices as increases in their own wealth and purchasing power, and therefore in their savings. They know that they can sell their homes at far more than they paid for them, unless housing prices fall sharply in the future. Then they can spend the money thus received to make purchases that seem quite real to them. This view is surely reflected in both the borrowing and spending behavior of millions of home-owners as well as in the desire of so many current renters to become homeowners.

Economists have bemoaned the declining levels of savings by American house-holds as a weakness in the U.S. economy, because low savings provide fewer resources for investment in production-expanding equipment and education. Savings as a percentage of disposable personal income are shown in Figure 3-11. The graph shows an irregular but consistent decline from 7 percent in 1980 to about 2 percent from 1999 to 2004, and then a drop to a slightly negative level in 2005. But households who own homes regard increases in the net equities in their homes caused by rising prices as true savings. In their minds, the national savings rate should include this element and therefore should be much higher than that shown by official statistics.

CONCLUSION

Rising home prices clearly have had profound effects—both positive and negative—on the American economy and the lives of millions of American households. In general, rising prices have benefited households who owned homes during the period of rising prices and harmed renters and those households who bought homes well into that period. Because over 60 percent of American households owned their own homes before the Niagara of capital began, a large majority has benefited from rising home prices. But heavy penalties have been placed upon millions of other households who could not afford to buy homes at all or at least until housing prices had risen substantially. Further analysis of some of these effects is presented later.

Notes

1. The nations are Austria, Belgium, the Czech Republic, Denmark, Finland, France, Germany, Greece, Hungary, Ireland, Italy, the Netherlands, Norway, Poland, Portugal, Romania, Spain, Sweden, Switzerland, Turkey, and the United Kingdom. United Nations Economic Commission for Europe, Environment and Human Settlements Division, http://w3.unece.org/stat/scriptsdb/DomainSelection.asp (accessed January 13, 2007).

2. French Ministry of Transportation, Infrastructure, Tourism and the Sea, Office of Economics, Statistics, and Forward Planning, http://www.insee.fr/en/ffs/ chifcle_fiche.asp?ref_id=NATTEF11401&tab_id=233 (accessed January 22, 2007).

3. Royal Institute of Chartered Surveyors, Table 201, Housebuilding: Permanent Dwellings Started and Completed, by Tenure: United Kingdom.

4. "Government Confirms 24% Increase in Housing Units" and "Number of Properties in Spain Not Excessive," *Spanish Property Insight*, December 2006, www.spanishpropertyinsight.com/spanish_property_news_bulletin_latest.htm (accessed January 15, 2007).

5. Data from Statistics Sweden, Official Statistics of Sweden, http://www.scb.se/templates/tableOrChart____143197.asp.

6. "Big Builders Improve Operations and Reap Big Profits," *Nation's Building News*, June 26, 2006, http://www.nbnnews.com/NBN/issues/2006-06-26/Front+Page/3.html.

7. Seiders is quoted in Blanche Evans, "Realty Times Outlook: Precarious Market for New Homes," *Realty Times*, January 31, 2007, http://realtytimes.com/rtapages/20060227_outlook.htm (accessed January 31, 2007).

8. Parts of this paragraph were taken from Anthony Downs, "How Rising Home Prices Have Stimulated U.S. Consumption," *Wharton Real Estate Review* 10, no. 2 (Fall 2006): 81.

9. Nationwide, "Quarterly Regional Review," *House Prices*, http://nationwide.co.uk/hpi/historical/UK_Q4_06.pdf.

10. The total number of homeowning households rose from 15.848 million in 1993 to 18.605 million in 2006, and the percentage of homeowners among all households rose from 66 to 70 percent.

11. Donna McCormick, "Field Guide to National Association of Realtors Membership Statistics, 1908 to Present," http://www.realtor.org/libweb.nsf/pages/fg.oo3 (accessed May 2007). The 2005 membership data are from the same site but a different subsection.

CHAPTER FOUR

Effects of the Niagara of Capital on the Filtering Process in Housing Markets

One of the biggest effects of the Niagara of capital in American housing markets has been on the process by which older housing units, originally built for high-income households, gradually come into the possession of much lower-income households. This process, known as *filtering*, was long the main source of supply of decent housing units for low-income households in the United States. This chapter discusses how the Niagara of capital has both hampered and accelerated that process.

THE BASIC IDEA OF FILTERING IN HOUSING MARKETS

Filtering is a process in which housing units originally built for high-income residents slowly decline in relative economic value compared to even-newer units and are therefore gradually taken over first by middle-income, then by moderate-income, and finally by low-income residents after the original high-income owners and their successor occupants move to newer units. At the end of these chains of moves, housing originally built for high-income residents who initially paid high prices or rents for it is eventually occupied by low-income households who pay much lower prices or rents for it. Thus, initially high-priced units gradually *filter down* through the income distribution to the point where they become affordable to low-income households.

In the United States, such filtering down of housing units—and its accompanying filtering up of households—has in the past been the main source of housing affordable to low-income households. It provides housing affordable to such households without government subsidies. One reason filtering has been so important in the United States is that our local housing laws require builders to construct new units that meet high-quality standards of size, amenities, and quality of construction. Therefore, most low-income households cannot afford to buy or occupy any newly built housing units in America without subsidies. In much of the rest of the world, both builders and households themselves are permitted to construct, or at least are not prevented from constructing, new low-quality housing—often just shacks. Hence, very-low-income households can build shelters for themselves directly without public subsidies. But that construction is almost universally illegal in the United States, and the laws against it are usually enforced quite rigorously.

FIVE CONDITIONS NECESSARY FOR THE FILTERING PROCESS TO FUNCTION EFFECTIVELY

In 1988, I wrote an article in which I identified the following five conditions necessary for filtering to provide housing affordable to low-income households:[1]

1. *An overall housing surplus.* The total usable supply of decent-quality housing in a metropolitan area must be larger than the total number of households living there. If the total supply of housing units in the metropolitan area is smaller than the total number of households living there, housing markets will be tightly occupied. That situation will put upward pressure on housing prices and rents, hindering housing from becoming less costly as it filters downward through the income distribution.

2. *A surplus of new housing construction over new household formation.* In any given period, the *net* number of new units being added to the inventory each year (net of demolitions and removals) must exceed the *net* number of additional households being added each year within the metropolitan area (net of deaths and out-migration). If the total number of new housing units built each year in the metropolitan area is smaller than the total net number of additional households formed there or entering each year, the overall housing supply will become tighter each year. That situation will gradually put upward pressure on the prices and rents of housing units in the area—the opposite of filtering.

3. *No major nonprice barriers to mobility among low-income households.* The housing market must not exhibit serious discrimination against minority-group or other low-income households seeking to move upward in the hierarchy of neighborhoods. If low-income or other households from minority racial or ethnic groups are prevented by discrimination among brokers and homeowners from moving freely among neighborhoods within a metropolitan area, or even just believe they cannot so move, the filtering process may be subverted. In that case, housing vacancies opened up in primarily white neighborhoods through the filtering process may

not be accessible to low-income African Americans, Hispanics, or Asians. This condition is becoming more important because the percentage of all newly formed or newly arrived households in the United States consisting of members of those three minority groups already exceeds one-half and will reach over 75 percent in the near future.

4. *Moderate operating costs for most newly built units.* The type of housing typically added to the housing inventory by new construction must not be so costly to operate as to be beyond the ability to pay of low- and moderate-income households. Such costly operating expenses could arise from very large housing units serviced by air conditioning and expensive heating systems and absorbing large amounts of electric power, as well as generating high property taxes.

5. *A limited number of very poor households.* The number of households in the metropolitan area who cannot afford to support occupancy of even minimally defined decent housing units must be quite small and should be declining over time. If a metropolitan area contains many more very-low-income households than the net surplus of housing units over total households in the region, then the filtering process will not make enough older units available to those very-low-income households each year to provide shelter for all those who need it. Even in such a case, however, filtering could still provide a significant number of low-income households with decent units.

ONE OTHER CONDITION NECESSARY FOR FILTERING TO WORK WELL

Since writing the 1988 article, I have realized that one other condition is necessary for filtering to succeed in providing affordable housing to low-income households:

6. *If nearly all housing prices in a metropolitan area are rising instead of falling, the ability of low-income households in that area to pay for housing must be increasing faster than the market prices or rents of the housing they seek to occupy.* Rising ability to pay among low-income households can occur in spite of increasing home prices if (a) their household incomes are increasing, (b) interest rates are falling, (c) other requirements for borrowing money are improving, or (d) some combination of the first three factors exists.

Because of the Niagara of capital, this condition has become important since 1995 and particularly since 2000. In those two periods, housing prices (and rents) rose much more rapidly than usual. In the past, when housing units initially built with high prices at the edges of a metropolitan area were surpassed in desirability by newer units, then the prices of those older units declined. They usually fell both absolutely and in relation to the prices of the newer units. In most cases, those newer

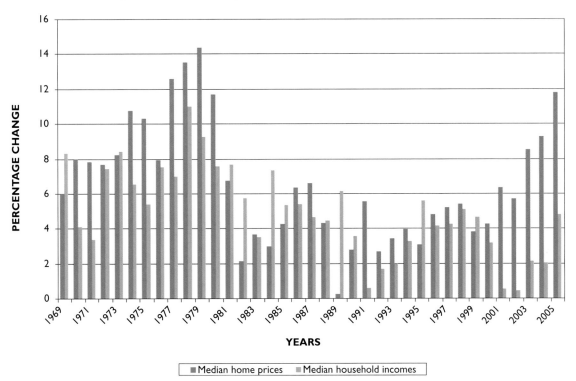

Sources: Home prices: California Association of Realtors, *Trends in California Real Estate*, various monthly issues, and National Association of Realtors, *Insights*, various monthly issues; median incomes: U.S. Census Bureau, "Historical Income Tables, Households, Race and Hispanic Origin of Householder, 1967–2005," Table H-5, http://www.census.gov/hhes/www/income/histinc/h05.html (accessed July 2007).

units were located farther outward from the metropolitan area's downtown than were the initially built units, because nearly all regions have historically grown outward from their original centers. In particular, prices of the older units declined in relation to the incomes of all groups of households in the metropolitan area. This decline in relative prices is what enabled households to filter upward in the inventory by moving to units newer than those they had been occupying.

But since about 1995, housing prices in the United States—and most other developed nations—have risen much faster than in previous periods, when inflation rates are taken into account (see Figures 4-1 and 4-2). The first graph is in current dollars, and the second graph is in constant 1982–1984 dollars. I calculated the average annual rates of change for both variables in both current and constant dollars for the two periods 1968–1995 and 1995–2005. Stated in current dollars, both vari-

FIGURE 4-2. **ANNUAL RATES OF CHANGE IN U.S. MEDIAN HOME PRICES AND HOUSEHOLD INCOMES, 1969–2005 (CONSTANT DOLLARS)**

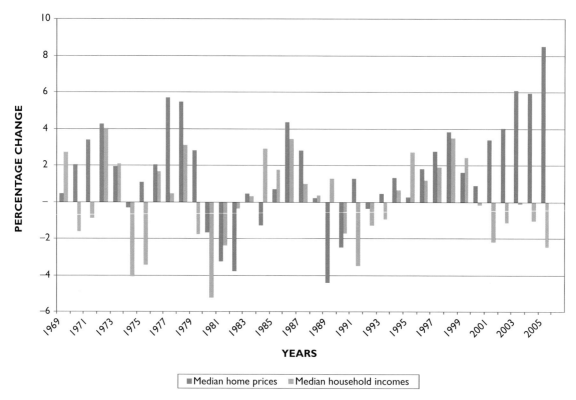

Sources: Home prices: California Association of Realtors, *Trends in California Real Estate*, various monthly issues, and National Association of Realtors, *Insights*, various monthly issues; median incomes: U.S. Census Bureau, "Historical Income Tables, Households, Race and Hispanic Origin of Householder, 1967–2005," Table H-5, http://www.census.gov/hhes/www/income/histinc/h05.html (accessed July 2007).

ables increased throughout the period shown, but median home prices rose much more, both in the 1970s and since 2001. Stated in constant dollars, median home prices declined in 7 of the 37 years, but median household incomes fell in 17 of those same years. Moreover, from 2001 onward, median home prices soared in real terms, whereas median household incomes were lower in 2005 than they had been in 1998. In short, U.S. household incomes have not kept pace with U.S. housing prices since 1970—and especially since 1995.

At first glance, one would conclude from these facts that the traditional housing filtering process did not work well in the past decade. Since about 1995, the market prices of housing units that became older did not fall. Instead, those prices rose—and much faster than household incomes. Therefore, instead of becoming more affordable to households with incomes lower than those of the original occupants of such housing, those older units seem to have become less affordable as they got older and their prices rose.

HOW CHANGES IN INTEREST RATES AND CREDIT TERMS OFFSET RISING HOME PRICES

Nevertheless, that conclusion is erroneous. Why? Because it does not take into account simultaneous changes in financial conditions that often more than offset rising home prices. As noted in Chapter 3, those changes included falling interest rates, lowering downpayment requirements, permitting borrowers to devote higher percentages of their incomes to paying off home mortgages and other credit bills, using negative amortization mortgages, and permitting borrowers to declare what their household incomes were without having the lender confirm that declaration with the sources of income. Each such change increased a household's ability to pay for a home out of a given income, thereby expanding its reach into higher-priced homes.

The dramatic results of this credit-easing process can be illustrated by a hypothetical example whose results are shown in Table 4-1. It presents 14 cases with differing incomes, home prices, interest rates, and downpayment arrangements. These cases are described in detail in the accompanying box.[2]

This analysis shows that falling interest rates, plus lenders' ingenuity and willingness to take risks, greatly expanded the ability of households to buy homes from 1990 to 2005, even if their incomes did not rise nearly as much as home prices. Table 4-1 shows that median household incomes in current dollars rose 48.6 percent from 1990, whereas median home prices in current dollars rose 125 percent. Yet a household whose 1990 income did not rise at all in 2005 could still afford to pay for a home costing more than the national median home price in that year—if that household made use of several easier-credit devices simultaneously. That finding is a testament to the effects of both interest rates and credit terms on household ability to pay.

The combined effect of all these changed conditions upon the filtering process has been dramatic. From 1990 to 2005, the total number of U.S. households rose by 19.1 million,[3] but 81 percent of that increase consisted of more homeowning households and only 19 percent of more renters—even though homeowners were only 69 percent of all U.S. households in 2006 and renters were 31 percent.[4] In other words, during the 15 years from 1990 to 2005, American households rushed into buying homes at record rates rather than renting. Yet that was a period when housing prices were rising much faster than incomes. In theory, filtering should not have worked very well under such conditions, because prices of even older housing were rising instead of falling. But in reality, falling interest rates and easier credit terms

TABLE 4-1. **FILTERING ABILITY-TO-PAY ANALYSIS**

Year	Case	U.S. Median Household Income ($)	Percentage Gain over Base Case	Percentage of Income Used for Housing Loan	Housing Share of Income ($)	Monthly Payment ($)	Mortgage Interest Rate (%)
1990	1	29,943	0.00	30	8,983	748.58	9.75
1995	2	29,943	0.00	30	8,983	748.58	7.47
2000	3	29,943	0.00	30	8,983	748.58	7.58
2005	4	29,943	0.00	30	8,983	748.58	6.39
2005	5	29,943	0.00	30	8,983	748.58	6.39
2005	6	29,943	0.00	30	8,983	748.50	6.39
1995	7	34,076	13.80	30	10,223	851.90	7.47
2000	8	41,900	39.93	30	12,570	1,047.50	7.58
2005	9	44,503	48.63	30	13,351	1,112.58	6.39
2005	10	44,503	48.63	30	13,351	1,112.58	6.39
2005	11	44,503	48.63	30	13,351	1,112.58	6.39
2005	12	29,943	0.00	40	11,977	998.10	6.39
2005	13	44,503	48.63	40	17,801	1,483.43	6.39
2005	14	44,503	48.63	40	17,801	1,483.43	6.39

Source: Author's calculations using mortgage payment data from Power One Finance computer program.

almost fully offset the adverse impact of rising prices upon the filtering process—at least in the nation as a whole. In some regions where home prices rose more than twice as fast as in the entire nation—as in California—filtering was seriously disrupted. But in other metropolitan areas where housing prices rose more slowly than in the nation as a whole, filtering still may have worked effectively.

The consequent flood of capital into housing and commercial property then began to take on some of the aspects of a self-fulfilling prophecy. As housing prices rose sharply, especially in certain high-amenity markets like California, households realized they could make large gains in the net equity in their homes—if they were homeowners. This opportunity helped persuade millions of Americans to eschew renting and embark on homeownership. Consequently, homeownership rose from

Year	Case	Percent Down-payment	Down-payment ($)	Years of Mortgage	Mortgage Supported by Monthly Payments ($)	Housing Price Supported ($)	Price Percentage Increase over Base Case	Actual Median Home Price Price That Year ($)
1990	1	20	21,788	30	87,153	108,941	—	92,000
1995	2	20	26,844	30	107,375	134,218	23.20	110,500
2000	3	20	26,557	30	106,227	132,783	21.89	139,000
2005	4	20	29,947	30	119,789	149,736	37.45	207,000
2005	5	15.39	21,788	30	119,789	141,577	29.96	207,000
2005	6	0	Int. only	7	119,789	119,789	9.96	207,000
1995	7	20	30,549	30	122,196	152,744	40.21	110,500
2000	8	20	37,161	30	148,645	185,806	70.56	139,000
2005	9	3	5,600	30	181,079	186,679	71.36	207,000
2005	10	20	45,270	30	181,079	226,349	107.77	207,000
2005	11	0	Int. only	7	178,055	178,055	63.44	207,000
2005	12	20	40,612	30	162,447	203,058	86.39	207,000
2005	13	20	60,359	30	241,437	301,796	177.03	207,000
2005	14	3	7,467	30	241,437	248,904	128.48	207,000

64.2 percent of all U.S. households in 1990 to 69.0 percent in 2006. Between 1990 and 2005, the number of households rose by 19.1 million, and 15.47 million of them, or 81 percent, were added homeowners. No wonder the current-dollar median price of U.S. homes sold rose by 125 percent in that same period!

Some observers believe that this large increase in home prices was entirely caused by a relative shortage of housing in U.S. markets. They argue that total demand in the form of households plus household growth must have risen faster than total supply in the form of both existing and newly built homes, or prices would not have risen. But the data do not support that view. From 1990 to 2005, even though the U.S. Census Bureau counted that the total number of households increased by 19.143 million, 28.372 million new housing units were started in the same period, or 48.2

Description of Terms for Filtering Ability-to-Pay Analysis

Case 1: The base case—The hypothetical household in the base case for Table 4-1 has the national median household income in 1990 of $29,943. I assume that each household could devote 30 percent of its income to making monthly payments on a home (except for some cases described below). That amounts to a monthly payment of $748.58 on the mortgage, plus a 20 percent downpayment. In 1990, the mortgage interest rate on a 30-year fixed-rate mortgage, according to the Federal Reserve Board, was 9.75 percent. Therefore, the household could use its $748.58 monthly payments to support a mortgage of $87,153. If that household could make a downpayment of $21,788, it could therefore buy a home priced at $108,941 (the downpayment equals 20 percent of that price). In 1990, the national median price of existing single-family homes sold was $92,000, according to the National Association of Realtors, which tracks that price yearly.

Case 2: Lower interest rate—By 1995, the median price of existing homes sold had risen to $110,500, which initially seems to be beyond the ability of this household to pay. But the mortgage interest rate had fallen to 7.47 percent. Even if the household's income did not rise at all, that drop in interest rates allowed the household to buy a home costing $134,218, if it could manage the downpayment of $26,844. Thus, a 23.4 percent fall in interest rates increased the household's ability to pay for a home by 23.2 percent.

Case 3: Higher interest rate—By 2000, the median-priced home had risen to $139,000, or 51.0 percent above the 1990 median of $92,000. The mortgage interest rates also actually rose slightly to 7.58 percent in 2000, so a home priced at the national median was slightly out of reach of this household—again assuming its income did not rise.

Case 4: Lower interest rate again but higher downpayment—This case uses the interest rate prevailing in 2005—6.39 percent—but keeps the household's income frozen at the 1990 level. That lower interest rate permits the household to buy a home costing $149,736—if it can scrape up a 20 percent downpayment of $29,947.

Case 5: Lower interest rate but same downpayment as in Case 1—If the household can pay the same $21,788 downpayment as in the base case, it can still support the same sized mortgage, but the maximum amount it could afford to pay for a home would be $141,577. Therefore, the household could not afford the median-priced home in the year 2005, which was $207,000.

Case 6: Interest-only mortgage and zero downpayment—Ingenious lenders overcame the problem in Case 5 by offering potential homebuyers interest-only, no-downpayment mortgages for the first five to ten years. With such a mortgage at the 2005 interest rate of 6.39 percent, the household could initially afford to buy a home costing $119,789—or 30 percent higher than the price it could afford to pay in 1990, even though its income had not increased! Unfortunately, the monthly payment would go up substantially as amortization was added in, so that outcome was probably not sustainable.

Case 7: Higher income—In reality, median household incomes also rose over this 15-year period, further increasing the average household's ability to pay for a home. By 1995, the median household income had risen to $34,076. With a 20 percent downpayment and the then-prevailing interest rate of 7.47 percent, the household could pay $851.90 per month for a mortgage, which would support purchase of a home costing $152,744. That amount was well above the actual national median home price of $110,500 in 1995.

Case 8: Higher income and higher interest rates—By 2000, median household income was at $41,900, but the interest rate had risen slightly to 7.58 percent. So the household could afford to buy a home costing $185,806. That was well above the 2000 national median price of $139,000.

Case 9: Higher income, lower interest rate, and 3 percent downpayment—In 2005, the median household income was $44,503, and interest rates had fallen to 6.39 percent. Moreover, homes could be bought with downpayments of only 3 percent! Those conditions enabled a household with the median income to afford a home costing $183,562, which was only 11.4 percent below the actual 2005 national median price of $207,000.

Case 10: Higher income, lower interest rate, and 20 percent downpayment—If the buyer was able to make a 20 percent downpayment of $45,270, he or she could buy a home costing $226,349 with the same monthly payment of $1,112.58. That home was well above the national median home price of $207,000 in 2005.

Case 11: Higher income, interest-only loan, and no downpayment—If the buyer could not make any downpayment, he or she could use an interest-only loan to purchase a home costing $178,055.

Case 12: 1990 income, higher share paid for interest, low interest rate, 20 percent downpayment—A buyer whose income remained fixed at the 1990 median income level of $29,943 could nevertheless buy a home costing $203,058 if (a) the buyer was permitted to raise the share of income devoted to loan repayment from 30 percent to 40 percent, (b) the 2005 interest rate of 6.39 percent prevailed, and (c) the buyer could raise $40,611 for a downpayment. Thus, easier credit terms allowed a household with a 2005 income fixed at the 1990 level to buy a home in 2005 costing 99.98 percent of the actual 2005 national median-priced home—if it could swing the larger downpayment.

Case 13: Higher income but spending 40 percent on debt repayment with 20 percent downpayment—A buyer whose income had risen to the 2005 median income of $44,503 could easily afford to buy a home costing more than the 2005 median-priced home ($207,000) if the household could spend 40 percent of its income repaying housing debt, rather than 30 percent, and could make a full 20 percent downpayment.

Case 14: Higher income but spending 40 percent on debt repayment with 3 percent downpayment—Exactly the same as case 13, except for a lower downpayment.

percent more than the number of households added. Also, the nation's total housing inventories as measured by the Census Bureau rose by 22.258 million in the same period. Because 28.372 million new units were built (if all starts were completed) but the inventory rose by only 22.258 million, that implies 6.114 million older units were removed from those inventories—an average removal of 407,600 units per year. That would still result in a net housing gain in the inventory 3.115 million units, which is greater than the total number of households added from 1990 to 2005. That net gain equals the additional number of vacant units counted by the Census Bureau from 1990 to 2005.

These numbers imply that no overall shortage of housing in the United States occurred during the period 1990 to 2005 when housing prices rose sharply. True, internal migration of millions of households from the Midwest and the Northeast to the West and South may have caused relative housing shortages in the latter regions. But housing prices rose almost as much in coastal portions of the Northeast, which had major out-migrations of population, as in the West or South. No doubt the desire of renter households and new households to become homeowners helped increase housing prices, especially in regions with high in-migration from abroad or the rest of the nation. But the magnitude of housing price increases and their appearance all over the nation indicate that additional factors are required to explain those increases. The most important factor was the Niagara of capital into real estate of all types, including housing. This conclusion is borne out by several issues of the *Economist* magazine, which featured cover articles on the worldwide boom in housing markets caused by massive inflows of capital.

THE SUBPRIME MORTGAGE MARKET

A major effect of the Niagara of capital on residential markets was a large increase in the use of *subprime mortgages*. Such mortgages are loans to borrowers with relatively poor credit histories made by lenders who are willing to risk a greater chance of delinquency or default in return for higher interest rates on the loans they make. The typical subprime mortgage loan has an interest rate about 300 basis points (three percentage points) higher than a prime mortgage (that is, one made to a borrower with a good credit history). The flood of capital into housing markets generated much more willingness among lenders to make subprime loans. That willingness arose because lenders had so much capital to place and found returns from prime loans less profitable than in the past because of lower interest rates in general. In addition, renter households with poor credit records were eager to become homeowners because of the "American dream" of homeownership and the potential profitability from rising home prices. Finally, because home prices were rising rapidly until 2005, both lenders and borrowers thought there was less risk in making questionable loans because those prices would provide more collateral for each loan. With greater loan capital supply among lenders, greater demand for homeownership among subprime borrowers, and rising home prices, the volume of subprime lending reached record levels after 2000.

Unfortunately, reliable data about home-mortgage originations, in general, and subprime lending, in particular, are difficult to obtain. In 2005, the Federal Reserve Board conducted a special study of home-mortgage origination, written in part by Chairman Alan Greenspan, to provide reliable information on that subject from 1991 through 2004.[5] Figure 2-1 presented at the beginning of Chapter 2 shows the results of that study, plus later data for 2005 from Fannie Mae and subprime data from Credit Suisse. The line indicating total originations for one-to-four-family home mortgages shows the spectacular increase in home mortgage lending that resulted from the Niagara of capital in U.S. housing markets. Total home mortgages originated quadrupled in dollar value from about $1 trillion in 2000 to $4 trillion in 2003. Most of that home lending was refinancing of existing home mortgages, which constituted 28 percent of all mortgages originated in 2000 but then shot up to 72 percent in 2003. Total originations dropped to under $3 trillion in 2004, but rose again to $3.033 trillion in 2005 and then fell to $2.761 trillion in 2006, according to Fannie Mae.[6]

Subprime lending volumes are even harder to measure or estimate than total mortgage originations. Data from Credit Suisse quoted in Hammond Associates' *Research Report April 2007* indicate that subprime loans were only about 13.0 percent of all mortgage originations in 2000 (using the Federal Reserve Bank and Fannie Mae estimates), but then rose to 19.2 percent in 2004 and 21.3 percent in 2005. Before 2004, most subprime loans were adjustable-rate loans or hybrids combining adjustable- and fixed-rate components. From 2004 onward, interest-only loans were more prominent among subprime mortgages; in the third quarter of 2005, about 30 percent of all subprime loans were interest only.

The likelihood of delinquency or default among subprime borrowers was naturally much greater than among other borrowers, given that the former had poor credit records and were paying higher interest rates on their loans. The Mortgage Bankers Association conducts national delinquency surveys, which showed that subprime borrowers had delinquency rates above 10 percent from the fourth quarter of 2000 through the third quarter of 2003, compared with delinquency rates of less than 2 percent in the same period among prime borrowers. Foreclosures were also much higher among subprime borrowers than prime ones. When the U.S. economy in general slowed down in the first quarter of 2007, problems among subprime lending firms became acute. More than 50 such firms went out of business in 2006. They were mostly small firms, but some very large ones also were suffering from acute financial pains in 2007. Several large hedge funds were also badly hurt by rising delinquencies among subprime borrowers in 2007; at least one had to be rescued by a $3.2 billion loan from its major sponsor, Bear Stearns, in June 2007.

As a result of difficulties in the subprime market, federal financial regulators began pressing lenders of all types to tighten their credit standards and stop encouraging so many borrowers with poor credit to make risky interest-only or adjustable-rate mortgage loans. In 2006 and 2007, this regulatory pressure to improve underwriting standards spread to banks and other lenders who were making loans mainly to prime borrowers. The same pressure caused many lenders, both prime and subprime, to edge their interest rates upward and tighten other credit standards.

It should be emphasized, however, that most subprime borrowers—probably 80 percent or more—were not delinquent or defaulting, at least as of August 2007. So the subprime market successfully enabled large numbers of households with poor credit records to attain homeownership and apparently to sustain that benefit. Just how severe the problems of such borrowers would become in a serious economic downturn remains to be seen.

In mid-August 2007, defaults among subprime borrowers became serious enough to cause a near panic among various funds and individuals who had been supplying loans and credit to hedge funds, mortgage funds, and other financial intermediaries who had been lending to subprime homebuyers. Those initial lenders began to refuse to extend further credit to such financial intermediaries, some of whom were therefore caught in great financial difficulty. This situation even affected some financial intermediaries in Europe who had been acting in the American subprime lending market. Credit markets in general began to freeze up, and stock values plunged for fear of a major crisis in financial markets worldwide. In a surprise response, the Federal Reserve Board decided to increase liquidity in U.S. financial markets significantly. It also reduced the rate at which it would lend money to banks and other intermediaries—a major change in its preceding policy stance on interest rates. The Fed believed such steps were necessary to prevent a general credit panic that might notably slow the growth of the American and world economies.

A REVISED VIEW OF THE FILTERING PROCESS

Because housing prices in the United States have been rising for many years, and especially rapidly since 1990, the traditional view that falling housing prices will enable low-income households to buy better homes through filtering must be reexamined. From 1968 through 2006, the yearly median price of all existing single-family homes sold in the United States rose continuously, according to the National

Association of Realtors (NAR), which tracks that statistic. The average increase in the national median was 6.59 percent per year in current dollars, and the total increase from 1968 to 2006 was 1,039.8 percent! The lowest annual price increases were 0.22 percent in 1989 and 1.05 percent in 2006. This measure is based on all existing homes sold, no matter how old they are, not just on newly built homes. It would therefore appear at first glance that filtering has not worked since 1968! But several factors contrary to this conclusion must also be considered.

The most important contrary factor is that rising prices were often offset by improving credit conditions, including lower interest rates, as discussed earlier. When credit conditions change in ways favoring borrowers, effective prices to those borrowers can actually fall in relation to their purchasing power, even though those prices are rising in current-dollar terms. That clearly happened in the period from 1990 through 2005. Moreover, from 1981 through about 2003, mortgage interest rates were gradually declining, though not without interruptions. That decline increased the homebuying reach of even static incomes over the same period. Clearly, however, the same interest-rate decline was not happening in all those other years from 1968 through 2006, as can be seen from Figure 2-3. Although mortgage interest rates for a 30-year loan fell from 10.79 percent in 1987 to 6.03 in 2003 and 6.23 percent in 2006, such rates also rose in four of those 20 years. In many of those years, credit conditions for borrowers were worsening.

Another point is that the prices that were constantly rising were in current dollars, but prices in constant dollars did not rise continuously or as much. If current-dollar prices are converted into 1982–1984 prices by means of the Consumer Price Index based on those years, then the national median home price fell in 8 of the 38 years from 1968 to 2006, and rose 96.5 percent over that period. The average annual price change was plus 1.66 percent. Real median household incomes in the United States rose only 25.9 percent in the same period, so housing prices were rising much faster than household incomes even in real terms.

Another relevant factor is that housing prices have fallen in some communities during some time periods, in spite of the overall tendency of housing prices to rise. For example, from 2005 to 2006, median home prices fell in 26 metropolitan areas of 159 reported on by the NAR. That decline occurred, however, after many years in which home prices rose continuously in almost all metropolitan areas, up to 2005. In earlier periods, falling home prices in many regions permitted some filtering of the traditional type to occur. For example, between the second quarters of 1990 and 1996, median home prices fell in 14 of 114 metropolitan areas then tracked by the NAR.[7] Those areas included Albany, Nassau, New York City, Providence, and Hartford in the Northeast and San Diego, Riverside-San Bernardino, Honolulu, Los Angeles, Orange County, and Sacramento in the West.

The essential factor determining whether filtering will work effectively is whether the prices of older existing housing units have changed in response to new housing construction in ways that make those older homes more affordable to low-income households—regardless of whether those prices are falling or rising. If prices fall more than household incomes, that outcome would be the case, as in the traditional version of the filtering process. But if prices rise, homes could still be more affordable to low-income households if their incomes rose faster or if changes in credit conditions more than offset higher prices. The latter is what happened from 2000 to 2005, and even earlier. So filtering was working effectively in many regions at that time, in spite of rising home prices and relatively stagnant household incomes.

Thus, to determine whether filtering might work under given conditions, what is happening in a specific market to household incomes, housing prices, credit market conditions, and the five other specific conditions described earlier must be examined.

DOES FILTERING STILL HAVE ADVANTAGES AS A MEANS OF PROVIDING HOUSING TO LOW-INCOME HOUSEHOLDS?

In the past, filtering had three main advantages in providing housing for low-income households:

▶ *Economic efficiency.* Filtering was economically efficient, because it matched individual households with differing abilities to pay for housing with particular housing units they could afford. Hence it reduced the need to provide housing subsidies for households who lived in units they could not afford without assistance. Nevertheless, many households living in extreme poverty still needed subsidies to be able to live in decent-quality housing units.

▶ *Permitting low-income households to benefit from new construction.* Normally, most homebuilders concentrate on constructing relatively high-cost new housing units because they gain larger profits from such units. Low-income households usually cannot afford to occupy such costly units. Yet homebuilders' behavior could still indirectly benefit many households who could not afford to occupy the new units homebuilders were creating if either rising household incomes among low-income households or improving credit-market conditions more than offset housing price increases.

▶ *Administrative efficiency.* Filtering was administratively efficient because it allocated resources used in housing through a process of individual household choices in markets, rather than by having government bureaucracies make such choices for them. In the United States, Congress does not provide enough housing subsidies to serve all those households who technically and economically meet the requirements for such subsidies. Therefore, some noneconomic process must be used to allocate subsidized units among the many households eligible for them. That process is usually a waiting list run by a housing authority or other public bureaucracy or by a community development organization receiving government aid. Because filtering operates through markets, it does not generate the substantial economic and political costs of establishing and running large public bureaucracies.

I believe filtering still has all three of these advantages, assuming it operates under the necessary conditions described earlier.

DOES FILTERING STILL HAVE SIGNIFICANT DISADVANTAGES?

In the past, filtering also had several disadvantages, which are described in the following sections.

Inadequate Maintenance of Housing Units

Filtering required a decline in the relative price of existing housing units that sometimes caused their owners to underinvest in maintenance, permitting such units to deteriorate below socially acceptable minimum quality standards. This deterioration was particularly likely in the last stages of a housing unit's filtering down through the income distribution. At that point, the households then likely to occupy it had such low incomes that they could not pay rents sufficient to support adequate maintenance and refurbishing. Owners of such units were more likely to skimp on maintenance than when they could charge higher rents.

This disadvantage still exists in theory, but its importance has been diminished by local governments' more-rigorous enforcement of housing codes. When older housing units have become so deteriorated or undermaintained that they are no longer fit for human habitation, most local governments will condemn them or mark them for demolition. I have long argued that city governments should engage in differential degrees of housing code enforcement in different types of neighborhoods, in recognition of the residents' varying ability to pay. In very-high-income neighborhoods, rigorous enforcement of all codes is appropriate, because the occupants—many of whom own their homes themselves—can afford to pay to keep their homes up to very high standards of quality. But in much-lower-income neighborhoods, where most households are renters, local government officials should rigorously enforce only those elements of housing codes necessary to protect health and safety. Code officials can be more forgiving about elements of housing codes that are mainly decorative in nature and thus have no direct bearing on the health and safety of the occupants.[8] Such differential code enforcement is in fact almost universal in very large cities with many very poor residents, even though it is technically illegal. I realize my recommendation is quite controversial; some of my apartment-owner friends strongly favor all-out code enforcement in all neighborhoods, regardless of income. In the past few decades, however, local governments have more effectively removed the most deteriorated and dilapidated housing units from the scene through strong code enforcement regarding units in such deplorable condition. Professor John Quigley of the University of California at Berkeley pointed out recently in a 2006 paper on housing that:

> In 1975, there were about 2.8 million renter households who lived in "severely inadequate housing," representing almost 11 percent of renter households. By 2001, the last year for which comparable data are available, the number of inadequately housed households by this standard declined by 60 percent. And the fraction of renters living in severely inadequate housing was less than 3.5 percent.[9]

Encouraging Neighborhood Socioeconomic Segregation[10]

A second past disadvantage of filtering was that it was often accompanied by, and was a major cause of, neighborhood socioeconomic segregation, because a whole neighborhood often contains housing of approximately the same age, physical condition, or design, especially if it was created by a single homebuilding firm during a relatively short period. If this housing differs in these respects from housing in surrounding neighborhoods, the housing market may treat this neighborhood as a sociological unit. All the housing therein will be perceived as belonging to a single neighborhood. In fact, such perceptions often define neighborhoods, because many have no clear-cut physical boundaries.[11] As this housing in a neighborhood gets older, it becomes occupied by persons with lower incomes and social status than those who initially occupied it, as explained earlier. To some extent, its transition to lower and lower socioeconomic status results from a self-fulfilling prophecy by key actors in the metropolitan area's housing market.

This de facto socioeconomic segregation occurs because American households have a strong desire to live in neighborhoods occupied primarily by other households with incomes and social status either roughly the same as, or greater than, their own. The converse of this tendency is their desire to avoid living in neighborhoods occupied primarily by other households with incomes or social status lower than their own. When a neighborhood becomes occupied primarily by households at any given socioeconomic level, most households at higher socioeconomic levels will try to avoid living there. Those high-income or high-status households remaining in the area will gradually move out through normal turnover, caused by death, job transfers, or household composition changes. But because of the area's reputation, they will not be replaced by other high-status households.

This overall behavior pattern tends to create a socioeconomic hierarchy of neighborhoods within each major metropolitan area. At one extreme of this hierarchy are a few very expensive, high-status areas in excellent condition occupied by affluent households. Some are in the central city, but most are in the suburbs. At the other extreme are many more relatively inexpensive, low-status, often deteriorated areas occupied by very poor households. Most are older areas within the central city. Almost anyone familiar with the housing market of any metropolitan area can readily identify the specific neighborhoods at these two extremes. In between are many more areas with less clearly defined socioeconomic status. Each neighborhood is roughly homogeneous in physical quality and socioeconomic status, although it may contain considerable diversity around the mean.

This arrangement of residential neighborhoods into a socioeconomic hierarchy provides good-quality housing for a majority of American households, ranging from those at the high-cost end of the hierarchy well down toward those at the low-cost end. Hence, a majority of American households and local government officials approve of and sustain it.

But the hierarchy emanating from this process also compels most of the very poorest households to live together in the oldest, most deteriorated, worst-quality neighborhoods along with other very poor households. They must do so because they are excluded by high costs from higher-status areas. These lowest-status neighborhoods are usually dominated by very poor households. Hence their environment becomes heavily influenced by certain conditions associated with poverty, although not invariably found in poor areas. Those conditions include high rates of unemployment, crime, broken homes, alcoholism, gang dominance, drug abuse and drug traffic, mental illness, poor-quality schools, and physical deterioration. Plagued by such conditions, those residents able to move away do so, leaving the areas concerned dominated by residual households with the lowest levels of capability in society. These areas clearly do not offer their residents—especially the children growing up there—the same opportunities for personal development and economic advancement that are found higher up in the neighborhood hierarchy, particularly in the suburbs. Hence, they create conditions of unequal opportunity that are unjust—especially to children. This undesirable and unfair outcome is not caused solely by filtering, but the whole filtering process certainly contributes to it.

The evidence is strong that neighborhood socioeconomic segregation is still widespread in U.S. metropolitan areas.[12] Therefore, this disadvantage remains in effect.

Gentrification

Such segregation is offset to some degree in many urban neighborhoods by another process known as *gentrification*, the upgrading of the socioeconomic status of the area—and its physical quality—by an in-migration of higher-income and higher-status households than initially or recently lived there. In this process, a relatively rundown neighborhood occupied mainly by low-income households that neverthe-less has some locational amenities—such as proximity to downtown—is entered by a few higher-income households. They take advantage of the relatively low prices of housing to buy older homes and move in. Then they physically and aesthetically improve the homes they have bought. The arrival of a significant number of such households in a rundown neighborhood can change its reputation from being dete-riorated and undesirable to being fashionable and improving. This reputation may attract even more higher-income newcomers. Gradually, the entire area can be upgraded—or gentrified—in a process that resembles filtering in reverse. Gentrifi-cation, however, tends to remove many older housing units from the economic reach of low-income households, because as a neighborhood becomes gentrified, the prices of homes there rise significantly. Hence, gentrification tends to reduce the number of housing units in the area accessible to low-income households.

In recent years, significant numbers of empty nesters, gay households, child-less married households, single households, and newly married households without school-age children have been moving into central-city neighborhoods close to down-town employment centers. They do so partly to avoid traffic congestion going to and from work in those centers. But their ability to gentrify older neighborhoods has been greatly enhanced by the Niagara of capital flowing into residential real estate markets. Where gentrification is occurring to a notable degree, filtering is likely to be thwarted by rising home prices and increases in the average incomes and social status of the residents there. Therefore, in judging the effectiveness of filtering in any given neigh-borhood or community, determining whether gentrification is a major force there is necessary. Where it is, filtering is less likely to work well. The best source of informa-tion on the subject is local real estate brokers.

Neighborhood Instability

The filtering process implies that most neighborhoods will undergo massive changes in the character of their occupants as they progress through various stages of their life cycles. In all neighborhoods, the individual households living there constantly change through normal processes of movement, death, and shifts in household com-position. On average, from 15 to 20 percent of the households in a typical American neighborhood move each year. This percentage is much higher among renters (about

38 percent per year) than among homeowners (about 10 percent per year). But filtering also often causes the relative socioeconomic status of an area to change over time. That status usually declines as the housing in an area ages, except in well-maintained historic-preservation districts or a few close-in suburbs with strong locations and amenities. This process of constant or frequent neighborhood transition is a source of social instability and intergroup conflict within U.S. urban areas.

Nevertheless, the type of rapid and large-scale transition of neighborhoods from occupancy mainly by whites to occupancy mainly by African Americans that occurred in many U.S. cities in the 1950s and 1960s is no longer prevalent. It has slowed dramatically because of the much lower growth rates in the African American population in large cities. African Americans today are more likely to be migrating from big cities out to the suburbs than in-migrating from the countryside to big cities. In some cities, such transition has been replaced by transition from white to Hispanic occupancy, or from occupancy by one minority group to occupancy by another, with the latter usually consisting of recent immigrants from abroad. Such transitions are now found just as often in suburbs as in central cities, and more scattering of ethnic and racial groups and intermingling with white populations exist than in the past. Even so, in determining whether filtering will be effective in any given city or community, determining whether any large-scale neighborhood transitions from one group to another are underway there is necessary.

CONCLUSION

Filtering has long been a major source of housing for American low-income households. It provides them with homes at prices or rents they can afford without requiring subsidies from government agencies. The former prevalence of falling prices among older homes has more recently been replaced by steadily rising prices among nearly all American homes, however, except in metropolitan areas losing population or growing very slowly, such as Cleveland, Pittsburgh, and Rochester. This shift has the potential of making the whole filtering process ineffective at providing unsubsidized housing for low-income households. Under some circumstances—mainly rising household incomes and easing credit conditions—filtering can still work when housing prices are rising, if they are not rising faster than those other circumstances can overcome. But filtering can no longer be taken for granted as an automatic source of a major part of the housing needs of low-income households. Nor can it be assumed that filtering will act in just the same way in all the different communities within a metropolitan region or a state. Rather, determining whether filtering can supply much of the housing needs for low-income households requires investigation of a considerable number of conditions affecting housing markets in the communities concerned. Therefore, estimating what additional actions are necessary to meet a community's need for housing for low-income households is much more difficult than in the past. Nevertheless, such estimation should be an important part of each community's and state's planning to meet its future housing needs.

Notes

1. These conditions are quoted from Anthony Downs, "The Filtering Process as a Source of Housing for Low-Income Households," *Journal of Planning Literature* 3, no. 2 (Spring 1988): 127–52.

2. The relationships between incomes, interest rates, downpayments, and specific monthly mortgage payments in this table were calculated using the computer program Power One Finance with Commercial Real Estate templates, by Infinity Software. The mortgage template was used.

3. Data for 1990 and 2000 were taken from the U.S. Bureau of the Census Web site for those two decennial censuses, http://factfinder.census.gov/servlet/DatasetMainPageServlet?_program= DEC8_submenuId=datasets_08_lang=en, and for 2005 from the American Housing Survey for 2005, http://www.census.gov/hhes/www/housing/ahs/ahs05/ahs05.html, also on the U.S. Census Bureau Web site.

4. Data are from the American Housing Survey for 2005 on the U.S. Census Bureau Web site.

5. Alan Greenspan and James Kennedy, *Estimates of Home Mortgage Originations, Repayments, and Debt on One-to-Four Family Homes* (Washington, D.C.: Federal Reserve Board, 2005), on the Federal Reserve Bank Web site, http://www.federalreserve.gov/pubs/feds/2005/200541/200541pap.pdf. Mortgage-origination data from the Mortgage Bankers Association and the U.S. Department of Housing and Urban Development closely parallel the Federal Reserve estimates.

6. Fannie Mae, Economic Commentary for April 2007, on the Fannie Mae Web site, http:// www.fanniemae.com/media/pdf/berson/monthly/2007/041207.pdf.

7. Data from various monthly issues of *Metropolitan Area Home Price Sales* published by the National Association of Realtors.

8. Ignoring mainly decorative minor violations of housing codes contradicts the "broken windows" theory of law enforcement in low-income neighborhoods. According to that theory, any visible signs of deterioration or poor maintenance of properties contributes to a generally permissive attitude toward law enforcement that encourages more serious forms of crime. Hence, such visible signs should be immediately corrected. For a presentation of this theory, see George L. Kelling and Catherine M. Coles, *Fixing Broken Windows: Restoring Order and Reducing Crime in Our Communities* (New York: The Free Press, 1996).

9. John Quigley, "Just Suppose: Housing Subsidies for Low-Income Renters" (paper presented at a conference on rental housing sponsored by Harvard's Joint Center on Housing and the MacArthur Foundation, Cambridge, Mass., November 2006), 10.

10. This section is taken from my earlier paper "The Filtering Process as a Source of Housing for Low-Income Households."

11. For a discussion of how neighborhoods are defined, see Anthony Downs, *Neighborhoods and Urban Development* (Washington, D.C.: The Brookings Institution, 1981), 13–23 and *passim*.

12. For a review of the evidence, see Douglas S. Massey and Nancy A. Denton, *American Apartheid: Segregation and the Making of the Underclass* (Cambridge, Mass.: Harvard University Press, 1993).

CHAPTER FIVE

How the Niagara of Capital Has Affected Housing Affordability

The Niagara of capital flowing into real estate has aggravated already serious housing affordability problems in the United States and other developed nations. Yet, paradoxically, the same Niagara of capital also helped millions of American renter households become homeowners. This chapter discusses how the recent inflow of capital to housing markets produced both of these seemingly opposite effects.

EFFECTS THAT WORSENED HOUSING AFFORDABILITY IN GENERAL

The Niagara of capital was itself caused in part by the globalization of financial markets, which permitted capital to flow freely and rapidly around the world. Its effect on housing accentuated a basic problem worsened by such globalization. That problem is the increasing economic divergence within developed nations between the economic welfare of many low-and-moderate-income workers—especially manufacturing workers—and that of most high-ranking executives and professional workers. This divergence is illustrated by Figure 5-1. The share of total household income received by the highest-income quintile (20 percent) of all households rose steadily from a low of 43.2 percent in 1975 to a high of 50.4 percent in 2005. The percentage shares of all the other four quintiles declined in this same period. The exact relative shares of these quintiles is a subject of considerable argument by statistical experts.[1] But universal agreement exists that the share of the highest-income quintile has risen compared with the shares of the other 80 percent. Nor does anyone dispute the fact that the highest-income quintile receives many times more income every year than each of the lowest three quintiles.

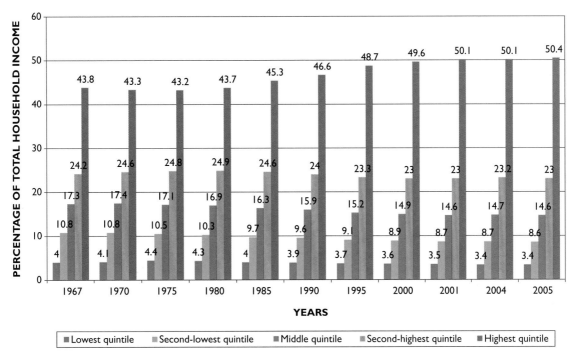

Source: C. DeNavas-Walt, B.D. Proctor, and C.H. Lee, U.S. Census Bureau, Current Population Reports P60-231, *Income, Poverty, and Health Insurance Coverage in the United States: 2005* (Washington, D.C.: U.S. Government Printing Office, 2006), Table A-3, 40.

American low-income households have faced low wages and incomes prevented from rising in part by competition from very-low-wage foreign workers. Two conditions have recently made such competition more important than ever before. First, many more very-low-wage foreign workers have become well-enough educated to compete in skill with workers in developed nations. Second, those foreign workers have been technologically empowered to compete effectively from long distances by computers, almost instantaneous Internet and satellite communications, and fast global shipping systems. Technological improvements in American manufacturing productivity have also caused U.S. manufacturing employment to decline steadily since peaking in 1979, thereby helping limit increases in manufacturing wages. Most high-level executives and professionals have not been subjected to similar foreign competition. So they have been capturing ever-larger shares of the overall wealth produced in economically developed societies. The resulting economic inequality threatens both the domestic tranquillity in developed nations and their willingness to continue politically supporting the free markets and free trade that form the heart of economic globalization.

Yet housing in developed nations is not a commodity that can be built cheaply abroad and shipped around the world. Nor can housing be cheaply built within America by foreign workers, because our building regulations prohibit construction of very small, inexpensive housing units with low levels of amenities. Therefore, housing might seem immune to the economic effects of globalization. But a flood of money into housing markets, some of it from outside the United States, has helped drive up housing prices at the same time that industrial and many other wages and incomes were stagnant, caused in part by the effect of low-cost foreign labor and in part by changes in technology and other factors. For homeowners who benefited from greater home equities caused by rising home prices, the effect of stagnated wages was notably diminished, even if they had relatively low incomes. But low-income workers who did not own their own homes were increasingly squeezed economically between stagnant incomes, on one hand, and soaring housing costs and rising rents, on the other.

This outcome has greatly aggravated previously serious housing affordability problems for many American low-income households. This same effect has appeared in other developed nations, such as the United Kingdom, Spain, and Australia. Because housing costs are the largest single item in the budgets of almost all households, intensified housing affordability problems greatly affect the overall welfare of any households involved—especially those with low incomes.

An understanding of the complex set of events and conditions that caused that result requires first analyzing what is meant by "housing affordability problems" and then connecting them to the Niagara of capital in the United States and around the world.

WHAT DOES "AFFORDABLE HOUSING" REALLY MEAN?

In plain language, a housing unit is affordable to the Jones family if that family can pay for the cost of occupying that unit without unduly reducing the resources it has left over out of its income to pay for other important necessities, such as food, clothing, transportation, education, and medical care. But this seemingly straightforward definition contains many ambiguities, including the following:

▶ *What level of shelter quality does the Jones family need to live a satisfying life?* Some minimum level of shelter quality must be required to meet the family's normal housing needs. How this level should be defined in practice varies immensely from one society or culture to another. My own experience is that the minimum quality of housing required in each society is almost entirely a matter of relative cultural values, rather than any absolute physiological necessities for healthy living. I reached this conclusion when I first visited Hong Kong in the 1970s. That city was housing more than 1 million refugees from China (then politically and legally separate from Hong Kong) in seven-story, walk-up apartment buildings containing one-room housing units with only 120 square feet of living space per unit. Inside those 10-foot by 12-foot units was electricity but no heat, no running water, and no bathroom. Each floor had one collective water pipe and one large collective bathroom for all persons living on that floor. These dwellings would even then have been considered drastically substandard in the United States or Western Europe, but the residents seemed to be suffering from no serious illnesses or drawbacks from their housing experiences. Yet such large differences in housing quality directly affect variations in the cost of the housing involved. These differences mean the quality of housing that American local governments consider the minimum necessary for a household is determined much more by American cultural values than by the physiological necessities of living.

▶ *What income does the Jones family have with which to pay for housing and other necessities and luxuries?* Reasonably considered, every household with an annual income above some specific level should have enough resources not to suffer from housing affordability problems. But what is that level?

▶ *What are the Jones family's requirements for nonhousing consumption?* The answer varies with the number of persons in the family; their ages; whether they have any health problems; and what specific needs they may have to develop their special talents, such as great musical ability, great skill at basketball or some other sport, or brilliant mathematical ability.

▶ *What does "unduly reducing resources" really mean in practice?* How greatly can the Jones family cut back on nonhousing spending to meet its minimum housing needs without drastically reducing its overall standard of living? This, too, is almost entirely a matter of subjective judgments or society's particular cultural standards.

In the United States, practical answers to all of these questions have been developed over time in the process of deciding which specific households should receive government assistance in meeting their housing needs. These answers can be roughly stated as follows:

▶ *Minimum shelter requirements.* These requirements include a dwelling unit with a waterproof roof; heating in the winter; electricity; a telephone; hot-and-cold running water; an indoor toilet and shower or bath; "adequate" lighting in the form of windows; doors and windows that can be secured against intruders; a kitchen with stove, refrigerator, and sink; at least one bedroom for every two persons; and preferably no more than one resident per total number of rooms. In America, a typical two-bedroom unit with all these elements would contain at least 500 square feet of total area and, more likely, 800 square feet. Moreover, the traits considered minimal for decent housing units have increased in number and cost over the years as social standards rose.

▶ *Low income levels.* The income level that the federal government considers a maximum for a household to be considered potentially eligible for government housing assistance is 80 percent of the locally measured median household income in the region where the household lives. Greater eligibility exists for households with incomes of 50 percent of that median income or less. In the United States as a whole, the 2005 median household income was $44,503 in 2005 dollars, according to the American Housing Survey of 2005; 80 percent of that amount was $35,602, and 50 percent was $22,251. According to the American Housing Survey of 2005, in that year 27.942 million U.S. households had pretax incomes of $22,251 or less, and 44.178 million had pretax incomes of $35,000 or less.[2] They constituted 25.67 percent and 40.58 percent, respectively, of all households in 2005. Clearly, however, millions of low-income households did not accurately report their incomes to the Census Bureau or anyone else. They omitted government in-kind transfers like food stamps and public housing, intergenerational transfers from their parents and grandparents, and illegal incomes or money earned legitimately but not reported to the Internal Revenue Service. That is why so many low-income households reported spending far more on consumption than they received as income, as discussed below. Those percentage figures for very-low-income households thus are way too high.

▶ *Nonhousing consumption requirements.* The household requirements for nonhousing consumption have been established by examining government statistics about actual household consumption spending over the years. The U.S. Department of Housing and Urban Development (HUD), which administers most federal housing subsidies, has concluded that households have a housing affordability problem if they both (a) have low incomes, as previously defined, and (b) spend 30 percent or more of their incomes for all housing expenses. That problem is considered severe if they spend half or more of their incomes on housing.[3]

Figure 5-2 shows the shares of total annual consumer expenditures spent for housing by members of nine income groups from 1984 through 2005 from the Consumer Expenditure Surveys of the Labor Department's Bureau of Labor Statistics. Two major conclusions can be drawn from this information. The first is that households with incomes below $20,000 per year tend to devote considerably more than 30 percent of their total spending to housing. In 1984, 53 percent of all households surveyed had incomes (in current dollars) below $20,000; in 2005, 23 percent did.[4] The second conclusion is that the percentage of total consumer spending devoted to housing has risen steadily from 1984 through 2005; in the latter year, it equaled or exceeded 35 per-

FIGURE 5-2. **HOUSING COSTS AS A PERCENTAGE OF CONSUMER SPENDING**

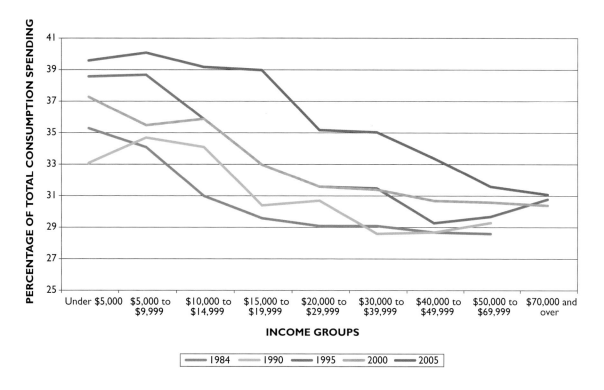

Source: Bureau of Labor Statistics, Consumer Expenditure Survey, 2005, Table 1. Quintiles of income before taxes: Average annual expenditures and characteristics, http://www.bls.gov/cex/2005/Standard/quintile.pdf.

cent for all households with incomes under $30,000 (who comprised 35 percent of all households surveyed), and exceeded 30 percent for households in all ten income groups, including those with incomes of $70,000 or more.

Translating these percentages of *total consumer expenditures* devoted to housing by each income group into reliable percentages of *income* devoted to housing by that group is almost impossible. Why? Because all the 30 income groups who reported pretax incomes below $40,000 per year also reported that they spent more than 100 percent of their incomes for consumer goods and services (except for households with incomes of $30,000 to $39,999, who spent 98.8 percent of their incomes in 1984, 99.7 percent in 1990, and 85.7 percent in 1984, according to published survey data). How people can annually spend more than they receive in income—up to 25 times as much for some very-low-income groups—is not explained by the Bureau of Labor Statistics, except for the obvious statement that low-income households were undoubtedly underreporting their incomes. Therefore, the relationship between housing costs and incomes estimated from Consumer Expenditure Surveys can hardly be considered a reliable measure of reality. Even if it were, that measure would indicate that 30 percent is far too low an estimate of how much of their incomes very-low-income households were spending on housing, at least from 1990 to the present. Yet 30 percent is the measure the U.S. government has officially adopted as the maximum amount poor households should be required to pay for housing, even though most such households already pay considerably more than that.

Thus, the basic idea of housing affordability is highly ambiguous and ill defined, and the U.S. government's official statistical approach to it is surely inaccurate. Nevertheless, the government's approach can be used to estimate the number and percentage of households who are suffering from housing affordability problems as defined by HUD. We need only assume that the percentage of total *spending* each household devotes to housing is the same as the percentage of its total *income* devoted to housing. In short, we must assume that people can spend only what they actually receive in income. This approach indicates that in 2005, 100 percent of American households had housing affordability problems, although that conclusion seems completely unrealistic. In contrast, in 1984, 42.7 percent had such problems. In any event, that percentage is both very large and has clearly risen significantly over time, especially after 2000 when the Niagara of capital was in full flood. A second implication of this assumption is that all households from 1995 through 2005 had actual incomes of at least $14,000 per year, regardless of what they reported their incomes to be, because they all spent at least that much annually. Thus, the Niagara of capital has greatly aggravated the severity of housing affordability problems within American society by directly causing a huge rise in the price of owner-occupied housing and indirectly causing a rise in rents too.

EFFECTS THAT REDUCED HOUSING AFFORDABILITY PROBLEMS FOR MANY

At the same time, by enriching all those homeowning households who have gained large increases in the equities in their homes, the Niagara of capital greatly or even fully offset their housing affordability problems caused by higher home prices. Furthermore, by flooding debt markets with capital, the Niagara of capital both drove interest rates down and motivated lenders to ease credit terms for households seeking to borrow money to buy homes. The resulting lower interest rates and easier credit terms enabled millions of renter households to become homeowners even though housing prices were rising faster than household incomes, as discussed at length in Chapter 4. Many such new homeowners were able to sustain their ownership roles in spite of monthly payment increases required by interest-only loans and other credit-easing devices. For many of them, becoming a homeowner early in the period from 2000 to 2005 enabled them to enjoy rising net equities in their homes.

Households who bought their first homes in 2005 or later, however, purchased them at close to the top of the housing price market. If their purchases were highly leveraged with debt, they will suffer declining net equities if housing prices decline significantly, as they began to do in many metropolitan areas in 2006 and 2007. That is especially likely concerning speculators who borrowed the maximum amount and bought late in the game in hopes of flipping at higher prices. So the net effect of the Niagara of capital upon housing affordability for such households remains to be determined by future events.

These developments mean that housing affordability cannot be realistically defined solely in terms of the relationship between housing costs and incomes. That definition must also take into account the effects of (a) rising home prices on home-owner equity wealth, (b) changing credit terms upon the ability of households to become or remain homeowners, and (c) intergenerational transfers of wealth from their parents or grandparents.

Another implication of the preceding analysis is that the Niagara of capital had much more harmful effects upon renter households who did not have homeowning parents or grandparents to help them buy homes than upon homeowner households or renters who had such benefited relatives. In the 2000 U.S. Census, 58 percent of all households with 1999 incomes below $35,000 were renters; in 2005, 44 percent of all households with incomes below $40,000 (about the same in real terms as $35,000 in 1999) were renters. That fraction declined because of the sharp rise in homeowner-ship between 2000 and 2005, which also resulted from the effect of the Niagara of capital on credit terms.

EFFECTS THAT WORSENED U.S. AFFORDABILITY PROBLEMS

The Niagara of capital has made American housing affordability problems notably worse for low-income renters without homeowning parents or grandparents, although it also helped reduce the proportion of renters in the entire population. This result can be seen by comparing American median household incomes from 1968 to 2005 with median housing prices in the same period. Figure 5-3 depicts these two variables after transforming both into 1982–1984 dollars to eliminate the effects of inflation. Between 1968 and 2005, median household incomes in 1982–1984 dollars as reported by the U.S. Census Bureau rose only 2.31 percent, an average annual increase of only 0.062 percent. But median home prices, also in 1982–1984 dollars, rose 83.3 percent— or 36 times as much. The ratio of median home prices divided by median household

FIGURE 5-3. **U.S. REAL MEDIAN HOME PRICES AND MEDIAN INCOMES**

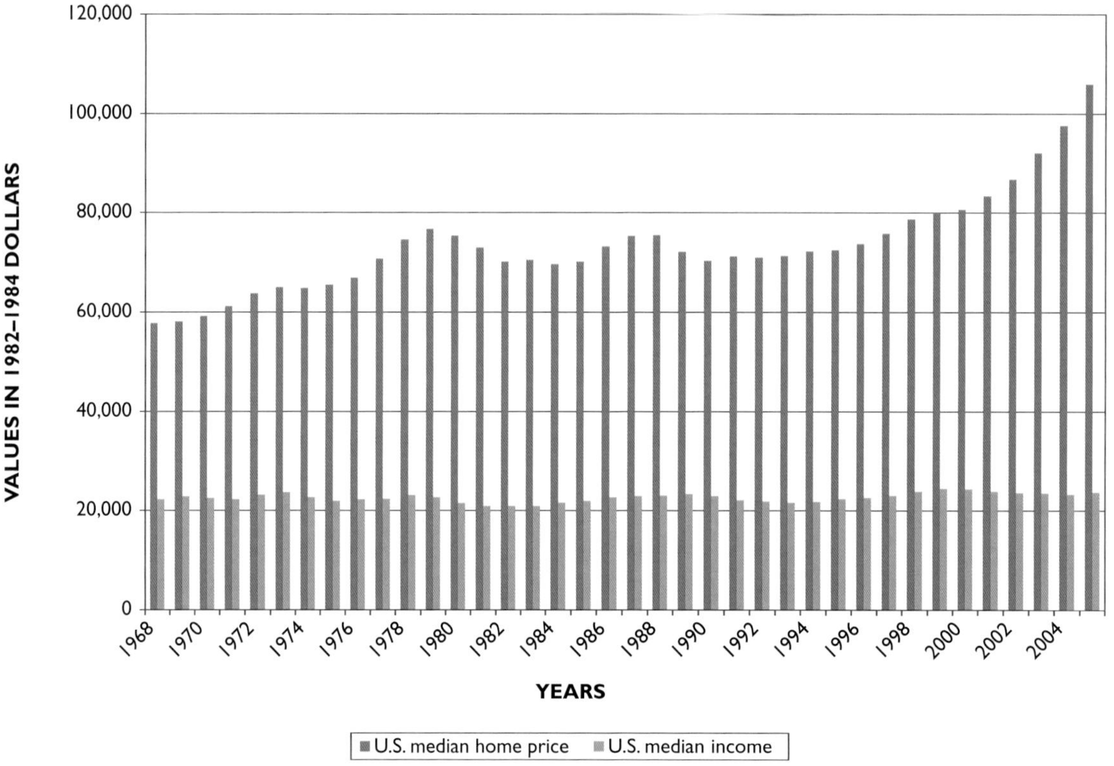

Sources: Home prices: California Association of Realtors, *Trends in California Real Estate*, various monthly issues, and National Association of Realtors, *Insights*, various monthly issues; median incomes: U.S. Census Bureau, "Historical Income Tables, Households, Race and Hispanic Origin of Householder, 1967–2005," Table H-5, http://www.census.gov/hhes/www/income/histinc/h05.html (accessed July 2007).

incomes is shown in Figure 5-4. That ratio started at 2.6 in 1968, rose slowly to 3.5 in 1980, fell to between 3.0 and 3.5 in the 16 years from 1984 to 2000, then shot up from 3.5 in 2001 to 4.5 in 2005—the very period in which the Niagara of capital was at its peak. This ratio increased 40 percent in five years, although it had remained relatively flat for the preceding 16 years. The increased ratio raised the monthly payments potential homebuyers had to make to become homeowners to levels many could not afford.

A second effect of the Niagara of capital on housing affordability concerns renter households. Median rents in constant-value 1982–1984 dollars remained between $270 and $300 per month from 1988 through 2000, as shown in Figure 5-5. Then the median rent in constant dollars rose to a peak of $324 in 2004, 12 percent higher than the median rent in 1988. Median household incomes, also in constant dollars, rose

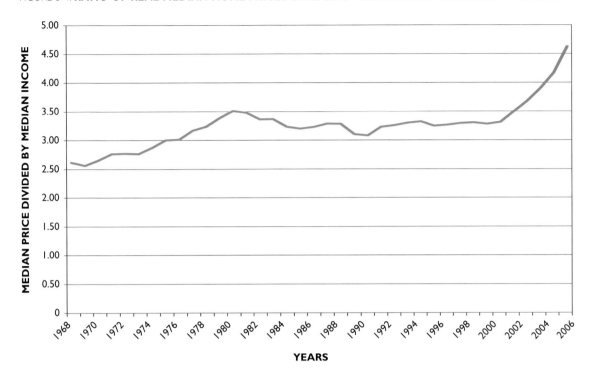

Sources: Home prices: California Association of Realtors, *Trends in California Real Estate*, various monthly issues, and National Association of Realtors, *Insights*, various monthly issues; median incomes: U.S. Census Bureau, "Historical Income Tables, Households, Race and Hispanic Origin of Householder, 1967–2005," Table H-5, http://www.census.gov/hhes/www/income/histinc/h05.html (accessed July 2007).

less than 10 percent in the same time period. Nevertheless, a household receiving the median income could easily have paid the median rent by spending less than 30 percent of its income on rent alone, because 30 percent would have equaled $1,105 per month in 2004 (in current dollars) when median rent was $636.

The rent-paying capacity of poorer households was much weaker, however, partly because so many marginally poor households have become homeowners. A household with an income equal to 60 percent of the national median could have paid the rent, although not leaving much else out of 30 percent of its income to pay for other housing-related expenses. But households with incomes equaling only 50 percent of the national median income could have paid the median rent in only one-third of the 18 years from 1988 through 2004. And households with incomes equaling only 25 percent of the national median could have paid less than half the median rent with 30 percent of their annual incomes in all 18 years. Yet in 2005, 7.2 million

FIGURE 5-5. **U.S. MEDIAN RENTS IN 1982–1984 DOLLARS, 1988–2006**

Source: U.S. Census Bureau, Housing Vacancy Surveys, Table 11, Median Rents.

renter households had incomes of 25 percent of the national median or less, while 14.185 million had incomes equal to or less than 50 percent of the national median.

The preceding statistics are misleading for two reasons, however. First, many low-income renters do not fully report their earned incomes or government transfers (which they are not required to report) or intergenerational transfers of wealth from parents or grandparents. Consequently, many have much greater abilities to pay median rents than reported income indicates. Reliably estimating how many are in that category is nevertheless impossible. Second, rents vary much more across the nation than household incomes. Rents on the West and East coasts are much higher than in much of the Midwest and South, and rents in rural areas are much lower than those in big cities and their major suburbs. Hence, conclusions derived from national statistics may not apply to many specific parts of the nation.

THE NATURE OF AMERICAN HOUSING AFFORDABILITY PROBLEMS TODAY

Just how bad has the housing affordability situation become for low-income renter households? From 2005 data presented earlier, 44.178 million U.S. households (40.6 percent of all households) appear to have had incomes at or below 80 percent of the national median income, and 27.942 million (25.67 percent of all households) had incomes at or below 50 percent of the national median. Nevertheless, the American Housing Survey of 2005 also indicated that 23.1 million households with incomes at or below 80 percent of the national median (52 percent of all such low-income households) were homeowners.

Many of those low-income homeowners can reasonably be assumed to have received significant benefits from greater home equities caused by the increase in U.S. home prices since about 1997. Hence, they have the ability to borrow against their higher home equities to help meet their housing expenses. That was true of households who became homeowners well before housing prices reached their peak in about 2005. However, some households who bought homes right when housing prices were peaking have not enjoyed increased net equities in those homes—especially if they used credit devices that involved negative amortization.

Therefore, the population groups suffering most from housing affordability problems are (a) current renters with incomes below 80 percent of the national median income or those at 50 percent of the national median income who do not have homeowning parents or grandparents, and (b) households who bought their first homes right when housing prices were peaking by using credit terms that imposed high repayment burdens upon them. Neither of these groups received significant benefits from increased equity in their own homes. Also, both groups have the disadvantage of having to pay much higher prices to buy homes, either when they bought them or when they try to buy them in the future. Moreover, median rents have risen faster since 2000 than median incomes, causing further disadvantages for low-income renters.

In 2005, according to the American Housing Survey in that year, 21.0 million renter households had incomes at or below 80 percent of the national median income, including 14.3 million renters with incomes at or below 50 percent of the national median. These 21.0 million are the households most in need of aid to cope with housing affordability problems. They constituted 62.0 percent of all renter households in 2005, or 19.3 percent of all U.S. households in that year. These renter households were in the income groups shown in Table 5-1.

These statistics also are somewhat misleading. Many of the lowest-income groups in Table 5-1 are young college students whose long-term income prospects are much greater than their present incomes. Other of the lowest-income groups

TABLE 5-1. **RENTER INCOME GROUPS**

Renter Income Groups	Number of Households	Percentage of All Renters
Under $5,000	3,164,000	9.32
$5,000–$9,999	3,367,000	9.92
$10,000–$14,999	3,292,000	9.70
$15,000–$19,999	3,026,000	8.92
$20,000–$24,999	2,969,000	8.75
$25,000–$29,999	2,809,000	8.28
$30,000–$34,999	2,426,000	7.15
Total	21,053,000	62.03%

Source: U.S. Census Bureau, "American Housing Survey of 2005."

were inaccurately reporting their incomes, as noted previously. Yet many truly low-income renter households exist who constitute a highly disadvantaged group. Clearly, the major housing problem facing these households is lack of income, not the cost of occupying "decent" shelter. In short, poverty—or at least poverty in relation to housing costs—is the central cause of housing affordability problems in America, rather than the absence of physically adequate dwelling units. Therefore, the single-most-important policy objective in attacking housing affordability problems is to raise the money purchasing power of low-income renter households.[5]

CONCLUSION

The Niagara of capital flowing into American housing markets has had a dual effect in those markets over the past 15 years or so. By raising housing prices spectacularly, it put home ownership out of the economic reach of millions of renter households. But at the same time, by flooding home lending markets with money, it drove down interest rates and encouraged mortgage lenders to loosen their underwriting standards to an unprecedented degree. Those results enabled other millions of renter households to achieve homeownership even though their incomes were not rising nearly as fast as home prices.

Even so, millions of low-and-moderate-income households, and even many middle-income households in high-housing-cost regions who want to become homeowners are still unable to do so. The next chapter discusses possible means of helping them overcome this disadvantage.

Notes

1. For example, see Robert E. Rector and Rea S. Hederman, Jr., *Income Inequality: How Census Data Misrepresent Income Distribution*, Heritage Foundation Center for Data Analysis Report #99-07 (Washington D.C.: Heritage Foundation, 1999), http://www.heritage.org/Research/Labor/CDA99-07.cfm (accessed April 28, 2006).

2. These household estimates were derived by calculating what share of each $5,000 income group was above the level of income bounding the group in which the boundary income was located. For example, an income of $23,163 is $3,163 into the income bracket of $20,000 to $25,000, or 63.26 percent. There were 6,804,314 households in that income bracket in 2005; 63.26 percent of them equals 4,304,409. There were also 22,980,934 households in income brackets below $20,000. Adding those last two numbers together yields a total of 27,285,343 households who had incomes of less than 50 percent of the national median income. Data from U.S. Census Bureau, "American Community Survey for 2005," table B19001, Household Income in the Past 12 Months (in 2005 inflation-adjusted dollars).

3. The 30 percent threshold has been derived from two sources. First, Sen. Edward Brooke of Massachusetts proposed in 1968 that no households living in public housing should be charged more than 25 percent of their incomes for rent, and this law was passed by Congress. The Reagan administration later raised that fraction to 30 percent to save money in running HUD. This fraction gradually came to be the threshold that HUD considered the maximum amount that poor households should be required to pay for their own housing without suffering hardship, regardless of how that housing was provided to them. Insofar as I can determine from HUD officials, no scientific, statistical, or physiological studies were specifically used to support this decision.

The second source of the 30 percent threshold is the Consumer Expenditure Surveys conducted yearly by the U.S. Labor Department's Bureau of Labor Statistics. Those surveys asked a large randomized sample of American households how much money they spent on various types of consumer goods and services each year. The surveys also asked those households to estimate the sizes of their incomes and then computed each type of expenditure as a percentage of both (a) the household's total consumer spending and (b) its after-tax income.

4. Those percentages are taken from the Consumer Expenditure Surveys for the years indicated.

5. The conclusion that raising incomes for poor households is a more important public policy than building new low-cost housing units was brilliantly analyzed and defended by Louis Winnick in his 1995 article, "The Triumph of Housing Allowance Programs: How a Fundamental Policy Conflict Was Resolved," *Cityscape: A Journal of Policy Development and Research* 1, no. 3 (September 1995): 95–121.

CHAPTER SIX

Trying to Improve Housing Affordability

The previous chapter analyzed how the Niagara of capital flowing into real estate markets has affected housing affordability in the United States. It concluded that the Niagara of capital aided many low-income renter households in attaining home-ownership by improving their credit conditions but simultaneously prevented many others from doing so by raising the prices of homes beyond their economic reach. That conclusion leaves two key questions unanswered: what actions might be taken to improve housing affordability for the second group of American renter households, and how effective are those actions likely to be?

This chapter deals with those questions. It is not a complete catalog of how to improve housing affordability for low-income renters. Rather, it explores the main means of doing so and their political feasibility. Because this chapter does not focus specifically on the actions and effects of the Niagara of capital in coping with housing affordability, readers interested solely in the financial capital aspects of this whole study may wish to skip this chapter and move directly to Chapter 7.

THE MAIN ASPECTS OF HOUSING AFFORDABILITY PROBLEMS AMONG LOW-INCOME U.S. RENTERS

The previous chapter ended with the unsurprising conclusion that the major housing problem facing low-income renter households is their lack of income compared to the cost of occupying "decent" shelter, rather than the absence of physically adequate dwelling units. Therefore, the single-most-important policy objective in attacking housing affordability problems is to raise the money purchasing power of low-income renter households.[1]

As identified by housing experts attending a November 2006 "National Policy Summit" on American rental housing, sponsored by the Joint Center for Housing Studies of Harvard University and supported by the John D. and Catherine T. MacArthur Foundation in Cambridge, Massachusetts, the following three other aspects of the housing situations of low-income renter households are also significant problems:

▶ *Concentrated poverty neighborhoods.* Many low-income renters reside in neighborhoods that contain high concentrations of other low-income renters, who often have incomes below the poverty line. Such concentrated poverty areas are mainly located within large cities. These neighborhoods are typically marked by high rates of crime, dilapidated buildings, unemployment, broken families, juvenile delinquency, gang activity, drug abuse, and low-quality public schools. The life opportunities of people living in such areas—including ready access to good jobs—are not nearly as beneficial as those of people living in areas with much smaller concentrations of poor households.

▶ *Exclusionary local housing regulations.* Many metropolitan suburbs with much more favorable neighborhood living conditions than the previously described neighborhoods—including ready access to good jobs—have adopted zoning and building code regulations that prevent developers from building relatively low-cost housing within their boundaries. Such regulation greatly reduces the ability of low-income renter households living in concentrated-poverty neighborhoods to move into more-desirable neighborhoods within the same metropolitan areas. That difficulty in turn blocks their chances of escaping from the adverse conditions where they now live.

▶ *Declining number of low-rent housing units.* The total supply of housing units in America with relatively low rents affordable for low-income renters is declining over time. One reason is that both the quality and the size of new housing units built in the United States over the past several decades have increased notably, thereby increasing the cost of occupying them. In its report *The State of the Nation's Housing: 2006*, the Joint Center for Housing Studies at Harvard University said:

> The nation has been losing affordable housing for more than 30 years. This is the housing stock that is affordable, at 30 percent of income, to the third of renter households with incomes of $16,000 or less. From 1993 to 2003, the inventory of these units—with inflation-adjusted rents of $400 [per month] or less, including utilities—plunged by 1.2 million. With such drastic losses to upgrading, abandonment, or demolition, the shortage of rentals affordable and available to low-income households was a dismal 5.4 million. . . . In 2001, owners of fully 12 percent of all rental properties with average rents of $400 or less reported negative operating income—an unsustainable condition that points to accelerating losses of low-cost units going forward.[2]

As the Joint Center pointed out, almost all new rental units being built are in large structures containing many units, designed to command high rents. So the economy must rely on downward filtering of older units to serve directly the low-income renter population. But rents have been rising fast enough to prevent many older units from moving into truly low-rent classifications. Also, many rental housing units have been converted to condominium ownership units in the past few years, reducing the rental supply.

All four of the major housing-related problems of low-income renters are extremely difficult to overcome. Moreover, the second, third, and fourth problems are fundamentally based on the first problem—the lack of adequate incomes among many renter households. Therefore, the remainder of this discussion of housing affordability problems focuses on potential approaches to remedying that lack of income in relation to housing costs.

HOW TO REDUCE THE RECENT WORSENING OF HOUSING AFFORDABILITY PROBLEMS

In theory, the recent worsening of housing affordability problems caused in great part by the Niagara of capital might be remedied or at least diminished in many ways, which are discussed in the following separate sections.

Raising Household Incomes

From 1976 through 2002, median housing prices in the United States were between 3.0 and 3.51 times as great as median incomes. To return to that 3.51 relationship in 2005, 2005 median incomes would have to have risen to $58,974 in 2005 dollars—an increase of 33 percent. That increase would be greater than all the annual changes in real incomes since 1968 combined, given that the U.S. median household income rose in constant dollars only 20.2 percent in those 37 years by some measures and only 2.7 percent by other measures, both from the U.S. Census Bureau.[3] In other words, household incomes would have to experience a sudden and large upward surge like that shown by American housing prices from 2000 to 2005.

No such surge in real household incomes has occurred since income records began to be kept in detail after World War II. Only three times since 1968 have real median household incomes risen a total of over 7 percent in any three-year period. That happened in periods ending in 1970, 1986, and 1989. That record is a far cry from the much greater gain they would need to catch up to home prices. In short, no such catch-up will occur from increases in real household incomes in the foreseeable future.

Because of competitive pressures from low-wage workers in foreign countries, any such sudden increase in American household incomes is virtually impossible—especially for households in lower-income brackets who suffer most from housing affordability problems. Even an immense increase in American protectionism against imports from abroad would not be likely to produce such a huge gain in incomes for low-income American households in the near future, if ever.

In the long run, the best way to raise the incomes of low-income households is to increase their earning power, mainly through better education and training. A major reason that the U.S. distribution of incomes has been experiencing a bifurcation between rising incomes at the top of the distribution and stagnant incomes at the bottom and in much of the middle is the difference in levels of education attained by households in those segments. And the surest way for any individual to improve his or her income-earning potential is by increasing his or her level of educational attainment through better schooling.

This conclusion is especially relevant to the prospects of low-income renter households living in big-city, concentrated-poverty neighborhoods. The public schools serving such neighborhoods provide much lower quality educations to most of their students than do public schools in most suburban communities. One reason is that so many of the students in schools serving concentrated-poverty areas come from low-income households. They often have no resident adult males or are headed by working mothers who have little time to spend with their children, or rely on teenage mothers to raise children, or provide inadequate diets, or are heavily influenced by gangs with antischooling attitudes. As Paul Peterson and Jay Greene recently observed in their analysis of big-city public school systems:

> Unfortunately, it is in these big cities that public schools fail their students most miserably and the costs of failure are most severe. According to a national survey carried out in 1996, only 46 percent of urban students read at a "basic" level, as compared with 63 percent of students in nonurban areas. Among high-poverty schools, the differences are even greater. Only 23 percent of students at urban high-poverty schools read at the basic level as compared with 46 percent in nonurban high-poverty areas. Similar performances for urban schools were reported in math and science. As columnist William Raspberry recently put it in the Washington Post, "Poor children desperately need better education. Yet the schools they attend—particularly in America's overwhelmingly black and brown inner cities—may be the least successful of all public schools."[4]

Yet repeated attempts to improve the educational performance of big-city school systems have so far largely failed. One reason is that these systems are so highly segregated by race and ethnic groups, with mainly minority enrollments. Also, they contain high proportions of children from very-low-income households. In 2001, 41 of

Public School District	Poor Primary Students	Total Primary Enrollment 2003–2004	Percentage of Enrollment Poor
Miami	125,078	177,499	70.47
Los Angeles–Long Beach	593,304	856,588	69.26
Riverside–San Bernardino	229,699	377,168	60.90
Houston	252,972	443,580	57.03
Tampa	94,749	172,296	54.99
Dallas–Ft. Worth	185,159	357,560	51.78
Phoenix	186,401	371,124	50.23
Chicago	372,505	787,579	47.30
San Diego, CA	113,439	241,243	47.02
Orange County, CA	117,916	256,978	45.89
Atlanta	166,970	378,289	44.14
Baltimore	74,564	189,470	39.35
Detroit	140,060	372,617	37.59
Philadelphia	130,710	364,363	35.87
Washington, D.C. area	135,829	410,323	33.10
Seattle–Bellevue–Everett	56,815	176,996	32.10
Minneapolis–St. Paul	70,405	245,638	28.66
Boston	119,889	444,478	26.97
Totals	**3,166,464**	**6,623,789**	**47.80**

* Poor students are those who qualify for a free lunch.

Sources: Diversitydata.org and Harvard School of Public Health, http://diversitydata.sph.harvard.edu/rankings.jsp?i=503.

the largest public school districts in the United States—all within big cities—contained 5.93 million students, of whom 24.9 percent came from households with incomes below the poverty level (compared with the overall average of 11.7 percent of poor persons within the entire United States in that year).[5] Table 6-1 shows that in 18 large U.S. cities containing 6.6 million public primary school students, an average of 47.8 percent were poor enough to qualify for free school lunches. In the Los Angeles–Long Beach school district, 69.3 percent of its 856,588 primary school children were from poor households. Most of the households from which these students came were renter households. Thus, improving the educational attainment of the children of many low-income renters is going to take a tremendous effort to turn around the performances of American big-city public school systems. This improvement is not likely to happen very soon, given the poor record of many past attempts to improve those systems and the fact that almost all of those systems are run as monopolies dominated by teachers' unions.

Providing Government Housing Subsidies

Another remedy would be providing government subsidies to low-income households to enable them to buy or rent more-costly houses without overburdening their incomes. In fiscal year 2005, the U.S. Department of Housing and Urban Development (HUD) spent $31.5 billion on all its activities.[6] (This amount does not include another $100 billion in revenues forgone by the federal government because of income tax benefits to homeowners.[7]) If HUD were to provide sufficient subsidies to permit all U.S. renter households with 2005 annual incomes below $30,000 to reduce their 2005 spending on housing to 30 percent of their incomes or of their reported total consumer spending, whichever was higher, HUD would have to aid 18.627 million households at an estimated total subsidy cost of $32.053 billion.[8] That amount would be more than its entire spending budget in fiscal 2005.[9] This solution is clearly not politically feasible in an era of large annual federal deficits and even larger future entitlement costs looming from Social Security and Medicare. Moreover, Congress has never been willing to provide housing aid to the poorest households as an entitlement available to all who qualify by income level or any other criteria, mainly because of the high cost of doing so.

Nevertheless, the federal government does provide what amounts to a housing-related entitlement benefit to homeowners who deduct their home mortgage interest from their taxable incomes. This benefit was originally an accidental result of federal income tax laws but has later been retained to encourage households to buy their own homes. If the federal government would follow the recommendations of almost every federal committee, commission, or other investigatory body that has recently studied the nation's housing policies, it would alter the nature of current tax benefits that go mainly to the wealthiest homeowners and use some of the money thus saved to benefit poor renters.[10] A recent analysis of homeowners' tax benefits showed that they amount to $100 billion per year (the amount of taxes saved by homeowners who use those benefits) and that 82 percent accrues to the highest-income quintile of tax-paying households. A disproportionate share of those benefits goes to homeowners on the West and East coasts, because housing prices and mortgages are largest there.

To make this tax system far more equitable, the present tax deduction of mortgage interest from taxable income should be shifted to a tax credit based on the amount of interest paid. That would give each homeowner the same dollar benefit for each dollar of mortgage interest paid, regardless of that homeowner's tax bracket.

Under the present law, a homeowner in the 45 percent tax bracket saves $45 per $100 of mortgage interest paid, whereas a homeowner in the 15 percent bracket saves only $15 even if he or she pays the same $100 of mortgage interest. So high-bracket homeowners receive much higher shares of total federal homeowner tax benefits than low-bracket homeowners making the same mortgage payments—though the latter need the assistance more. As a result, tax benefits among home-owners would be shared much more equitably than they are now. Furthermore, the total benefit now going to the highest-income 20 percent of taxpaying households—now about $80 billion—could be reduced by enough to pay all low-income renters a subsidy that would substantially reduce their costs of occupying adequate shelter. That simple reform could be adopted without costing the federal government one cent. Moreover, this change in policy has been repeatedly recommended by housing experts studying present homeowner tax benefits. Yet not one leading American politician in either political party has had the courage to propose such a change, even though it would be much fairer to all households. I strongly recommend this change, but I believe the political power of homeowners—especially the wealthiest ones—plus other beneficiaries of existing arrangements, such as Realtors and homebuilders—is too great to permit it to happen soon, if ever.

Lowering Prices of Existing Homes

Another possible approach would be to lower housing prices enough so that the U.S. median home price would be no more than 3.0 to 3.5 times as great as median house-hold income. That situation prevailed most of the time from 1968 through 1976 and again from 1982 through 2000. Those two periods contained 28 years, or 76 percent of the entire time from 1968 through 2005.

But how could society lower home prices by the required 27 percent when 69 percent of all U.S. households are homeowners? They would stand to lose large portions of their recent home equity buildups by such a policy—buildups they have greatly enjoyed as sources of household wealth. Politically, this objective seems impossible, because the vast majority of American households—and therefore of voters—would oppose it. Moreover, federal government policies—such as holding interest rates low and encouraging homeownership through many tax advantages—played a large role in causing those equity buildups since 2000.

Figure 4-2, showing the course of U.S. median home prices in real terms from 1968 to 2006, indicates that the largest declines in those prices in that period were 9.2 percent from 1979 to 1984 and 6.7 percent from 1988 to 1990. (In current dollars, the U.S. median home prices never declined from year to year in the 37 years from 1968 to 2005. However, median prices in current dollars did fall from year to year in some specific metropolitan areas.) Thus, even in the most severe recessions from 1968 to 2005, U.S. median home prices in real terms never declined anything like the 27 percent they would have to fall to eliminate the aggravating effect of the Niagara of capital on housing affordability problems. In view of this fact, and the likely immense political resistance from over two-thirds of all Americans who are homeowners to cutting home prices by any sizable amount, no democratically elected government would cause or permit such a drop in home prices.

Moreover, if a sizable decline in home prices began to appear, for whatever reason, millions of homeowners would withdraw their homes from the for-sale market rather than accept prices below what they believed their homes were "really worth." Those withdrawals would place a floor under any widespread price declines that would prevent anything close to a nationwide decline of 27 percent, even over several years.

Even if a politically insensitive national government concluded that large-scale home price declines were desirable, the only way it could bring them about would be to encourage massive production of new housing units. If such flooding of the housing market with new units were large enough, it could depress the prices of existing homes. But private homebuilders, who create nearly all the new housing built in America, would refuse to flood their own markets to the extent required to force prices downward significantly. And nearly all local governments would refuse to grant homebuilders permission to build such large numbers of new units within their borders. Overbuilding enough to depress prices of existing homes would greatly reduce local government property tax revenues and enrage local homeowners. Hence, this approach is triply unfeasible politically.

Federal Funding of New Low-Cost Housing Construction

A fourth approach would be for the federal government to finance, directly or indirectly, the construction of large numbers of new low-cost housing units in all parts of the nation where housing affordability problems appeared acute. This approach was used by Western European governments after the destruction of World War II created severe housing shortages throughout Europe—including in the United Kingdom. The British government set up local housing authorities and helped finance their construction of millions of multifamily apartment structures all over the United Kingdom. A similar strategy on a much smaller scale was used by the federal government in the United States in the Depression of the 1930s and after World War II through local public housing authorities.

In both cases, national governments were motivated to adopt unusual measures of direct public action because of what they perceived as dire absolute shortages of decent dwelling units for millions of low-income and moderate-income households.

The sense of urgency to provide immediate shelter in those circumstances caused national governments to bypass the purely private construction and ownership of housing that had previously dominated their housing markets. Therefore, a key issue concerning present housing affordability problems in America is: are those problems seriously thwarting the ability of enough households to obtain decent shelter to warrant at least a temporary use of public instruments to create many new housing units at prices that private builders are either unable or unwilling to construct?

In America, the key housing affordability problem for low-income households is not an absolute shortage of decent dwelling units but the high prices those households must pay to occupy those units when compared to their low incomes. Congress realized this fact many years ago and therefore shifted most housing assistance that subsidizes low-income households from financing the construction of new housing to paying for vouchers and other forms of income assistance to such households. The major reasons for this shift were the following:

▶ Housing allowances and vouchers are far less costly per low-income household aided than paying for the construction of new housing units.

▶ Providing households with vouchers lets them choose where to live, rather than requiring them to occupy newly built, federally financed housing units. In theory, this policy also permits greater dispersion of households away from high-poverty areas, although that has not proven very successful in practice.

▶ Past housing production programs have been marked by some fraudulent and wasteful practices plus subsequent mortgage defaults and scandals that undermined the willingness of Congress to continue supporting them.

▶ The concentration of very poor, underclass households suffering from many social problems in federally financed housing, especially in public housing projects, made many communities unwilling to accept such projects within their boundaries. Such resistance was especially great when those projects were at a large enough scale to change the character of entire neighborhoods. Congress preferred letting individual households choose where to live rather than requiring them to live in projects that the government had to assume the political responsibility for locating somewhere.[11]

For those reasons, the prospects for reviving any large-scale housing construction programs to alleviate affordability problems are indeed dim. In addition, many suburban communities have erected regulatory barriers against the creation of any new rental units within their boundaries. Hence, even if a federal construction program were started, it would have great difficulty locating new low-cost units in areas most beneficial to low-income renter households—that is, outside of present concentrated-poverty neighborhoods.

Implementing Inclusionary Zoning

A completely different approach to coping with housing affordability problems is inclusionary zoning or inclusionary housing. This approach cannot remedy all the housing affordability problems of America's low-income households. Rather, it is designed only to build low-cost housing units for a limited percentage of such households at relatively low costs to governments, and thus to taxpayers. The basic idea is for the government agencies administering housing construction permits in a community to require any firms that build new housing units there to make a certain percentage of those new units available to low-income households at low costs. In return for accepting the economic burden of selling or renting such units at below cost, the builders involved are granted special privileges to offset their resulting losses. Those privileges could be density bonuses for the number of units they can create on any given site, faster government processing of their permits and inspections, relief from some local taxes or building fees, the possibility of building the low-cost units on sites different from their market-priced units, and the ability to design and construct the low-cost units with smaller sizes and fewer amenities than their market-priced units. Such inclusionary zoning rules were first adopted in Montgomery County, Maryland. They have subsequently been adopted in more than 100 localities in California and in many communities in New Jersey, although each jurisdiction normally has inclusionary rules quite different from most others.

The fraction of all newly built units that must be available at relatively low prices is normally between 10 and 20 percent of all new units built. Higher fractions would impose such severe costs upon builders as to dissuade many from building at all. In some places, builders can avoid actually constructing such units by giving land for them at no cost to the local government or by paying fees-in-lieu. The government then offers the land or pays the fees to nonprofit organizations that actually construct new low-cost units. But the most successful inclusionary zoning programs require builders to create such low-cost units themselves, because that strategy guarantees such units will in fact be built by experienced operators.

Inclusionary zoning has several major advantages over doing nothing. First, if implemented at any significant scale—that is, by a large number of communities, counties, or states—and made mandatory for all the jurisdiction's builders, it could produce a lot more affordable housing than is now being constructed in America. Second, it would impose far less costs upon governments—hence taxpayers—than federal financing or subsidies. Third, its rules can be adapted to differing local conditions in housing markets across the nation. Fourth, it leaves housing production in private hands, thereby avoiding many complex rules and regulations that plague projects carried out under federal auspices—such as the requirement to use costly Davis-Bacon union wage levels that are mandatory when federal funds are used.

Inclusionary zoning also has some drawbacks, however. First, almost all homebuilders and owners of land suitable for homebuilding, and most Realtors, lenders, and other professionals in the housing industry, strongly oppose it. Homebuilders and landowners complain—correctly, I believe—that inclusionary zoning unfairly forces them to bear the full costs of carrying out a public policy adopted for the benefit of society as a whole, that is, providing shelter that low-income households can afford. They argue that, if a locality wants to have such a policy, everyone in that locality should contribute to paying for it, rather than forcing homebuilders and landowners alone to do so. If the locality provides enough offsetting benefits to homebuilders, much of this objection can be overcome, but rarely does that alleviate all the burdens placed on them.

Other instances exist in which society imposes burdens on some of its citizens but not all of them to meet pressing needs. Casualties in war are borne only by members of the U.S. armed services engaged in combat, not by the vast majority of Americans who are civilians (though their taxes pay for the war). Many hospital emergency rooms are obligated to provide free care to severely injured or sick persons who have no money or insurance with which to pay for medical treatments. If the need is pressing enough, and society compensates to at least some extent those who meet that need, some American precedents exist for programs like inclusionary zoning.

A second objection is that inclusionary zoning may raise housing prices for households who do not gain access to the low-cost units it creates. That will occur if homebuilders try to recapture what they lose on those low-cost houses by raising the prices they charge on their supposedly market-priced homes. Whether this argument is correct depends in part upon the degree of competition in the housing markets concerned. If the homebuilders are competing with others in similar nearby communities that do not have inclusionary zoning, they will be less able to raise prices on market-priced units in their own projects. But if inclusionary zoning with common rules is adopted everywhere in a region, that might cause higher prices to prevail on market-priced units.

A third drawback of inclusionary zoning is that the affordable units it would most likely create would not be low-cost enough to meet the needs of the very poorest households without some additional subsidies. Of the 21 million renter households with 2005 incomes under $35,000, 6.5 million had reported incomes below $10,000. That group could pay housing costs of only $250 per month or less without spending more than 30 percent of their reported incomes on housing. In 2005, according to the American Housing Survey of 2005, only 5.077 million rental units had monthly costs that low (excluding 2.1 million units with no cash rent). That was only 15 percent of all rental housing units. Newly built housing units would undoubtedly have to charge more than $250 per month rent, even if built under inclusionary zoning, to keep the losses sustained by homebuilders within reasonable bounds. Thus, a substantial percentage of all renter households suffering from affordability problems could not afford even the supposedly affordable units built under inclusionary zoning. This difficulty could be partially met by having the local government add subsidies to the low costs required by the builders of inclusionary units. Local governments have limited ability to subsidize income redistribution because their wealthier residents might move elsewhere. But adding even small subsidies to the low rents or costs of inclusionary units might bring such units within range of even very-low-income households.

Another drawback of inclusionary zoning is that it could not produce enough affordable units to meet the housing needs of anywhere near all the low-income households suffering from household affordability problems. Even if every homebuilder in America made 20 percent of its new units available at low costs, that would provide far fewer such units than the number of households suffering from affordability pressures. Those sufferers number in the many millions, almost certainly exceeding 15 million renter households alone. In average home construction years since 2000, new starts included about 300,000 units in structures with five or more units (of which 80 percent were probably for rent); 40,000 two- to four-unit starts; about 1,500,000 single-family starts, of which perhaps one-fifth might be rentals; and about 170,000 mobile homes. That totals roughly 2,010,000 units, of which 650,000 might be rental units. If 20 percent across the entire country were made affordable by nationwide inclusionary zoning (vastly more such zoning than existed in 2007), then about 130,000 more rental units and 272,000 more ownership units would be affordable each year. For rental units alone—the most important for combating affordability problems—this annual rate of production (which is high, considering total housing starts would exceed 2 million units) would take 115 years to produce 15 million more affordable rental units. In 2005, 13.757 million owner-occupant households had reported incomes below 50 percent of the national median income. If only 25 percent of them had affordability problems, that would be 3.439 million such households. At the annual rate of production of affordable ownership units through inclusionary zoning described, 12.6 years would be needed to create enough added ownership affordable housing units to meet their needs. In short, inclusionary zoning at any realistic scale cannot provide relief to anywhere near all American households with housing affordability problems within a reasonable time.

That drawback, however, has applied to all previous housing assistance programs passed by Congress and administered by the federal government or local housing authorities. None of those programs were adopted and funded at sufficient scale to assist all those households who were eligible in terms of incomes and household sizes. In spite of that drawback, many millions of American low-income households have benefited from receiving decent dwelling units through federal housing assistance programs over the past 50 years.

Yet another characteristic of inclusionary zoning that some citizens would regard as a drawback is that it would probably raise housing densities in the communities using it. That would increase some local expenditures for roads, schools, and other infrastructure while at the same time lowering the tax base per housing unit in the community. However, many citizens and most urban planners would regard higher densities as a strong advantage. In the long run, higher densities might reduce total auto travel, cutting air pollution that aggravates global warming and making wider use of public transit more feasible.

The final drawback of inclusionary zoning is that it requires continuous regulation and monitoring of the stock of affordable housing units created. Otherwise, those units would pass out of affordability too rapidly. Households who received the first affordable units under inclusionary zoning could not resell or rerent them at any prices they could get; they would have to do so only to other households who qualified as having housing affordability problems. This policy means organizations to monitor what happens to all such housing units must be created and operated far into the future—perhaps for as long as 50 years. To some extent, resale and eligibility restrictions can be put into the deeds of inclusionary units. Also, local housing authorities or state housing agencies could possibly monitor what happened to inclusionary units over time.

To summarize, inclusionary zoning has the potential to create a much larger number of new housing units affordable to low-income households than are now being produced in America, with relatively low costs to governments and taxpayers. But by itself, even if adopted on a massive scale, inclusionary zoning could not eliminate all housing affordability problems. Moreover, it has several significant drawbacks and would be strongly opposed by the very people whose efforts would be required to carry it out: homebuilders and landowners.

In spite of those problems, many localities are adopting inclusionary zoning, often with the support of Urban Land Institute member developers. Moreover, inclusionary zoning may be the only even partial remedy for housing affordability problems that has any political chance of being adopted in many jurisdictions. If local leaders realize their communities are no longer affordable to many of the workers they need to operate those communities and the firms in them, they may decide that inclusionary zoning is a useful and worthwhile tool. It certainly beats nothing at all as a response to the nation's difficult housing affordability problems.

Creating Local Workforce Housing Supplies

Another proposed remedy for housing affordability problems is creating so-called workforce housing. This term usually means low-cost housing for persons who work in the community; have modest incomes above low-income levels; and perform services vital to that community's economic, political, and social welfare. Because those workers cannot afford to buy or rent homes in that community's costly housing markets, they need help. "Workforce housing" often refers to housing for moderate-and-middle income workers that each community needs to operate its schools, hospitals, government offices, police forces, firefighting forces, and small businesses.

The basic problem with this concept is that local sources of financing such housing are so limited that they cannot supply anywhere near as much of it as local workforce members need. The federal government can legally raise taxes that apply everywhere in the nation, so no one can escape those taxes by moving unless they leave the country. But local and state governments can only tax people residing within their own borders. Those people can move somewhere else if they believe local or state taxes on them have become too onerous. That is why local government programs that redistribute incomes from wealthier to poor residents are necessarily limited to very small-scale redistributions. State governments can do better because their territories are much larger, making taxes harder to escape by moving away. But only the national government can finance truly large-scale redistribution programs like Medicaid and Social Security, because changing countries is much more difficult than changing communities, or even states.

In some communities, workforce housing is treated as a form of inclusionary zoning. In such cases, private developers of projects in certain types of locations—such as those very near metro rail stops or built on publicly furnished land—may be required to produce a certain fraction of the new units they create to be affordable to community workers.

As a result, workforce housing programs are generally restricted to very small-scale sponsoring of the construction of a few apartment projects within high-income communities to enable local civic servants to live as well as work there. In some cases, private employers of large numbers of workers in local plants or offices have also helped sponsor such projects to assist them in attracting or retaining workers vital to their operations. But almost all such projects are limited in size by the inability of local governments and private firms to pay for sizable subsidies. Consequently, workforce housing construction can make only tiny headway toward remedying the nation's widespread housing affordability problems.

Miscellaneous Other Programs

Some localities and states have adopted housing trust funds, in which fees charged against sales of housing units or other real estate are put into a special fund to be used to subsidize housing for low-income households. Still other places (such as San Francisco) exact low-income housing fees against all types of new construction and use the results to support low-income housing, on the assumption that any new job-holding building should contribute to housing the people who will work there. A completely different approach is expanding the reach of the federal earned income tax credit program, which provides subsidies to low-income families whose members are employed to raise their incomes. The variety of such additional remedies and their respective benefits and costs are too great to be discussed in detail in this book.

Reducing Regulatory Barriers to Low-Cost Housing Erected by Local Governments

As noted earlier, many local governments—especially suburban ones—have adopted regulations concerning zoning, building permits, setbacks, development fees, and other items that raise the costs of building or renovating housing. In my opinion, these regulatory barriers are often a deliberate result of homeowner desires in the local electorate to prevent the construction of any lower-cost dwellings—or sometimes any more high-cost ones either—within their communities. Homeowners fear such dwellings might reduce the market values of their homes or encourage unwanted lower-income households to move into the neighborhood. Therefore, they pressure their local governments to adopt regulations that block or inhibit the creation of lower-cost single-family homes or all rental apartments in their communities. This pressure is most commonly exhibited in zoning hearings involving requests by builders to create new subdivisions containing rental apartments or lower-cost ownership units. Neighbors of the proposed new projects show up in large numbers to protest such proposals. They often succeed in persuading their local zoning officials or city council members to block such proposals, greatly modify them, or seriously slow down their consideration.

Numerous academic studies have confirmed the preceding analysis. As a result, very few low-cost housing units, either ownership or rental, are being built in the United States, compared to the number of households who need to occupy such units. In the period right after World War II, thousands of relatively low-cost housing units were built in the suburbs to provide shelter for returning veterans and their families.

Many such units were small, bungalow-like dwellings containing less than 1,000 square feet. Others were boxlike two-story units built in subdivisions by the thousands. These units met a widespread need for low-cost shelter for millions of modest-income households.

Today, few homebuilders create such units. One reason is that local regulations make doing so difficult or impossible. Another reason is that most homebuilders have decided they can make greater profits by building much larger and more-luxurious units. They believe most American households want greater space and more amenities, and I think they are correct. But it is also true that millions of American households who might want such units cannot afford to occupy them and would therefore be happy with much smaller and less-luxurious homes. But builders can do better financially by focusing on the higher ends of the market.[12] And they generate much less resistance from local governments if they follow that strategy.

After years of observing this situation, I have come to the conclusion that the United States will not build any significant number of new housing units affordable to low-and-moderate-income households as long as sole power over the regulations governing home construction remains in the hands of individual local governments. Democracy at the local level is all too effective in preventing such construction for the reasons previously stated. Local democracy even prevents legalizing the creation of accessory apartments in large, older single-family homes occupied by elderly couples or individuals. Developing such add-on units for rental to households or individuals would greatly expand the supply of low-income rental units in suburbs all over the nation—at almost no cost to governments. It would also allow empty nesters or elderly people to increase their incomes and thus retain their longtime residences. Yet very few suburban communities permit such accessory units because many local homeowners protest that those units would increase traffic congestion and allow "undesirables" to live near them.

After all, low-income households are the minority in America, a condition for which we can all be thankful, because it means most households are better-off. But the minority status of low-income households—not only in numbers, but also often in their ethnic character—prevents them from exercising much political power in local communities dominated by more-affluent homeowners. Local government officials who control building regulations owe their continuance in office to gaining the support of the majority of their local voting residents, who are almost always homeowners. Those local officials receive no political credit or support from paying attention to the needs of low-income households who now live in other parts of the same metropolitan area, often in big cities. Nor do those officials get any political rewards for paying attention to the needs of the region as a whole, as opposed to the desires of their own voters. As a result, control over what kinds of housing will be built, where, and for whom is vested almost entirely in the hands of officials who have no effective political concern about their whole region or about the welfare of anyone who does not now live in their jurisdictions.

This arrangement results from the effective operation of local democracy in individual communities, but it leaves no one concerned about the welfare of each metropolitan region as a whole. Moreover, it means that low-income people who would greatly benefit from moving out of areas of concentrated poverty in large cities have no political representation in the suburbs concerned with their future welfare. In theory, the government of each state as a whole should be concerned about both its metropolitan regions and the welfare of low-income residents everywhere in the state. But state governments are dominated by people who were elected in localities in the past or are so elected in the state legislature. They are sensitive to the majorities that elected them, which in most states are predominantly in the suburbs. Therefore, even state governments are reluctant to scrutinize the building regulations in individual localities that block the creation of more low-cost housing there. They are even more reluctant to impose limitations on local powers that might simplify those regulations and reduce the resulting price-raising effects on housing costs. Yet until state governments are willing to recognize the importance of building more low-cost housing in suburban areas near where most new jobs are being created, very little such housing will be built anywhere in America.

Americans have not yet recognized the need for at least some regionwide planning of housing, as they have recognized the need for such planning regarding transportation, utilities, and environmental controls. That does not mean I believe local governments should have no role in influencing housing regulations that affect their own territories. But it does mean that until state governments put pressure on local governments to simplify and open up their building regulations, nothing much will be done to create more affordable housing where it is needed most—in the suburbs.

CONCLUSION

The Niagara of capital flooding real estate markets has exacerbated the basic American problems of housing affordability stemming from four basic facts:

1. Millions of American households have incomes too low to pay the costs of adequate housing. This problem seems to be an inherent part of our free-enterprise economy.

2. A large fraction of American suburban communities have adopted local regulations concerning development that raise the cost of building housing there far beyond what it could be.

3. Because owning one's own home is a key part of the "American dream," public policies concerning housing in America—especially tax policies—are strongly slanted in favor of encouraging and aiding homeownership, even though most households suffering enough from housing affordability problems to need help are renters.

4. Because 69 percent of all American households and large majorities in most suburban communities are homeowners, while most poor households and recent immigrants are renters, the American public as a whole supports pro-homeownership tax policies and opposes providing similar entitlements to renting households.

In contrast, the Niagara of capital has also allowed millions of former renter households to become homeowners. It did so by flooding home lending markets with capital, which helped reduce interest rates and liberalize home credit terms through ingenious instruments invented by lenders competing to make loans. Since 2006, rising problems with subprime lending defaults and delinquencies have caused many lenders in home markets to tighten their credit standards to avoid similar problems themselves.

The net result of these opposing effects of the Niagara of capital is that housing affordability problems in America are likely to remain widespread, seriously handicapping millions of low-income and even middle-income households, mainly renters. Remedial public policies are not likely to be adopted at any scale significant enough to greatly change this current situation.

Notes

1. The conclusion that raising incomes for poor households is a more important public policy than building new low-cost housing units was brilliantly analyzed and defended by Louis Winnick in his 1995 article, "The Triumph of Housing Allowance Programs: How a Fundamental Policy Conflict Was Resolved," *Cityscape: A Journal of Policy Development and Research* 1, no. 3 (September 1995): 95–121.

2. Joint Center for Housing Studies of Harvard University, *The State of the Nation's Housing: 2006* (Cambridge, Mass.: Harvard Graduate School of Design, 2006), 24.

3. Median incomes for the United States in these calculations were taken from the U.S. Census Bureau Web site, http://www.census.gov, "Income, Historical Income Tables, Households," Table H-10, for all races in both current and constant 2005 dollars. That table shows that median household income in current dollars rose from $7,743 in 1968 to $44,326 in 2005—a gain of 472 percent. In constant 2005 dollars, the median rose from $36,873 in 1968 to $44,326 in 2005—a gain of 20.2 percent. Other data taken from U.S. Census sources for current-dollar median incomes, deflated by Consumer Price Index scores based on 1982–1984 dollars equaling 100, show that national median household incomes rose only 2.37 percent between 1968 and 2005. If that is true, the challenge of returning household incomes to the same relationship to

home prices as in the past is much greater than indicated in this text. Some inconsistencies in the text of this book arise from using these two different data sources in different parts of the analysis.

4. Paul E. Peterson and Jay P. Greene, "Race Relations and Central City Schools," *Brookings Review* 16, no. 2 (Spring 1998): 33–37.

5. U.S. Department of Education, National Center for Education Statistics, NCES Common Core of Data (CCD), "National Public Education Financial Survey," 2000–2001.

6. Nancy M. Gordon, Assistant Director for Health and Human Services, Congressional Budget Office, "Statement before the Subcommittee on VA, HUD, and Independent Agencies, Committee on Appropriations, United States Senate," January 26, 1995, http://www.cbo.gov/ftpdocs/47xx/doc4771/1995doc20.pdf (accessed January 28, 2007).

7. Economic Policy Institute, "Rethinking the Tax Benefits for Homeowners," *Economic Snapshots*, November 21, 2005, http://www.epi.org/content.cfm/webfeatures_snapshots_20051121 (accessed January 28, 2007).

8. According to the Bureau of Labor Statistics Consumer Expenditure Survey for 2005, the households in the lowest income quintile (some 23.441 million households) had average annual consumer spending of $19,120 and spent 39 percent on housing, or an average of $7,456.80 per household. To reduce that amount to 30 percent of their spending, they would have to cut housing spending to $5,736, or $1,720 per household. Multiplying that amount times 18.627 million poor renter households equals $32.053 billion. The average reported income after taxes of households in that same quintile was only $9,688, which was far less than their total spending. Reducing their spending on housing to 30 percent of that clearly underreported income, or $2,906, would require a subsidy of $4,550 per household, or a total of $84.76 billion for 18.627 million households. That sum was more than double HUD's total spending for the year.

9. In fiscal 2005, the Bureau of Labor Statistics Consumer Expenditure Survey indicated that all households with incomes below $30,000 (and many with higher incomes) spent more than 30 percent of their reported incomes on housing, or at least the average amount for each income group under that amount was above 30 percent.

10. An example is the President's Advisory Panel on Tax Reform, "American Needs a Better Tax System," http://www.taxreformpanel.gov (accessed March 27, 2006).

11. These points are made especially convincingly by Lou Winnick his 1995 article, "The Triumph of Housing Allowance Programs: How a Fundamental Policy Conflict Was Resolved."

12. In addition, fixed impact fees per unit tend to encourage builders to focus on higher-cost units, because such fees are a much smaller proportion of the total costs of higher-cost units than lower-cost ones. Peter Linneman pointed out this relationship to me, as he did many other key points in this book.

CHAPTER SEVEN

Effects on Commercial Property Markets

The Niagara of capital into real estate profoundly affected commercial property markets of all types, especially in the United States. The money flooding into commercial real estate was initially all focused on buying existing assets, not on renovating existing structures or building new ones. In fact, huge inflows of capital into real estate took place while the overall U.S. economy was suffering a mild decline from the stock market crash of 2000 and from the aftereffects of the terrorist attacks of September 11, 2001. Those negative forces caused commercial property vacancies to rise and rents to fall, which reduced property net incomes. In all past economic declines in space markets, rising vacancies and falling rents also reduced the market values of the properties concerned, as a result of their decreasing net incomes. Moreover, liquidity quickly dried up and capital was hard to acquire. But in this unusual cycle, property values of well-occupied structures of all types—initially excepting hotels and motels—moved up, not down. For the first time in recent history, capital remained easily available in the face of sharp declines in the demand for space, occupancy rates, and rents.

In essence, the massive funds being put forth by investors fleeing from stocks and bonds drove up the prices of commercial real estate properties, even though their economic performances were deteriorating. This situation resulted in the greatest economic disconnect ever in U.S. commercial real estate between conditions in space markets, on the one hand, and conditions in investment markets, on the other.

THE DISCONNECT BETWEEN SPACE AND INVESTMENT MARKETS IN OFFICE AND INDUSTRIAL SPACE

The worsening of space market conditions was greatest in Silicon Valley in Northern California because that was where a large fraction of the firms involved in the Internet stock bubble were located. Figure 7-1 shows office vacancy rates by quarters for both downtown areas and suburban portions of major metropolitan areas from 1984 to 2005. Figure 7-2 shows the suburban office vacancy rates by quarters for the entire nation and the San Jose metropolitan area only. Most of Silicon Valley's high-tech office space is in the San Jose suburbs.[1]

Figure 7-1 shows that vacancy rates were quite high in 1990 both in downtown and suburban office space as a result of the real estate crash that year. But office vacancy rates fell steadily as the general economy improved in the 1990s, with vacancies reaching a minimum in 2000. Office vacancy rates began rising sharply in 2001,

FIGURE 7-1. **U.S. DOWNTOWN AND SUBURBAN OFFICE VACANCY RATES, 1984–2005**

Source: CB Richard Ellis.

FIGURE 7-2. **SUBURBAN OFFICE VACANCY RATES, NATIONAL AND SAN JOSE METRO AREA, 1990–2006**

YEARS AND QUARTERS

——— National suburban office vacancy   ——— San Jose suburban office vacancy

Sources: Coldwell Banker and CB Richard Ellis, Quarterly Vacancy Reports, various years from 1990 to 2006.

but that rise was interrupted briefly after 9/11. The destruction of the two giant office towers in New York City suddenly removed a lot of space from the market, cutting vacancy rates. Then vacancies resumed their skyward rise, reaching peaks in late 2003 in the suburbs and early 2004 in downtowns. After that, office vacancies started falling again as the U.S. economy improved.

This graph indicates that space market conditions were steadily worsening from the third quarter of 2000 to the fourth quarter of 2003. That was the same period when investment money was pouring into these markets and driving property prices upward. True, rising values were at first confined to well-occupied properties with long-term leases and strong cash flows, but values soon rose for less-desirable properties if they had potentials for good cash flows.

Figure 7-2 shows how drastically suburban office vacancy patterns in the San Jose metropolitan area (Silicon Valley) differed from those in the nation as a whole. From 1990 to mid-1995, Silicon Valley vacancy rates remained between 10 and 15

FIGURE 7-3. **NATIONAL INDUSTRIAL VACANCY RATES, 1990–2006**

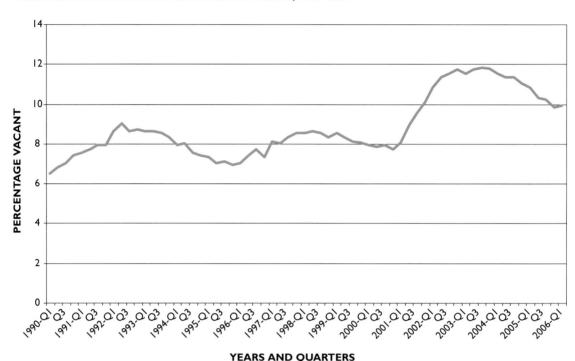

YEARS AND QUARTERS

Source: CB Richard Ellis.

percent, while those in the nation's suburbs as a whole were declining from 22 percent to 14.3 percent. Then, as the Internet bubble built up in the stock market, Silicon Valley vacancy rates plunged far below national suburban rates and remained under 5 percent from early 1997 until the last quarter of 2000. From 2001 to early 2004, as many Internet and other high-tech firms literally vanished from space markets, Silicon Valley vacancy rates shot upward to a peak over 25 percent, far above the national suburban average of 18.2 percent in that quarter. This large decline in occupancy also drove market prices of office and research space in Silicon Valley sharply downward after 2000. Some fell by 50 percent. Vacancies in other office-heavy regions laden with Internet and other high-tech firms showed similar patterns of moving from far below the national average to far above it, before returning to more normal levels in 2005.

Industrial vacancy rates reflected similar patterns in the same period but showed much less volatility in most regions. Figure 7-3 shows industrial vacancy rates for the nation as a whole. Industrial vacancy rates are generally much lower than office vacancy rates, partly because industrial space can be built more quickly and with smaller buildings, which allows industrial developers to avoid overbuilding markets more easily than office developers. Only after the stock market crash of 2000 and the terrorist attacks in 2001 did industrial vacancies rise to above 10 percent and stay there.

These figures show that for two of the most important types of commercial space in U.S. real estate markets, space market conditions were deteriorating in the periods right after 2000, and they remained in rather bad shape until the end of 2003. Yet that was the same period in which investors bidding intensively for well-occupied properties drove prices of some such properties upward dramatically, even though prices of many not-so-well occupied properties fell greatly, especially in Silicon Valley.

SOARING COMMERCIAL PROPERTY PRICES IN THE 2000s

The best proof of how much commercial property prices rose in the late 1990s and early 2000s is an examination of cap rates for different types of property over that period. As explained in Chapter 1, an income property's cap rate, or capitalization rate, is the percentage of a property's market value formed by its annual net income. It is computed by dividing a property's net income, usually unleveraged, by its market value. Thus, a property worth $1 million that produces a net income of $100,000 has a cap rate of 10 percent.

When a lot of people with a lot of money are competing to acquire profitable investments, they will drive up the price of acquiring any given net income. That price increase causes the cap rate to fall because the same net income is a smaller percentage of a higher price. Thus, if buyers bid up the price of the property just described to $1.25 million without any change in its annual net income, the cap rate falls to $100,000 divided by $1.25 million, or 8 percent. Thus, a 25 percent rise in the property's market price produces a 20 percent decline in the cap rate. Mathematically, each cap rate is the statistical inverse of the multiple that converts the property's net income into its market value. Thus, a cap rate of 10 percent is the same as a multiple of 10, and a cap rate of 8 percent is the same as a multiple of 12.5.

Therefore, changes over time in property cap rates are equivalent to changes in the market prices of those properties. When market prices rise without any increase in net incomes, cap rates are falling, and vice versa.

The National Council of Real Estate Investment Fiduciaries (NCREIF) keeps track of the cap rates its members pay to buy or sell the properties they report to NCREIF's analysts. Over time, these cap rate histories are the best evidence of systemwide changes in the prices of all types of real estate properties. However, NCREIF's portfolio consists mainly of "core" properties (high-quality properties, excluding highly risky ones), is relatively unleveraged with debt, and is evaluated by means of appraisals rather than direct observations of market prices. Figure 2-9 shows the cap rates for different types of properties held by NCREIF members by quarters from 1990 to 2006. Because these cap rates are highly volatile from quarter to quarter, the graph shows four-quarter moving averages rather than individual quarter cap rates. This simplification more clearly reveals the movements of cap rates—and thus property prices—over time. It also results in backward-looking numbers for each period, which are consistent with the inherent lag in NCREIF estimates because they are based upon appraised values rather than direct market-transaction values. In 1990, the graph reflects experience with 480 different individual properties; by the end of 2005, it is based upon 2,727 separate properties.

Figure 2-9 indicates a remarkable cycle of property price changes from 1990 through 2006. Cap rates for all four major types of properties—apartments, industrial, offices, and retail—were relatively low in the early 1990s, because of the time needed for appraisals of individual property values to decline after the crash of 1990. That means property prices were high at the start of the period shown on the graph—mainly because of a real estate development and investment boom in the late 1980s. Foreign investors in particular had entered U.S. property markets and bid prices up to record levels.

But then came the real estate crash of 1990. Net incomes began falling sharply because of the massive overbuilding of all types of commercial space that had occurred in the late 1980s and because of higher interest rates. Falling incomes were shortly thereafter accompanied by large declines in how investors were valuing net incomes, as shown by fast increases in cap rates from 1991 through about 1995. Table 7-1 sets forth what price declines were caused just by cap rate increases from 1990 to around 1995. These price changes are illustrated through analysis of a sample property producing a net annual income of $100,000, without any debt leveraging.

The negative effects upon property prices of rising cap rates were intensified by lower net incomes because of falling general liquidity and plunging occupancies and rents. So the actual declines in property prices were much greater than those shown in the table. An extreme example is the Waikoloa Hotel on the Kona Coast of the Hawaii's Big Island. It is a huge resort containing 1,249 rooms and suites in several buildings that are connected by a small railway and a small-boat canal that meanders through its 62-acre site, which has no beach on the ocean. The Waikoloa was built in the 1980s, partly financed by Japanese investors, for a total cost of about $360 million. After the Japanese economic bubble burst in 1989 and American property values crashed in 1990, the same resort was sold for about $60 million in 1993 and is now operated by Hilton. That is a drop in market value of 83.3 percent!

Then economic conditions in general improved, occupancy rates rose, and net incomes stopped dropping. So cap rates began a long process of declining over time as investors became more optimistic about future prospects for real estate. A sharp

TABLE 7-1. **PROPERTY PRICE DECLINES CAUSED BY CAP RATE INCREASES, 1990–1995**

Property Type	Annual Income	Cap Rate Low	Property Value	Cap Rate Peak	Property Value	Percentage Decline
Apartments	$100,000	.065966	$1,515,932	.089602	$1,116,048	−26.4
Industrial	$100,000	.071576	$1,397,116	.098094	$1,019,430	−27.0
Offices	$100,000	.058191	$1,718,479	.097504	$1,025,599	−40.3
Retail	$100,000	.069333	$1,442,315	.100717	$992,881	−31.2

Source: Author's calculations using cap rates from sources cited in accompanying text.

acceleration in that decline took place after 2001 for apartments and after 2002 for the other three types of properties. By 2006, cap rates for all four property types were well below their lowest points in the 1990s. The Niagara of capital had driven property prices up dramatically, especially after 2002. Moreover, rising net incomes in all types of properties as vacancies fell meant actual property price increases were substantially larger than shown by cap rate declines alone. Appraisers estimate that the Waikoloa Hilton is today worth about $400,000 per room, or a total of $503.6 million. That price is 40 percent above its original cost and 88 percent above what its current owners paid for it (without taking into account improvements they have made).

Table 7-2 shows the effect of falling cap rates on property prices for each type of property in Figure 2-9 from their cap rate peaks around 2001–2002 to the fourth quarter of 2006. These price changes are again illustrated through analysis of a sample property producing a net annual income of $100,000, without any debt leveraging. Offices increased most in price, rising by 65.9 percent in about six years, with retail not far behind. Moreover, for those properties that also had rising net incomes, market price increases were larger than shown in this table. That group probably included most of the properties bought or sold in this period. Why? Because after about 2003, the economy began to recover strongly from the negative effects of the stock market crash and 9/11. Office vacancy rates had soared after bottoming out in 2001 at 6 percent downtown and 8 percent in the suburbs. They leveled off at 15 and 18 percent, respectively, in 2004, then began falling. Even some rents then began rising, doubly improving property net incomes from their low points.

Cap rates for other types of properties not shown moved in similar patterns. Hotels did not recover quite as fully because they suffered more than most other property types from the disruption of airline and tourist travel after 9/11. But by 2004 to 2006, hotels were booming and their prices were rising notably.

TABLE 7-2. **PROPERTY PRICE INCREASES CAUSED BY CAP RATE DECLINES, 2001–2006**

Property Type	Annual Income	Cap Rate Peak	Property Value	Cap Rate Low	Property Value	Percentage Increase
Apartments	$100,000	.0808	$1,237,623	.0510	$1,960,784	58.4
Industrial	$100,000	.09138	$1,094,331	.05984	$1,671,122	52.7
Offices	$100,000	.09329	$1,071,926	.05622	$1,728,726	65.9
Retail	$100,000	.09403	$1,063,490	.05875	$1,702,128	60.1

Source: Author's calculations using cap rates from sources cited in accompanying text.

In sum, Figure 2-9 reveals a striking cycle of property values from very high levels at the end of the 1980s through a trough in the mid-1990s and back to record levels by 2006. In reality, because net incomes fell and rose in the same period, actual movements of property values were even more dramatic than those shown by cap rates alone.

CHANGES IN CREDIT CONDITIONS PRODUCED BY THE NIAGARA OF CAPITAL

Just as homeownership—and housing prices—in housing markets were greatly stimulated by an easing of credit requirements on homebuyers, commercial property prices were similarly stimulated by an astonishing increase in the ease of borrowing for investors seeking to buy commercial properties. This greater ease—and both lower actual risks and perceptions of risks by lenders concerning their own risks in making loans on real estate—were caused by the factors discussed in the following sections.

Securitization and Lender Risk

As pointed out in Chapter 2, the securitization of lending, which is now pervasive in most debt markets, has greatly expanded the flow of debt into real estate—and other investments—in two ways. First, it reduced the degree of risk associated with lending by breaking up large blocks of debt into smaller segments that could be sold separately to many different investors. This factor slashed both the actual and the perceived risk of investing in real properties, compared to past practices of each lender's having to bear the entire risk of each loan. Second, by reducing the risk of real estate lending, securitization greatly expanded the pool of financial firms and investors willing to put their funds into real estate. Previously, many investors had been reluctant to do so because of their unfamiliarity with real properties and their skepticism about the profitability of such properties.

Commercial Mortgage–Backed Securities

These securities embodied a specific form of securitization focused on commercial real estate properties. In the late 1990s and after 2000, a whole new industry of specialists in all phases of creating commercial mortgage–backed securities (CMBSs) sprang into existence. They developed the ability to raise large amounts of money at relatively low interest rates by spreading risks, as discussed earlier. This lending vehicle enabled real estate deals of unprecedented size to be financed relatively rapidly and easily. Because the securities involved were essentially nonrecourse loans (that is, the lender had only the property itself as collateral and could not seize any of the borrower's other assets in case of default), they appealed to developers and other borrowers who wanted to expand their purchasing power without risking being wholly wiped out if something went wrong. As a result, the amount of real estate financing based upon CMBS instruments grew rapidly, especially from 2003 to 2006. Total CMBS lending of over $360 billion in just the two years 2005 and 2006 exceeded the combined total in the preceding five years from 2000 through 2004 and was 35 percent larger than the combined total from the eight years before that.

Mezzanine Financing

Another whole industry that greatly expanded in the past decade is mezzanine financing. Mezzanine financing refers to loans made on properties that do not have the repayment standing of first mortgages, or even second mortgages, but which can be used to reduce the amount of equity that the borrower must put up in return for the borrower's paying higher interest rates to get such financing. Thus, mezzanine financing stands between mortgage financing and equity. Many more sources of mezzanine financing have come into being because lenders were so eager to get higher returns on their funds than they could get from straight mortgage financing, with its ability to foreclose on the properties in case of default. The *National Real Estate Investor* reported that the origination of "mezzanine loans, second mortgages, and preferred equity deals skyrocketed 296 percent in 2005 to $12.84 billion, up from $3.24 billion the previous year . . . according to the Mortgage Bankers Association."[2]

Lowered Underwriting Standards

Lending officers from some of the biggest banks, insurance companies, and pension funds engaged in real estate investing in America have told me they have been under immense pressure to reduce the quality standards they use for underwriting property loans. This pressure arose both because their superiors were paid on the basis of each firm's total lending volume and because of intense competition among sources of funds eager to make deals. Furthermore, as soon as they sell their loans off to other people through securitization, most of their risk shifts to other people! At the beginning of the Niagara inflows, their prevailing underwriting standards might actually have been too high, based on the very low default rates they were experiencing. But as time passed, they were pressured to keep lowering those standards. In some cases, they were offered participation in large deals but not given enough time to carry out adequate due diligence investigations of the properties concerned before having to declare their willingness to participate. In other cases, they had time to conduct due diligence, but the terms they were offered did not compensate them adequately for the risks they thought they were taking. If they did not accept those terms, however, they would be replaced by other lenders who would accept the same terms. They felt that if they did not make such loans, they would not be able to place all the money that they had to invest, because so many other lenders were willing to accept such terms. These lenders agreed almost universally that their own underwriting standards—and those prevailing throughout the real estate lending industry—had greatly deteriorated under the pressure of so much money looking for real estate investments. This result is similar to that which occurred in the late 1980s among savings and loan associations concerning home mortgages.

Rapid Growth of REIT Stock Prices

One of the most spectacular results of the Niagara of capital in real estate was the escalation of real estate investment trust (REIT) stock prices compared to the prices of all the major stock indexes (see Figure 7-4). REIT stock prices, as measured by the line for the National Association of Real Estate Investment Trust (NAREIT) index, rose steadily from the left side of the graph (the last day in 1998) to the right side on February 7, 2007. In contrast, the other three major stock indices rose in 1999 but then suffered serious declines in the period from 2000 to 2002 before recovering to various degrees in 2003 and thereafter. The NAREIT index rose faster than the other three stock indices until February 7, 2007, when the NAREIT index hit its all-time peak. Since then, it has lost ground against the other three indices but is still way ahead in terms of overall performance since 2000. The differences between these stock price measures are set forth more precisely in Table 7-3.

From the beginning of 1999 to February 7, 2007, the NAREIT index more than tripled in value, and some individual REIT stocks increased to more than seven times their initial values. In contrast, all three major stock indices fell sharply from their highs in 2000 to their lows on October 9, 2002, with NASDAQ dropping the most, by

FIGURE 7-4. **NAREIT INDEX AND THREE MAJOR STOCK INDICES, 1999–2007**

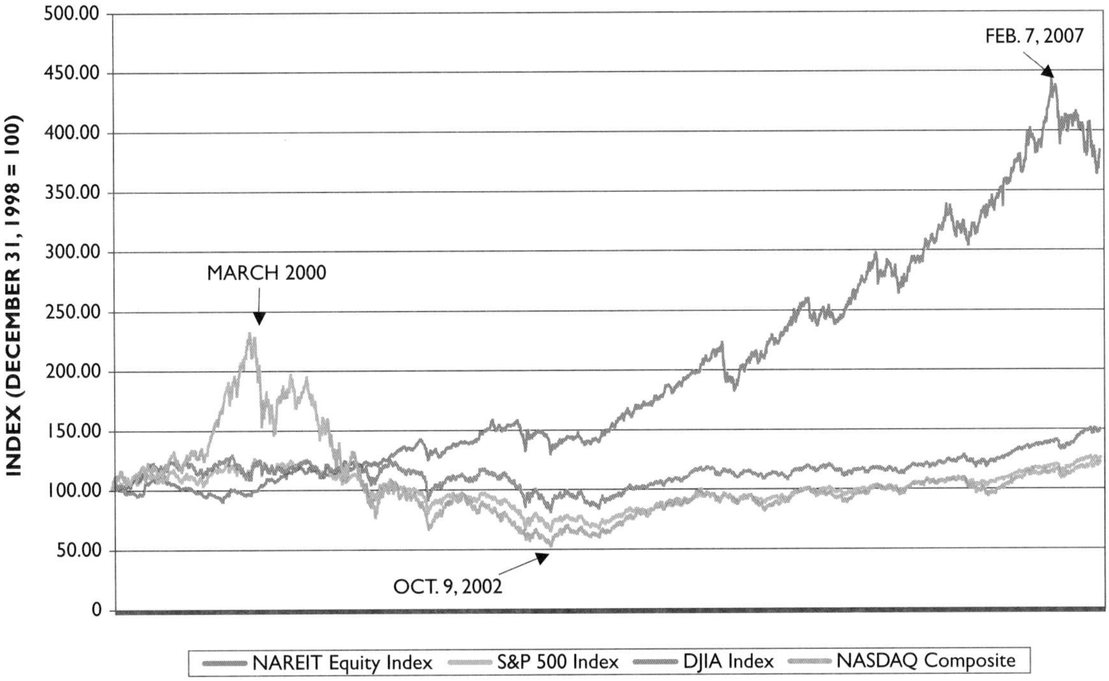

Sources: NAREIT Index: NAREIT and Bloomberg.com; major stock indices: Yahoo Finance, http://finance.yahoo.com.

78 percent. By February 7, 2007, the Dow Jones Industrial Average (DJIA), which includes only 30 stocks, and the Standard & Poor's (S&P) 500 Index had both surpassed their initial 1999 values by modest amounts of 38 percent and 18 percent, respectively. The DJIA was also above its high in 2000, but the S&P 500 (which contains the broad-est array of stocks in this analysis) was still about 5.07 percent below its 2000 high. The NASDAQ Composite had suffered the largest loss after 2000 because it was heavily loaded with Internet and high-technology stocks. By February 7, 2007, it was still a shade below 50 percent of its all-time high point in 2000 and only 13.59 percent above its value at the start of 1999.

After February 7, 2007, however, the NAREIT index began declining while the other indices kept rising, although erratically. From February 7, 2007, to August 10, 2007, when this chapter was written, the NAREIT index fell 21.1 percent, but the DJIA rose 4.52 percent, the S&P 500 rose 0.25 percent, and the NASDAQ rose 2.19 percent. Although the NAREIT index had still risen much more than the other three indices since those three hit their lows on October 9, 2002, the NAREIT index seemed to re-

TABLE 7-3. **COMPARISON OF NAREIT INDEX AND MAJOR STOCK INDICES**

Items	NAREIT Index	Dow Jones Industrial Average	S&P 500 Index	NASDAQ Composite
Value on Dec. 31, 1998	2,491.53	9,181.43	1,229.93	2,192.60
High Value in 2000	—	11,722.98	1,527.46	5,048.62
Low Value, Oct. 9, 2002	3,187.46	7,286.27	776.76	1,114.11
Percentage Decline from High to Low	—	–37.85%	–49.15%	–77.93%
Value on Feb. 7, 2007	10,980.62	12,666.87	1,450.02	2,490.50
Percentage Change, Dec. 31, 1998, to Feb. 7, 2007	340.71%	37.96%	17.89%	13.59%
Value on Aug. 10, 2007	8,663.09	13,239.54	1,453.64	2,544.88
Percentage Change, Feb. 7, 2007, to August 10, 2007	–21.10%	4.52%	0.25%	2.19%
Percentage Change, Oct. 9, 2002, to Aug. 10, 2007	171.78%	81.71%	87.14%	128.39%

Sources: NAREIT Index: NAREIT and Bloomberg.com; major stock indices: Yahoo Finance, http://finance.yahoo.com.

flect a shift of some funds out of REIT stocks into more-traditional types of stocks. When this chapter was being written, although too early to be sure, a repricing of real estate assets in relation to other types of equity assets seemed to be underway. Some stock market analysts believe that if a stock falls 20 percent or more in price, a bear market exists in that stock, and that had happened to the NAREIT index by August 10, 2007. However, the market prices of individual commercial real estate properties had not yet begun to show any such withdrawal of funds from real estate. So how this shift in direction in the NAREIT index will play itself out in the future remains uncertain.

Clearly, the Niagara of capital had its most positive effect on REIT stocks, which did not suffer any marked decline in the stock market crash of 2000. A few other stocks that continued to offer strong cash flows similarly prospered. True, the continuation of large capital flows into the U.S. economy after 2002 helped the rest of the stock market recover significantly from its 2002 low points. But REIT stocks were the star performers in those seven years by a wide margin. This fact is even more impressively illustrated by Figure 7-5, based on data from NAREIT. As of 2006, the capitalized value of equity REITs constituted 91.4 percent of the capitalized value of all listed REITs. The capitalized values of equity REITs were insignificant until 1993, but did not really take off until 1999. Then they soared, especially after 2002. The total capitalized value of all equity REITs in 2006 reached $400.7 billion, which was

FIGURE 7-5. **TOTAL CAPITALIZED VALUE OF EQUITY REITS, 1980–2006**

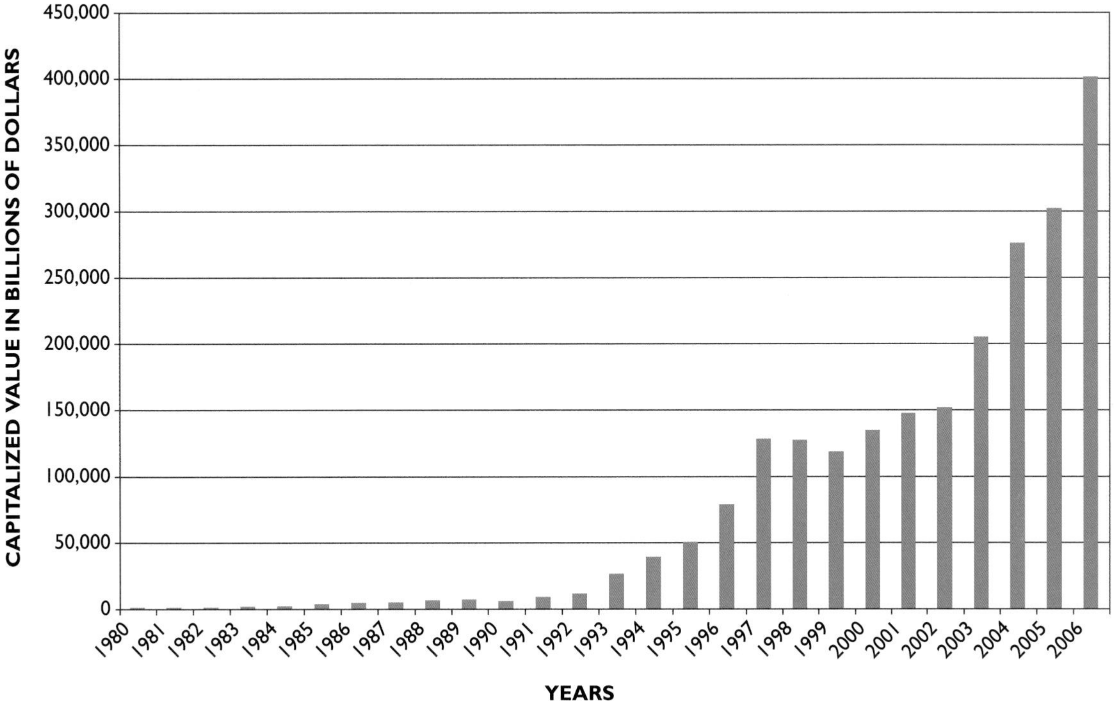

Source: National Association of Real Estate Investment Trusts, Data Library, Market Capitalization of the REIT Industry, http://www.nareit.com/library/industry/market.cfm.

239 percent higher than it had been in 1999. That value rose by $99.2 billion or 32.9 percent in just the year 2006 alone. Even so, the entire REIT industry remains relatively small in total capitalized value compared to such large individual firms as Exxon-Mobil ($410 billion), General Electric ($359 billion), and Microsoft ($276 billion).[3]

Many observers believe that REIT stocks were overvalued at the beginning of 2007 and are due to decline in price in the near future relative to the prices of other stocks. This belief has been voiced continuously for several years while REIT stocks have consistently outperformed the other stock averages. But recently, as noted, the NAREIT Equity Index has been declining from its high on February 7, 2007, and has therefore been losing ground to the other three stock indices. It seems likely to me that any dramatic takeoff of stock prices in general, or in some one outstanding sector other than real estate, might drain off some of the money that has stimulated such a huge rise in REIT stock prices. I do not believe, however, that anywhere near all the funds that have flowed into real estate in the Niagara of capital are going to flow out of it soon, thereby causing a sharp and prolonged plunge in REIT stock values. Too much of a paradigm shift favoring more long-term investments in real properties has occurred for that to happen. Only an immense collapse in real property prices in general could cause that paradigm shift to disappear, and I do not see such a prospect in view.

The Rise of Private Equity Funds

One prospect that is in view is the rising significance of private equity funds in real estate investment. The easy availability of low-cost debt capital has been stimulating the creation of many new private equity funds, some of which have aimed their acquisitive tactics at real estate in particular. In early 2006, Blackstone led the purchase of Equity Office Properties, the world's largest owner of office buildings, for about $36 billion, including the assumption of debt. Blackstone's 1 percent acquisition fee on that deal was $360 million! The avowed purpose of private equity funds in making such deals is to sell off their investments at a profit within five to seven years. A key incentive for such a short-term horizon is that profits earned operating purchased firms are taxed at the full corporate rate of 35 percent, whereas profits earned from reselling those same firms are taxed at the capital gains rate of 15 percent. This differential provides a strong motivation to resell purchased firms rather than hold and operate them over a long period. Blackstone thus planned to break up the collection of more than 500 office buildings that Sam Zell and his partners had put together into a single group with centralized management. Whether that can be done at a profit depends upon four key factors.

One is whether Blackstone can somehow improve the management of those office buildings so the buildings can earn higher net incomes than they did under Equity Office Properties. That, in turn, depends heavily upon improving conditions in office space markets generally. It also depends upon Blackstone's being a better manager than Equity Office Properties has been. Blackstone has been selling off buildings in the Equity Office Properties portfolio so fast, however, it has not had much time to affect how they are managed. The second vital issue is whether the easy availability of capital and prevailing low cap rates will remain in five to seven years. If so, buyers would be able to pay higher prices for the office buildings even if their profitability did not improve much, and especially if it did. The third key aspect is whether other developers of office buildings will flood the market with new buildings within the next five to seven years, driving vacancies up and rents down. The fourth factor is whether private equity firms will continue to enjoy certain income tax benefits compared to other property owners. This advantage is in danger of being taken away or at least reduced in scope by Congress. In theory, Blackstone is betting that those four conditions will remain favorable long enough for it to unload all those office buildings at a huge profit.

In reality, Blackstone seems to have adopted a somewhat different investment strategy regarding Equity Office Properties: sell as much as possible as fast as possible! Within a single year after the Equity Office Properties acquisition, Blackstone had already sold 60 percent of the individual properties in that portfolio. At least in this case, Blackstone's behavior clearly demonstrates its lack of commitment to operating the properties that it purchased or treating the whole firm it purchased as an ongoing operation. For Blackstone and other private equity firms, real estate is clearly not a long-term investment, but rather a vehicle for reaping as large a profit as possible, selling as fast as possible, and paying as few taxes as possible on the resulting profits. In fact, the concept that private equity firms "take public firms private" is often a myth. Many buy public firms with very little private equity but instead mainly with public debt offerings like CMBSs, which they borrow themselves. Then they sell the properties involved to new buyers who are also largely financed with borrowed funds, often some form of public debt. In the long run, the firms thus bought often move from being financed mainly with public equity to being financed mainly with public debt and very little private equity. The cash flows from the real properties involved no longer go primarily to equity investors but to holders of CMBSs and other similar public debt securities. And the firms that are purchased often no longer exist in anything like their original forms, because they are frequently broken up and sold off in many pieces.

A major factor in favor of Blackstone and other private equity firms is that REITs in general have kept their leveraging with debt down to much lower levels than traditional real estate developers did in the 1980s and earlier. REITs kept debt leverage low under pressure from Wall Street stockholders who wanted to avoid the real estate debacles that occurred in 1990. Then, many property owners went broke because they had such high leverage ratios they could not cover their debt service when rents fell and vacancies rose in adverse economic conditions. As a result, most REITs have debts that average about 40 percent of their total capitalized value. Blackstone and other private equity funds are relying on their willingness to increase debt leveraging on those office buildings as high as they can—as high as 90 percent. With debt service costs low because of low interest rates, such leveraging could raise the net gains to their equity stock significantly, if they can eventually sell those properties at prices equaling or surpassing what they paid for them.

Thus, the very availability of low-cost debt capital allows private equity firms like Blackstone to consider buying out REITs, increasing the debt loads on the properties involved to raise the net returns on their equity, and then selling off those properties. Up to mid-2007, when this was being written, such a strategy had been tried on REITs by only a few private equity funds. How many more such acquisitions and subsequent debt-loadings will occur remains to be seen. Its extent depends heavily upon the continued ability of private equity funds to borrow at low interest rates, both to raise the initial capital to buy out REITS, and then to increase the debt leverage on the properties they acquire. If the Niagara of capital were to slow down or stop altogether, this whole strategy might become extremely difficult to carry out successfully.

In August 2007, considerable turmoil in financial debt markets caused by the spreading effects of defaults among subprime home mortgage loans resulted in much less availability of low–interest rate lending to support high-risk investments in general. To bolster confidence among lenders and borrowers that adequate funds would remain available at reasonable costs, the U.S. Federal Reserve injected $38 billion of additional liquidity into debt markets in a single day. European central banks followed a similar strategy, because lending problems from U.S. subprime mortgage loans had spread to many European investors. How seriously these volatile conditions will restrain overall low–interest rate lending over the long run remains to be seen. In the meantime, spreads for higher-risk investments will very likely remain notably higher above Treasury rates than they were before 2007.

The Enrichment of Real Estate Operators, Developers, and Financiers

One of the most dramatic effects of the Niagara of capital in commercial property markets has been a huge enrichment of real estate operators, developers, and financiers. As money poured into commercial properties and drove their prices upward, fat profits were made by operators at all stages of real estate transactions. The most dramatic profit was attained by the owners and operators of Blackstone, the private equity firm that bought Sam Zell's apartment REIT, among many real estate and other properties. When Blackstone went public in June 2007, Stephen Schwarzman, the chief executive officer, received stock worth over $7 billion, and another principal partner, Peter Peterson, received over $1 billion in stock. The total value of Blackstone's assets under management rose from about $15 billion in 2001 to over $85 billion in 2007, an increase of over 467 percent in six years.[4] Schwarzman cleared over $600 million on the stock offering and had been paid over $400 million per year as salary and bonuses.

The broader effect of the Niagara of capital on the prosperity of commercial property markets can be seen from the expanded number of members in the Urban Land Institute (ULI), a national organization of real estate developers, managers, tenants, financiers, architects, owners, and consultants. In 1987, ULI had 11,221 total members. Ten years later, following the collapse of real estate prices in 1990 and shortly thereafter, ULI's membership had risen only to 13,057, or by 16 percent. Then, in the next ten years, ULI membership soared to 37,196, an increase of 185.5 percent, as shown on Figure 7-6. This huge increase in membership reflects the general prosperity of the commercial and residential property businesses, both of which are represented in ULI. Moreover, by 2007, ULI had established District Councils in several foreign countries as well as in most of the largest U.S. metropolitan areas.

Why Hasn't the Niagara of Capital Stimulated a New Development Boom?

A surprising aspect of the U.S. economy's general recovery starting in 2003 is that—at least up until early 2007—it has not been accompanied by a major boom in new real estate development of commercial properties.

My own theory is that the normal real estate cycle exhibits three different phases, almost always in the same order: the *development boom phase*, the *overbuilt phase*, and the *gradual absorption phase*. No one phase can truly be called "first," because that depends upon where in the general economic cycle one starts to look for the real estate cycle. The basic causes why the general economy shifts from a recession or slowdown into the beginning of a general expansion are not clearly established, so all specific identifications of such causes are controversial. Even so, I will try to describe roughly what happens in those two cycles: one in the general economy, and one in commercial real estate markets.

Typically, as the general U.S. economy starts into a recovery phase from a recession or sharp slowdown, the general economy first generates rapidly rising corporate profits with quite stable wages. This growth occurs because interest rates have been reduced and the money supply expanded at the behest of the Federal Reserve Bank to combat a recession. Wages are kept from rising, however, by relatively high unemployment rates. In addition, the costs of occupying productive space are still depressed by the overbuilding generated during the previous cycle, which normally produces rising vacancies and falling rents. Hence, the costs that profitable corporate businesses face are relatively low.

If increases in business investments in plants and equipment have generated rising demand, those firms that produce such elements experience rising profits first. If increased government spending, such as during wars, has generated rising demand, those firms that provide goods and services to the government experience rising profits first. In some cases, rising demand is stimulated by greater housing production

FIGURE 7-6. **URBAN LAND INSTITUTE MEMBERSHIP, 1996–2007**

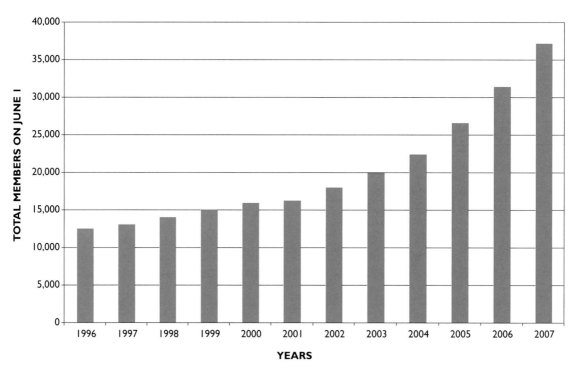

Source: Urban Land Institute.

encouraged by low interest rates. Then, rising profits occur first in homebuilding, home furnishings, and other services provided in connection with more housing.

In any case, those firms that first experience rising profits tend to raise their outputs and to invest in expanding their output capacity. This growth stimulates more-widespread prosperity and can launch the economy into a general recovery. During the early phases of such a general recovery, commercial property markets are still suffering from the excessive vacancies and low rents caused by overbuilding in the previous general economic recovery. The real estate cycle is then in its *overbuilt phase*. Property values tend to decline because of lower rents and higher vacancy than in the preceding phase. Few developers build more space because markets are already overbuilt, and the low potential returns from new structures cannot generate enough revenue to justify building them. This is the low point of the real estate cycle.

But as the general economy shifts into stronger recovery, demands for space rise, so space markets experience falling vacancies and stable or rising rents. Rents are not yet high enough, however, to justify developers' starting to build more offices, shopping centers, and industrial buildings. This is the *gradual absorption phase*. Conditions in space markets gradually improve as tenants expand their activities and earn higher profits, but little new development starts yet.

Eventually, the economy in general is in a full recovery phase, with levels of activity rising in all sectors. Expanding demands for space have already absorbed a lot of vacancy in the gradual absorption phase, so further increases in space demand begin driving up rents and cutting vacancy rates even more. Sooner or later, improved space market conditions persuade many developers to begin building new structures because they can now obtain rents high enough to make a reasonable return on such investments. Thus begins the *development boom phase* in the real estate cycle. That phase almost always starts at the peak of the general economy's full recovery phase.

No explicit overall coordination occurs among either developers or their financing sources. As a result, too many individual real estate development projects are launched in the development boom phase. This outcome is encouraged by two factors. One is the inherently optimistic and egotistical nature of real estate developers. Each believes that his or her own project will succeed even if the total number of projects of that type in that market being built is too great for the space market there to absorb them all without adverse consequences. Such a highly positive viewpoint is a necessary characteristic of real estate developers. From the viewpoint of society as a whole, developers' main function is to overcome the basic inertia of the world—its desire to perpetuate the status quo—by creating something sufficiently different to prosper in spite of heavy competition. Only people who are unusually optimistic and egotistical can successfully carry out such a function. But the very optimism and egotism that motivate them to start building also tend to make them insensitive to possible signs that their market will soon be overbuilt by both themselves and other developers. Thus, new construction projects started in the development boom phase have an inherent tendency to overshoot the capacity of space markets to absorb them all without creating an excess of supply.

The second factor encouraging developers' tendency to overshoot capacity consists of the long lead times required for developing large-scale real estate projects. Examples are regional shopping centers or super-sized office and mixed-use projects. When each such large project is started, discovering whether other developers are also starting similar projects is often difficult. Once a developer commits to starting such a project, stopping can also be difficult because the sponsors have already committed so much money to get it going.

Then the economy in general slows down for some reason, reducing demands for additional space. This occurs at the same time that a lot of the space on which construction began in the demand boom phase is just coming onto the market, since building large real property structures often takes several years. The arrival on space markets of all that new space just as demands for space are slackening produces an overbuilt phase again. Vacancies rise sharply, rents are driven downward, and buildings become less profitable. In past cycles, the market prices of commercial properties also declined as their incomes fell. Then the whole cycle starts all over again.

However, the Niagara of capital disrupted the normal operation of this three-phase real estate cycle. When the stock market crash of 2000 occurred, the resulting sudden decline in demands for space—especially office, industrial, and hotel space—created an instant version of the overbuilt phase in real estate markets. Many firms that had been occupying space disappeared almost overnight, especially in those markets specializing in high-technology and Internet-related activities. They included Silicon Valley, Austin, and parts of the Boston area. But the simultaneous massive inflow to real estate markets of money fleeing stock and bond markets prevented the prices of reasonably well-occupied real properties from falling, in spite of rising vacancy rates and declining rents in space markets generally. Although many existing office and industrial buildings were doing very badly in terms of their operating profits, their market prices did not plunge, as had usually happened in the past. Instead, prices of those properties remained stable or began rising rapidly in the case of those structures that were still well occupied with few leases about to roll over. So the overbuilt phase took place without any decline in most property prices. Surprisingly, that phase included a marked rise in the prices of many existing properties. This situation encouraged many owners of such properties to sell them to escape from their own operating losses, especially because they could get buyers to pay handsomely for such properties.

As shown in Figure 7-1, office space markets experienced falling vacancy rates from about 1993 through 1999 and even some of 2000. Then vacancy rates started upward in 2001, with a brief interruption in the last quarter of that year because of the destruction of the Twin Towers in New York City. Office vacancies continued to rise until mid-2004, even though the general economy had begun expanding before that date. These CB Richard Ellis data show that office vacancy peaked in the first quarter of 2004 at 14.9 percent in downtowns and in the last quarter of 2003 at 18.2 percent in suburban offices. After those dates, office vacancies began declining in both types of markets in the nation as a whole. At that point, the real estate cycle had moved from the overbuilt phase into the gradual absorption phase. No clear demarcation exists between those two phases, however, so exactly when that shift occurred cannot be pinpointed exactly. It probably took place at quite different moments in different locations.

In the previous real estate cycle in the 1980s, office vacancy rates had been rising for at least five years before the real estate cycle moved from its development boom phase to its overbuilt phase around the years 1989 to 1990. We know that is when the overbuilt phase became obvious because (a) in 1989 the Japanese stock market collapsed, and Japanese investors stopped buying U.S. properties, especially in Hawaii, and (b) in 1990, U.S. federal regulators pressured all banks, insurance companies, and savings and loans to stop making real estate loans on commercial properties—especially construction loans. Yet downtown office vacancy rates kept rising until late 1992, when they peaked at 17.6 percent as projects in the construction pipeline that had started three years earlier finally came on the market. Suburban office vacancy rates peaked earlier at 21.6 percent in the fourth quarter of 1989. Then vacancy rates began a long steady decline to the end of 1998 and the beginning of 1999, followed by another short period of decline in 2000.

Figure 7-7 shows when development booms in office space construction, industrial construction, and hotel and motel construction took place. By far the biggest office development boom the figure shows occurred in the 1980s, peaking in June 1985 at $62.4 billion in 1996 dollars. That boom was fueled by major tax breaks for real estate investors and developers passed in 1981 under President Reagan that lasted until the 1986 Tax Act ended them. Shortly thereafter, the real estate crash of 1989–1990 took place, cutting office space construction by two-thirds. A second office space development boom occurred in the 1990s as the stock market rose rapidly until the 2000 crash in stocks. In terms of total value of space built, this boom was considerably smaller than the one in the 1980s. However, office construction did not drop as drastically from 2001 to 2003 as in the 1990s, and a recovery in office construction began after 2003. This recovery does not yet appear to constitute a genuine development boom.

Industrial construction moved with a timing quite different from that of offices. The former enjoyed a development boom in the late 1970s, but then faltered in the 1980s when offices were going up everywhere. Industrial construction recovered in the early 1990s when office construction was plummeting. Another industrial construction boom occurred in the late 1990s but collapsed with the stock market in 2000. According to CB Richard Ellis data, industrial construction remained relatively low in 2003 and 2004 but surged in 2005 to levels 65 percent higher than in 2004. This upswing might be the beginning of another industrial development boom, but it is too early to be sure.

Hotel and motel construction has remained at much lower levels than the other two types of property discussed. It showed an overall movement pattern similar to that of office space, but at lower levels and with less volatility.

FIGURE 7-7. **NONRESIDENTIAL CONSTRUCTION PUT IN PLACE, 1964–2002**

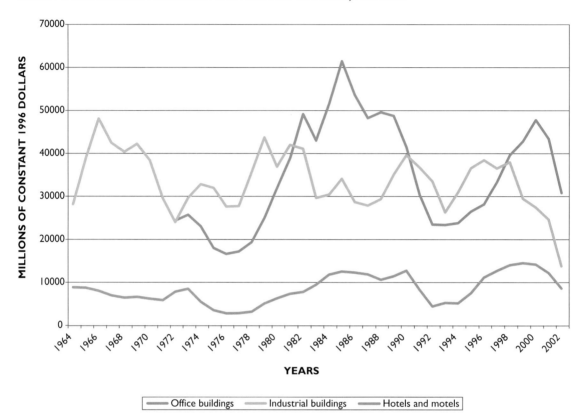

Sources: CB Richard Ellis and U.S. Census Bureau, "Value of Construction Put in Place Statistics," historic records of C30 Construction Reports, http://www.census.gov/const/C30/oldtc.html (accessed February 28, 2007).

A crucial issue in the near future is whether the easy availability of loan funds resulting from the Niagara of capital, plus continuing expansion of the U.S. general economy, will soon start another commercial property development boom period. The chance that this will happen is being encouraged by the very high prices—and thus low cap rates—on existing office and other commercial structures. Yields from buying existing buildings have steadily been driven down by rising prices fueled by the easy availability of loan funds from many private sources. In the past, developers have reacted to this phenomenon by building new projects, because they thought they could earn higher rates of return on new projects than they could get from buying existing properties at high prices. But up until 2006, new project construction has not happened at the kind of large scale that might precipitate another overbuilt phase in the real estate cycle.

FIGURE 7-8. **U.S. OFFICE VACANCY AND NEW SPACE COMPLETED, 1988–2006**

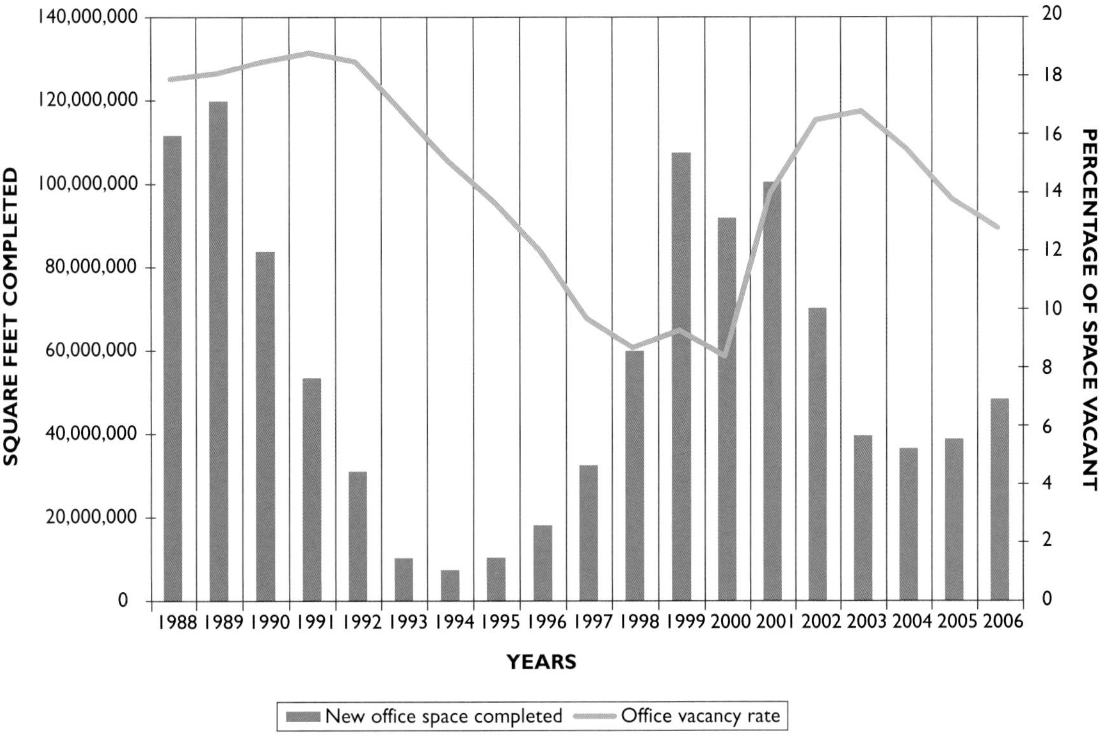

Source: CB Richard Ellis quarterly office vacancy reports.

Given that property prices have been high, and yields low, for some time, why have developers not started a new development boom already? Some observers believe developers have started into a new boom phase, as shown by the upward movement of new office space completed in Figure 7-8 after 2004. Office vacancy rates have been declining recently, however, which indicates that new additions to supply have not yet saturated the demand for space.

In spite of low yields from purchasing existing buildings, developers have been reluctant to start building massive amounts of new office space for several reasons. The first is that office vacancy rates at the national level are still relatively high—10.8 percent in downtowns and 13.9 percent in suburban markets as of the first quarter of 2007, according to CB Richard Ellis. As shown on Figure 7-9, those rates are considerably higher than they were in 2000, which indicates that a lot of vacant office space would still compete with any new space built by developers.

FIGURE 7-9. **NATIONAL VACANCY RATES FOR COMMERCIAL SPACE, 1990–2006**

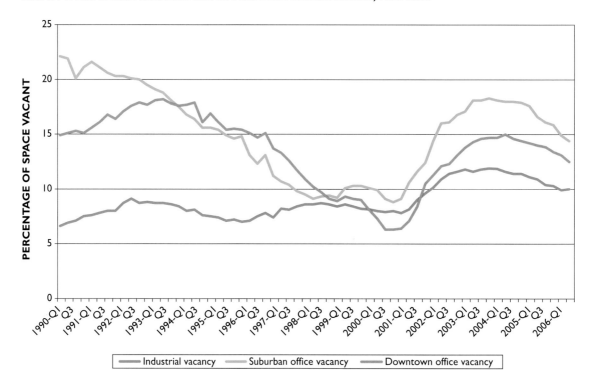

Source: CB Richard Ellis data from various monthly vacancy surveys.

The second reason is that construction costs have risen significantly in the past few years, partly because so many resources have been flowing into China to fuel its booming economy. Costs of steel, oil, and cement have been particularly affected, and all three are key ingredients in building new commercial buildings. Up to now, rapid increases in reproduction costs have kept many developers from starting enough new projects to constitute a true development boom.

The third reason is that sources of information about what is happening in real estate markets have improved greatly in the past decade. Now, developers can much more easily track how many other new buildings are being planned or built in any given market, and their likely effects upon vacancy rates, before committing to add to their number. As a result, the chance of any given developer starting a new project in a market that is already being overbuilt has fallen compared to what it used to be. True, developers are still inherent optimists who believe their own projects will be superior to any built by others; therefore, the better availability of information about competitors will not stop all overbuilding. But it will reduce the amount of accidental or unplanned overbuilding compared to what happened in the 1980s.

Finally, even though many investors are desperately looking for high-yielding projects, they are often reluctant to commit their funds to new projects being built in markets already burdened by significant vacancy rates and high construction costs.

All these factors have up to now constrained both developers and their money sources from launching a truly massive, across-the-board office space development boom similar to that which prevailed in the 1980s. True, a rise in the development of new office space seems to be appearing in 2006. CB Richard Ellis estimates that 6 million square feet of new space were started in both the fourth quarter of 2005 and the third quarter of 2006, with over 5 million having started in each of the first and third quarters of 2006. That is substantially more office projects than were started in several preceding years; however, these levels of office construction are still much lower than the levels that prevailed in 1999 and 2000 (see Figure 7-7). It indicates that construction of industrial buildings has increased sharply since 2003, but that has not happened concerning office space.

CONCLUSION

In my opinion, the longer money is readily available for borrowing at low interest rates and with easy credit terms, the more likely that developers will start large numbers of new commercial building projects. Doing so will seem likely to produce higher yields on their equity capital—or that of whoever is financing them—than using that capital to buy existing properties. In essence, the effects that the Niagara of capital has had on existing property prices, which are way up, and yields, which are way down, are undermining the willingness of investors to continue buying existing properties on those conditions. If money remains easily available, more investors and developers will decide that building new projects will produce better results than buying existing ones. The more people who make that decision, the more likely that a new development boom will arise.

I believe a real danger exists that a new real estate development boom could appear strongly in late 2007 and all of 2008 if the Niagara of capital continues to provide cheap debt money to developers and investors. This boom would be a danger because it might lead to another heavily overbuilt phase in the real estate cycle, especially if the general economy were to slow down for some reason in 2008. In contrast, if borrowing money becomes much more costly because of higher interest rates and wider rate spreads over rates on Treasury securities for risky investments, emergence of a strong new development boom will be much less likely.

That conclusion focuses attention on the subject of the next chapter: what might cause the Niagara of capital that has dominated American real estate markets since 2000 to slow down significantly or stop altogether?

Notes

1. Data for both figures were taken from quarterly vacancy reports prepared by Coldwell Banker and CB Richard Ellis, which in 1999 merged Coldwell Banker's commercial activities and Richard Ellis (outside the United Kingdom). Because my personal records of these vacancy reports were missing a few years, I extrapolated the values for which I had reports to produce the missing values. Such extrapolations involved mainly the years 1998–1999 and 2003–2004 and involved only 17 quarterly observations of a total of 64. I am confident they did not distort the meaningfulness of the resulting graph.

2. Matt Hodgins, "Mesmerized by Mezzanine," *National Real Estate Investor*, August 1, 2006, http://nreionline.com/mag/real_estate_mesmerized_mezzanine (accessed February 20, 2007).

3. Data on capitalized values of individual firms from Forbes.com, "The Global 2000," March 7, 2007, http://www.forbes.com/lists/2007/18/biz_07forbes2000_TheGlobal2000_Rank.html.

4. Henny Sander and Monica Langley, "How Blackstone's Chief Became $7 Billion Man," *Wall Street Journal*, June 13, 2007, pp. 1 and 12.

CHAPTER EIGHT

What Might Stop the Niagara of Capital into Real Estate?

For several years, especially since 2000, huge amounts of financial capital have flooded into real estate markets around the world, including those in the United States. Those inflows have caused a major restructuring of real estate markets and their relationship to the markets for other assets, such as stocks and bonds. But how long can these massive inflows of money continue? What factors might cause these inflows to slow down or even reverse themselves into outflows of funds away from real estate markets?

No one can answer those questions with much certainty. But I have formulated several alternative scenarios that might alter, stop, or reverse the recent flows of capital into real estate. This chapter analyzes the nature, likelihood, and effects of each of those scenarios.

WHY THE NIAGARA OF CAPITAL WILL NOT CONTINUE INDEFINITELY

The first thing to be said is that the current Niagara of capital into real estate cannot continue indefinitely. The present high availability of funds at relatively low interest rates is not really an equilibrium position of financial and production activities in real estate and other markets. Therefore, although that situation might continue for a while, it cannot be expected to prevail as normal throughout the future. Past history strongly implies that economic forces have an inherently changing and often cyclical nature. That nature prevents any set of conditions from prevailing without interruption over long periods of time. Sooner or later, some set of factors becomes seriously out of balance with others. Such imbalance always precipitates a significant change in prevailing conditions. Even the long rise in U.S. stock market values in the 1990s eventually crashed in 2000, and the long depression of the 1930s was ended by World War II. In economics, as in life generally, nothing in this world lasts forever.

The Niagara of financial capital into real estate was launched by three radical economic changes that produced imbalances in world financial conditions. The first was a huge generation of financial profits by firms and individuals in nations that had inadequate targets for investing those profits within their own borders. These nations included China, India, many former Soviet-dominated countries like Poland, Ukraine, Czechoslovakia, Romania, and Kazakhstan; oil-exporting nations like Russia, Iran, Saudi Arabia, and the Middle East emirates; and even successful firms and individuals in much of Western Europe and Japan. The firms and individuals controlling large profits in those nations wanted to put large shares of their capital into investments protected by a well-established rule of law and strong political and economic stability. Hence, many of their funds found their way into the United States and other major Western European nations.

The second change—partly supported by the first—was a series of rapid increases in U.S. international trade deficits, beginning in about 1998 and becoming steadily larger thereafter. This excess consumption by the United States helped absorb a corresponding imbalance of excess savings by the rest of the world, which was accentuated by rapid increases in oil prices that enriched oil-exporting nations.

The third radical change was a widely perceived fall in the minds of pension fund officials, other financial institutions, and investors in general in the attraction of investing in non–real estate stocks and bonds that took place in 2000 when stock values plummeted. In 1990, a similar flight of capital out of real estate had occurred because of massive overbuilding of property markets in the 1980s. The financial imbalance caused by that overbuilding and its consequences generated massive changes in real estate markets, including a collapse of commercial property values and development of wholly new financing sources, as described earlier.

Some changes in economic conditions are so profound, of course, that they become almost permanent fixtures that continue for long periods. The expansion of the U.S. national government into the nation's economic affairs in World War II was such a change. It permanently altered the role of government in the U.S. economy. I believe the Niagara of capital into real estate has had some similarly permanent effects. The most important is a much broader view among pension funds and other financial institutions that holding a significant fraction of their assets in real properties is a good idea. But exactly how those major institutions will carry out that idea is certainly subject to changes over time.

Moreover, most powerful economic trends tend to change conditions in ways that reduce the desirability—and likelihood—of their continuing indefinitely. The Niagara of capital has caused investors to drive the prices of commercial real estate properties up very high. That has driven yields on those properties abnormally low, compared to past American experience. These changes have reduced the relative attraction of buying real properties compared to that of buying other types of assets. Up to early 2007, however, the relative attractions of most non–real estate stocks and bonds have remained quite weak, reducing their ability to attract funds away from real estate. But those weak attractions could be changed by new economic conditions, as is discussed below.

Therefore, I do not believe that large amounts of capital will always be readily available for investment in real estate or that interest rates, yields, and cap rates on real properties will always remain low compared to their past levels, just because those conditions have prevailed for the past few years. But the question remains: what specific factors might cause those conditions to change, and how soon?

SCENARIO ONE: SHORT-RUN CONTINUATION OF THE NIAGARA OF CAPITAL

The most commonly made prediction of the future by experts and nonexperts alike is that tomorrow will be just like today. This prediction is popular because it is easy to make and describe, because the human mind is dominated by considerable inertia, and because people's thinking about the future is heavily influenced by what they have recently experienced. Therefore, many people in real estate markets think conditions created by the Niagara of capital will remain in effect for a long time. Those conditions are (a) investors controlling large amounts of financial capital seeking to invest it in real properties, (b) low interest rates on debt of all types, (c) low yields or cap rates on commercial real estate properties, (d) relatively high prices on such properties, and (e) easy transfer of funds from one nation to another around the globe. Low interest rates, in turn, depend on the continuation of relatively low rates of inflation in the world economy in general.

I believe this scenario is likely to prevail in the rest of 2007 because the world economic forces restricting inflation are still powerful. In my opinion, the most significant such force is the continuing entry into the world's industrial labor force of many well-trained, very-low-wage workers in China, India, and other developing nations. Their influence will help keep wage rates from rising greatly even in the developed world unless unemployment rates fall to even lower levels than they have been from 2005 through 2007. Figure 2-12 shows that U.S. inflation in general has been relatively low since 1993, although it has crept upward slightly since 2002. As long as central bankers around the world feel no great need to raise interest rates in order to slow down inflation, low interest rates are likely to remain in force as a stimulus to further economic growth. However, any widespread upward surge in inflation might change that view quickly.

A second factor supporting the continuation of present conditions is the reluctance of both investors and business firms to invest their profits and savings into expanding their own productive capacity. Enough uncertainty exists about the future course of economic growth to inhibit those persons and firms from committing all their profits to additional expansion. This reluctance will help sustain the surplus of investable funds that has fueled much of the Niagara of capital into real estate. Nevertheless, rates of investment in productive facilities have recently risen.

Moreover, this scenario cannot last for many years because it will eventually generate a renewed round of new property construction by real estate developers. Investors will be willing to finance that new construction to obtain what they believe would be higher yields on their capital than they can get from buying existing properties now selling at very high prices—and very low yields. As discussed in Chapter 7, if money availability remains unchanged, this situation will eventually lead to a new development boom across the nation. If such a boom continues for several years, it could create enough new property to depress the space market by increasing vacancies and putting downward pressure on rents of both existing and newly built properties. That would reduce the relative attraction of investing in real properties compared with investing in non–real estate stocks and bonds. Thus, the initial continuation of current conditions shaped by the Niagara of capital will, if sustained, generate results that will undermine further continuation of those conditions.

A preliminary indication of the changing attraction of real estate is that real estate investment trust (REIT) stock values, as a group, stopped rising on February 7, 2007, and have steadily declined since then, although the other major stock indices kept rising until about mid-August. This slump is not yet an absolutely conclusive sign of a long-term decline in REIT shares' attractiveness, but it may be a harbinger of things to come.

If no unexpected international events occur, a shift from current conditions to what would amount to an overbuilt phase of the real estate cycle may take several years. Figure 7-7, which is based on U.S. Census Bureau records of C30 reports on the values of construction of various types put in place in each year, shows that the overbuilding that occurred in office markets in the 1980s took many years to develop.[1] The recession of 1974–1975 was the low point of office space construction in the 1970s, which then shot upward almost continuously to a peak in 1985. Office construction remained quite high until 1989, after which it plummeted in the real estate

crash of 1990 to about 1994. Thus, the massive overbuilding of the 1980s that precipi-
tated the collapse in 1990 had occurred over almost a whole decade. I doubt if current
conditions of low interest rates and massive lending availability will last that long
before adverse repercussions begin to be felt in real estate and other markets.

This analysis illustrates the potentially self-limiting nature of a continuation
of current capital market conditions, almost regardless of what those conditions are.
All three of the basic phases of the real estate cycle are similarly self-limiting. The
overbuilt phase is self-limiting because construction of new space ceases during that
phase, but the general economy eventually recovers and drives up both occupancy
and rents to surpass the capacity of the overbuilt structures to contain burgeoning
demand. The gradual absorption phase is similar. Little construction occurs in that
phase, but rents are rising and vacancy is falling. Eventually, those changes create sufficient profit possibilities so developers start building again. The development boom
phase is self-limiting because all the new space created in that phase eventually drives
vacancies up and rents down—reducing profits and launching the overbuilt phase.

I believe the continuation of current conditions until a new development boom
begins is the most likely of the scenarios described in this chapter, unless some major
but unpredictable world event introduces one of the other scenarios described below.

SCENARIO TWO: A BIG RISE IN INTEREST RATES

If interest rates were to rise sharply, that could certainly inhibit continuation of the
Niagara of capital into real estate and other economic sectors. Interest rates are especially crucial to real estate because so many real property investments are for relatively long terms and involve high fractions of borrowed money. Hence, interest expenses are a key part of the profit potential of almost every real estate deal. A huge proportion of all real estate deals made with funds from the Niagara of capital has involved
borrowed funds. Furthermore, low interest rates have been a major element in the
Niagara of capital. They have rewarded people for borrowing money, because they
could invest that borrowed money in real estate at higher rates of return than the
cost of borrowing, even though those rates of return became relatively low in historic terms.

The Federal Reserve Bank in Washington has been trying to push interest rates
upward since the middle of 2004 to forestall possible inflation. It did so by gradually
raising the rate it charges banks to borrow money from the Fed. The federal funds
rate has been increased by 0.25 percent intervals, rising from about 1 percent in mid-
2004 to 5.25 percent in August 2006, where it remained until the time of this writing
(August 2007).[2] As a result of this pressure, the rate of interest on ten-year Treasury
notes rose from 4.01 percent in 2003 to 5.2 percent in May 2006, but then declined to

4.43 percent in December 2006; they increased again to 5.26 percent in June 2007, but declined to 4.64 percent on August 20, 2007. Thirty-year mortgage rates rose from 5.77 percent in mid-2004 to 6.81 percent in July 2006, then declined to 6.69 percent in June 2007 and further declined in August 2007 to under 5.0 percent. Thus, the Fed's attempt to push long-term interest rates upward has been only partly successful, although credit spreads on both junk bonds and investment-quality assets have recently widened somewhat.

Moreover, the Fed has stopped increasing its federal funds rate since August 2006 when it reached 5.25 percent. Apparently, the Fed believes inflationary forces have abated somewhat, especially since the rate of growth of gross domestic product (GDP) has slowed in 2007 and appears likely to be below that of 2006. If this behavior by the Fed persists, interest rates are not likely to rise much in the rest of 2007 unless something else causes a sharp increase in inflation.

What could that "something else" be? It is not likely to be a rapid increase in the wages of industrial or other workers because of the competitive pressure from low-wage foreign workers. It could be a big jump in oil prices because of an interruption of international oil shipments or production caused by violence in the Middle East or Nigeria, or a dispute between the United States and Venezuela, or some other improbable event. It could also be the spreading of investor reluctance to invest in debt securities caused by rising defaults and foreclosures in the subprime mortgage market in late 2006 and early 2007.

In my opinion, however, a sudden rise in interest rates not caused by one of the other scenarios described below is very unlikely to occur in 2007 or even 2008. With the U.S. economy clearly slowing down in 2007, inflationary pressures are likely to abate—again assuming no disruptive international events. Even though economic activity seems to be speeding up somewhat in both Japan and Europe and continuing strongly in China and India, a slowdown in the U.S. economy would inhibit any big increase in inflation likely to cause rapidly rising interest rates.

Therefore, this scenario seems unlikely. Interest rates may rise sharply, but only because of one of the other disrupting but improbable activities described in other of the following scenarios.

SCENARIO THREE: A SHARP DECLINE IN THE VALUE OF THE U.S. DOLLAR

The United States has been running large international trade deficits—that is, importing more than it is exporting—for many years. To pay for its imports, the United States has been selling Treasury securities and other forms of IOUs to foreign creditors. The U.S. trade deficit in 2006 was $856.7 billion—equivalent to 6.47 percent of the U.S. GDP of $13.247 trillion. Foreign creditors may become tired of selling their goods for our IOUs in dollars that keep shrinking in value. From January 2000 to May 2007, the U.S. dollar declined 24.8 percent compared to the euro and 18 percent compared to the British pound.[3]

If the dollar falls further in trading value, as seems likely, the prices of our imports will rise in U.S. dollars. In addition, exports of U.S.-manufactured goods and services to foreign buyers will increase because our prices will be lower to those buyers in their own currencies. Hence, U.S. unemployment rates will decline, putting some upward pressure on wages. Both developments would cause the rate of inflation in the United States to rise. That would in turn motivate the Federal Reserve Board to raise interest rates. Higher interest rates would make debt used in real estate transactions more expensive. They would also reduce the profitability of operating real properties heavily financed with debt, especially floating-rate debt. These developments would reduce the relative attractiveness of U.S. real estate compared to non–real estate stocks and bonds.

This chain of events would greatly affect the Niagara of capital into U.S. real estate only if the decline in the value of the U.S. dollar was both large and sudden. Then, the Federal Reserve would be pressured into raising interest rates quickly to stem any large outflow of dollars. The decline of the dollar's international trading value could possibly be gradual enough to avoid causing the Federal Reserve to raise interest rates rapidly. In that case, financial and trade markets would adjust without causing great disadvantages to real estate investment.

SCENARIO FOUR: A SUDDEN DECLINE IN WORLD ECONOMIC UNCERTAINTY

Another global event that could affect the Niagara of capital would be a sudden fall in global uncertainty because of the settlement of current intense conflicts. If peace were to break out between the Israelis and the Palestinians, or North Korea were to stop building nuclear weapons in a binding deal with other powers, or the Iraqi government decisively defeated the insurgents and established relative law and order, or Iran decided to stop building nuclear weapons and settle with Western powers, any or all of those developments would greatly change the future outlook of the investment community. In that case, stocks other than REIT shares might take off in another bull market because world commerce would be stimulated by greater chances of peace and prosperity. Such a stock-market takeoff would draw a lot of financial capital away from real estate and back into the non–real estate portions of the world's stock markets. That might occur even though a generally rising stock market would probably improve the operating performance of many commercial real estate properties by creating higher rents and occupancy. Even in that case, I do not believe that all of the capital that has migrated into real estate since 2000 would leave it. Since 2000, the financial institutions of the world have definitely decided that real estate is an asset class in which they ought to keep a significant portion of their total assets. Nevertheless, a notable share of all the capital that fled from stocks and bonds into real estate after 2000 would return to those other asset classes. That would greatly reduce the total amount of financial capital that flowed into real estate after 2000, causing a basic change in the Niagara of capital.

The probability of any of the uncertainty-reducing events described here actually occurring in the near future seems very low. Therefore, this scenario must be considered in the very-long-shot category and given little weight in decision making.

SCENARIO FIVE: SOME TYPE OF GLOBAL FINANCIAL DISASTER

Much more likely—but difficult to predict with any reliability—is the possibility of some major financial disaster occurring in the near future that would disrupt economic activity in many major developed and developing nations. An example would be a revolution in Saudi Arabia in which radical Islamic forces overthrew the Saudi monarchy and drastically cut back exports of oil to the rest of the world, sharply raised oil prices, or both. Another example would be an economic collapse or a civil war or political revolution in China. If oil prices soared on global markets, the resulting high costs to many developed nations, including the United States, could slow their economic growth and increase their chances of suffering recessions.

Another financial disaster would be the collapse of many major hedge funds, REITs, or private equity funds that have bought large real estate firms—followed by rapidly spreading bankruptcies of many American banks and other financial institutions. In 2006 and 2007, such a trend began among firms specializing in subprime residential mortgage lending when defaults on such loans soared and several subprime lenders went bankrupt. Then, subprime problems spread across the globe because such loans were included in many complex—and therefore opaque—collateralized debt obligations (CDOs) and securitized bond issues. Suddenly, real estate lenders and investors in CDOs and commercial mortgage–backed securities (CMBSs) of all types began to realize how poorly many of these loans had been underwritten and how badly they had been underweighting and mispricing the sizable risks involved. Their uncertainty caused mortgage interest rate spreads over Treasuries to increase and also led to more-stringent underwriting standards. Many lenders temporarily ceased lending, and many investors ceased buying CDOs and CMBSs until risks were better understood and priced more realistically. This fear threatened a widespread seizing-up of global credit markets that jeopardized the world's financial markets and the prospects for continued economic growth.

Responding to those fears, in August 2007, the European Central Bank, the U.S. Federal Reserve Bank, and the Bank of England increased liquidity in euros, dollars, and pounds and offered to lend extensively to banks at low rates. Moreover, in mid-September, the Federal Reserve Bank reduced both the federal funds interest rate (at which banks can borrow reserve funds from each other) and the discount rate (at which the Fed will lend money to banks) by 50 basis points each—a major policy change. This step caused an immediate short-run rise in stock prices around the world. But whether those actions will quell the spreading uncertainty and tightening lending conditions in world credit markets was not yet clear when this book was being written. In my opinion, such a return of stability in real estate credit markets is likely to take at least several months and could take much longer. A lot of potential lenders and investors with capital are still out there looking for something in which to invest, so there is no shortage of money. Nevertheless, any extensive and long-lasting general reduction in lender and investor confidence in world credit markets could generate higher interest rates over a longer period and thereby slow down or disrupt the continuation of large-scale capital fund investment in real estate.

Still another adverse financial development would be a substantial fall in the prices of housing units throughout the developed world, including in the United States. American housing prices have declined slightly but have not come close to collapsing, as did office space prices in 1990 to 1993. I do not believe such a widespread "bursting of the housing bubble" is likely. Most U.S. homeowners now trying to sell their homes at high prices do not have to move or sell rapidly. Hence, if housing prices start to decline sharply, they can just withdraw their homes from the market and keep living where they are now until the economic situation is more favorable to sellers. This withdrawal possibility places a floor under housing prices that is not present in other types of real property markets. In some nations, however, such as Spain, where many homes are owned by absentee households who use them for resort purposes and population growth is very slow, housing prices could fall much further than they will in the United States, where most homeowners live in their homes full time and total population is continuously rising.

The chance of any such financial disaster occurring is not trivial, although it is by no means a certainty either. That chance is probably much greater than the chance of a large decline in global uncertainty about the future. Assigning even a rough probability to the appearance of any global financial disaster that would slow, stop, or even reverse the Niagara of capital in real estate markets in the next few years is extremely difficult; however, the longer that Niagara continues, the greater the probability that it will be disrupted by some type of financial disaster.

SCENARIO SIX: AN AMERICAN RECESSION

The sixth scenario included in this analysis is the onset of a recession in the American economy in the near future. Although the U.S. economy slowed sharply in 2001 after both the stock market crash of 2000 and the terrorist attacks on September 11, 2001, the last year in which U.S. GDP actually declined in real terms was 1991—and that was a decline of less than 1 percent. The last recession before that was in 1980 and 1982, with declines in real GDP of 0.2 percent and 1.9 percent, respectively. Thus, the United States has not had a serious recession for 25 years. In fact, in the 68 years from 1939 to 2007, in only 12 years did real GDP decline. In the 47 years from 1960 to 2007, real GDP fell in only five, and in only one of those (1982) did it fall more than 1 percent. For many decades, the U.S. economy has been mostly free from recessions or even near recessions.

Yet at least some chance exists that the U.S. economy could experience a recession in the near future that could slow or stop the Niagara of capital that has been flowing into real estate in the past decade. One sign that a recession might occur is what has repeatedly happened to the U.S. economy since 1945 shortly after its housing production hit 2 million units per year or more. On five occasions after World War II, housing starts in America surpassed 2 million units per year for at least one year. On the first four occasions, in the four years following the last year of 2 million starts, new housing starts per year declined by an average of 40.9 percent. In three of those cases, one of those four following years was marked by a decline in real GDP for the economy as a whole. Those years of 2 million housing starts (including mobile homes) were 1950, 1971–1973, 1977–1979, 1984–1986, and 2004–2005. The years of negative real GDP following each of those spurts of high housing starts were 1954, 1974–1975, and 1982. The 1991 year of slightly falling GDP was five years after the last 2 million–start year, 1984–1986.

If this pattern repeats itself after the 2 million–start years in 2004 and 2005, the United States will see another year of negative real GDP between 2006 and 2009. Of course, in reality nothing requires past cycles to repeat so exactly. I certainly do not believe the U.S. economy will experience a recession in 2007, and no certainty exists it will do so in the next two years either. But it is at least a possibility that, if it took place, would discourage investors from continuing to pour capital into U.S. real estate.

SCENARIO SEVEN: A GLOBAL NONFINANCIAL DISASTER

The most damaging scenario that might disrupt the Niagara of capital into real estate would be another type of disaster that was not primarily financial, although it would have immense financial consequences. I am referring to a terrorist-caused nuclear explosion in a large U.S. city, or a major war in the Middle East that completely disrupted the flow of oil to the United States and forced it to spend more billions and lives on military operations there, or a global outbreak of bird flu that killed millions of people, or the earth's being struck by a large asteroid that disrupted the climate for years, or some other highly improbable event with catastrophic consequences for much of the world. Obviously, the likelihood of any such event is impossible to forecast, although I believe it is very small. But the probability of a tsunami that killed more than 229,000 people was very small too—yet it happened in December 2004.

CONCLUSION

Nothing in this world goes on forever, and that includes the Niagara of capital into real estate. In fact, the longer that Niagara continues, the more it undermines the very conditions that made it happen and that have sustained it for so long. Even so, no reason exists to believe those conditions will disappear almost immediately, unless some hard-to-predict global event causes major economic disruptions in worldwide flows of money and goods.

The most imponderable aspect of trying to decide when the Niagara of capital might end is that it was started, and then continued, more because of events outside real estate markets than those inside them. It was the sudden collapse of stock market values (except for REIT shares) in 2000, the terrorist attacks of 9/11, the long-run effect of millions of low-wage workers becoming better educated, and the efficiency of global communications and transportation that made assets other than real estate look far less attractive than they had in the 1990s. Those factors therefore made real estate look a lot more attractive relative to other assets than ever before—and that newfound attractiveness started the Niagara of capital into real property markets. Some similar set of factors will probably have to occur that makes other assets look a lot more attractive than real estate to slow down or end the Niagara of capital. But real estate itself will contribute to that end, too, because the longer the Niagara continues driving property prices up and yields down, the less attractive real estate will seem—other things being equal. If that seems a rather vague forecast of how the Niagara of capital will eventually end, it has to be vague because of the inherent uncertainty of the whole question.

Notes

1. Figure 7 7 docs not continue the series past 2002 because the Census Bureau stopped issuing the underlying data in the same form in 2002. Data issued later are not sufficiently comparable with those in the figure to enable its extension past 2002.

2. The federal funds rate first surpassed 5.25 percent on July 27, 2006, when it was set at 5.27 percent. However, it was not actually set to 5.25 percent until August 2, 2006. Data from the Federal Reserve Board Web site, http://www.federalreserve.gov/releases/h15/data.htm (accessed June 30, 2007).

3. Data on currency exchange rates from the Federal Reserve Board for 2003 to 2007, and from x-rates.com, http://www.xrates.com/cgibin/hlookup.cgi, for periods before 2003 (accessed June 23, 2007).

CHAPTER NINE

The Long-Term Effects of the Niagara of Capital

Because the Niagara of capital into real estate was still occurring when this book was being written, analyzing its long-term effects may seem premature. Nevertheless, the Niagara of capital has affected the U.S. economy and real estate in many important ways, some of which are likely to be permanent. This chapter examines those effects.

LONG-TERM EFFECTS ON HOUSING MARKETS

Because all of these effects have already been described in earlier chapters, this section has some of the traits of a summary, but it focuses only on those elements likely to survive over the long term.

Broader Gap between Household Incomes and Housing Prices

The most important long-term effect of the Niagara of capital on U.S. and other housing markets is the greater gap it produced between the incomes of households in the bottom half of each society's income distribution and the market prices of housing there. The higher prices of U.S. housing produced in part by the Niagara of capital will probably decline somewhat below their 2005 levels. That has already begun to occur under the impact of a huge oversupply of housing units for sale everywhere in 2006 and 2007. Many homeowners who finally decided to cash in on high prices in 2005 and 2006 by selling found that the number of buyers willing to pay those record prices had greatly shrunk. One reason is that the U.S. economy in general slowed down in 2007. Major causes of that slowdown were that new housing construction fell sharply after 2005 and home prices began to decline in many regions, which undermined the past practice among homeowners of borrowing against their higher-priced homes to finance consumption often not related to housing. Also, default and foreclosure problems—mainly among subprime homebuyers—began to plague housing markets and even affected several large hedge funds that had specialized in subprime lending. Those problems discouraged many potential subprime buyers. The same problems also reduced the number of mortgage lenders willing to make loans on super-easy credit terms and encouraged federal regulators to urge banks to tighten credit standards. With home sales off, but millions of homes on the market, sellers were less successful in disposing of their homes quickly.

Nevertheless, I do not believe U.S. housing prices will collapse under the weight of all those unsold homes. As prices decline gradually, many owners will withdraw their homes from the market rather than accept amounts they believe are less than what they think those homes are worth. As a result, the huge gap between high housing prices and stable incomes in the bottom half of the income distribution has become a permanent feature of many U.S. housing markets. Moreover, credit terms for borrowing to buy a home have begun to tighten from the extremely easy terms that prevailed from 2000 to 2005. Those easy credit terms enabled many low-income households to overcome the large gap between their incomes and the costs of buying a home. But with a sharp rise in defaults and slow payments among subprime borrowers, lenders began to tighten their credit standards in 2007. That trend is likely to continue for at least several years. As a result, households with low incomes will find buying homes more difficult.

Therefore, housing affordability problems will afflict much larger fractions of all households than in the past. The rate of homeownership is likely to decline slightly, and the overall demand for rental apartments will rise. Politicians may make some gestures toward helping renters become buyers with various forms of government aid. But higher housing costs have greatly increased the cost of doing so through public subsidies. Therefore federal, state, or local governments are unlikely to launch any truly effective publicly financed means of reducing housing affordability problems.

Greater Wealth among Homeowning Households

Rising home prices have, nevertheless, made a majority of American households wealthier. Sixty-nine percent of Americans owned their own homes as of 2006—and most experienced rising home equities in the past decade. Although their net equities will diminish somewhat as home prices decline, for most households, those equities will still be much greater than they were ten years ago. That will give such households a cushion against economic adversities.

Stronger Political Powers of Homeowners

Enhanced wealth in the form of higher home equities will also help sustain efforts of many homeowners to act as a powerful political force concerning government housing policies. Suburban homeowners in particular are likely to keep pressuring their local governments to inhibit or block the construction of any low-cost single-family homes or rental apartments in their communities. Homeowners—fortified by political support from homebuilders and Realtors—will also strongly oppose any changes in the currently unjust structure of homeowner tax benefits. That structure amounts to a homeownership entitlement that channels a huge fraction of all homeowner tax benefits to a few very wealthy homeowners. Many low-income renters receive some direct subsidy aid, but no aids to renters are entitlements paid to everyone who qualifies to receive them.

Another unfortunate political result will be the continued reluctance of state government leaders to pressure local governments to reduce existing regulatory barriers against lower-cost housing and all rental housing.

Increased Emphasis on Sprawl Development

In the United States, homeownership is associated in the minds of millions of households with owning a single-family, detached housing unit with its own lawn. As a result, the greater degree of homeownership among U.S. households promoted by the Niagara of capital has essentially increased the tendency of American households to live in sprawl-dominated settlement patterns rather than in higher-density developments. Over the long run, this pattern causes longer average commuting travel, more use of private automobiles rather than public transit, greater emission of air pollutants, and greater public expenditures on infrastructures than would occur if settlement patterns were higher in density and less spread out.

Over time, the percentage of all new homes started each year consisting of single-family units has risen notably since the Niagara of capital appeared, as shown on Figure 9-1. That percentage rose from 62.0 in 1997 to 77.9 in 2005 and 76.2 in 2006, both record highs, at least since 1960. Among all single-family homes started, about 91 percent are detached, based on U.S. Census Bureau inventories of all types of housing in every census year since 1940 (data on percentage detached are not readily available annually).

Thus, one of the long-term results of the Niagara of capital may be to increase or at least maintain the current dominance of sprawl development patterns in U.S. metropolitan areas, even though many urban experts believe the nation should shift toward more-compact, higher-density patterns.

FIGURE 9-1. **PERCENTAGE OF TOTAL HOUSING STARTS THAT ARE SINGLE-FAMILY HOMES**

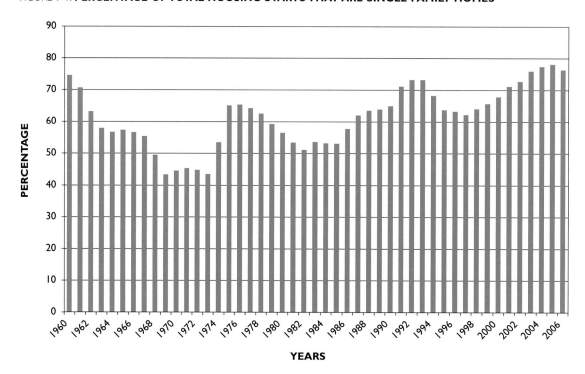

Source: Council of Economic Advisers, *Economic Indicators* (Washington, D.C.: Government Printing Office, various months), New Private Housing and Vacancy Rates.

Lowered Underwriting Standards among Housing Lenders

The Niagara of capital into U.S. housing markets also pressured institutions that lend money to potential homebuyers to reduce their underwriting standards to such households, but that is probably not a long-term effect. Escalating defaults and foreclosures among subprime borrowers in particular have already caused some bankruptcies among firms that lent money to such borrowers and could cause more. That outcome will lead federal regulators to pressure such lenders to raise their underwriting standards, and it will eliminate the worst offenders from doing business. Even so, some reduction in mortgage underwriting standards compared to what they were before 1990 is probably justified by the reduced risk of mortgage lending resulting from widespread securitization of both residential and commercial real estate lending.

Higher Property Taxes on Housing

An indirect long-term effect of the Niagara of capital has been to raise property taxes as a result of higher home evaluations by appraisers and assessors. This effect will increase the total share of public school funding that local property taxes pay across the nation. Consequently, differences in the amount of school funding per pupil among communities will become greater than ever. True, quality of education is affected by many factors other than the amount spent per pupil. Nevertheless, richer communities will be able to improve their schools more than poorer ones, aggravating the already large disparity of educational qualities offered students, to the disadvantage of those students who need help most.

Weakening of the Housing Filtering Process

Traditionally, most low-income households in America live in housing units they rent or have bought through the housing filtering process. In that process, older units decline in value as new ones are built, causing a chain of moves that eventually permits low-income households to buy or rent units that were originally built for higher-income households. But the large rise in home prices stimulated by the Niagara of capital meant that most older homes also rose in price, rather than declining with time—except in some slow-growing metropolitan markets. Even so, during the period from 2000 to 2005, when credit terms for homebuying were drastically reduced, many low-income households could still rent or buy well-built older homes, although the prices and rents of those homes were rising. But with credit terms returning to more-normal standards, such reaching upward in the home-price distribution will no longer be as easy. If enough capital is still flowing into real estate to keep home prices rising in the future—as they have at the national level since 1968—then the traditional filtering process will not work as well as it did when the prices of older homes were falling.

Accelerated Gentrification

Possible undermining of the filtering process will be further aggravated by the gentrification of older in-city neighborhoods. Gentrification occurs because the particular older neighborhoods involved have some attractive amenities—such as proximity to the region's downtown—in addition to relatively low housing prices. High-income newcomers typically invest in improving the older units they have bought, which raises the market value of those units and often attracts more higher-income households to move into that area. As more do so, the prices of housing in that neighborhood are driven upward, even though the units concerned are relatively old. In effect, gentrification reverses the traditional process whereby older units decline in price as time passes and newer, more modern units are built. It therefore undermines the entire filtering process, as discussed earlier in Chapter 4. Gentrification upgrades the housing stock of the neighborhoods where it occurs, however, so it benefits cities in the long run.

In many large cities, the gentrification process has been intensified by several ongoing demographic and other trends in American society. One such trend is the rising number of empty-nester households formed as the baby-boomer generation's children grew up and moved away from their parents. Those empty nesters often tire of caring for large suburban homes with big lawns. Many move to smaller quarters closer to their jobs or to the more-bustling lifestyles near downtowns. In addition, the hassles of coping with ever-greater traffic congestion in commuting to downtown jobs have motivated many households of all ages to move closer to those jobs. Hence, gentrification is a growing process in many large American cities, especially those in metropolitan areas with strong economies and prosperous downtown areas.

Gentrification is not primarily caused by the Niagara of capital, however; it is a social and economic trend that existed long before those capital flows began, and it will continue even if the Niagara of capital slows down. But as long as the Niagara of capital continues, it will accelerate such real estate investment trends as gentrification.

Greater Role of Housing in Household Balance Sheets

The last long-term effect of the Niagara of capital on U.S. housing markets is a shift in the balance sheets of American households toward having a higher share of their net wealth in the form of real estate ownership and a lower share in the form of stocks and bonds. This shift could be undermined in the future if the U.S. economy experiences another long period in which stocks outperform real estate, as happened in the 1990s. But the recent period in which real estate has outperformed stocks and bonds—as has happened since 2000—has impressed many American households with the importance of maintaining a significant fraction of their net assets in real estate, primarily in their own homes.

LONG-TERM EFFECTS ON COMMERCIAL PROPERTY MARKETS

Several major changes in commercial property markets seem permanent effects of the Niagara of capital. Therefore, those changes are likely to continue even when the Niagara itself slows down or disappears.

Lower Loan Underwriting Standards

I believe the recent decline of investment underwriting standards by real estate financing institutions caused by intense competition among lenders trying to place their huge supplies of funds is partly cyclical and partly structural. Because it is partly cyclical, it will probably diminish as soon as the huge capital flows in the Niagara of capital slow down sharply or stop, or when some large financial setback among real estate operators increases defaults and bankruptcies. Similar declines in underwriting standards have occurred before, although perhaps not as dramatically, and they have almost always vanished when markets got tight again.

But I also believe that part of the recent decline in underwriting standards results from structural changes in real estate finance. Those changes involve the securitization of lending instruments, which has reduced both the actual and the perceived risks of making real estate loans. Lenders who think the risks of property-based loans are lower tend to accept lower underwriting standards when making such loans. In particular, they have reduced the strength of the covenants that they have written into their loan documents, easing the pressure on borrowers to restrict their own behavior. Hence, that portion of lower underwriting standards caused by perceptions of reduced lending risks will survive at least some cyclical downturns in property markets. To some extent, this reaction is rational: truly lower risks ought to produce somewhat lower underwriting standards. But it is easy for lenders to go too far in cutting underwriting standards whenever huge surpluses of money to be invested put all of them under tremendous competitive pressures.

Will U.S. Real Estate Markets More Closely Resemble European Markets?

Some expert observers believe that the Niagara of capital has permanently altered the structure of U.S. commercial property markets. They foresee lower U.S. current yields and cap rates—thus higher property prices—similar to those long prevailing in Western Europe. They also think this change will occur because of the ever-increasing resistance among U.S. voters and local governments to new developments likely to disrupt local community life at least temporarily. Greater local resistance to new projects tends to raise development costs substantially and to lengthen the time required to add to capacity—two more similarities to Western European development. A final factor supporting their case has been higher construction costs because of the strong demands for key building materials from expanding economies in China, India, and other developing nations.

This argument has some plausibility. It is especially relevant to a few very large U.S. metropolitan areas where foreign investors and major U.S. financial institutions like to focus their U.S. real estate investments. Those areas are the San Francisco, Los Angeles, New York City, and Washington metropolitan regions, and especially their downtowns. But I believe such changes will not hold true over the long run or in the vast majority of other U.S. metropolitan areas. Interest rates have been kept low in part by low-wage competition in world manufacturing markets from Chinese and

FIGURE 9-2. **INTEREST RATES ON TEN-YEAR TREASURY BONDS, 1962–2006**

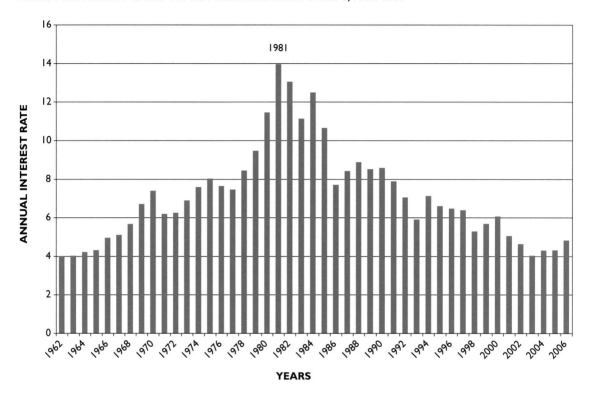

Source: Federal Reserve Board, Selected Interest Rates, Historical Data, U.S. Government Securities, Constant Maturities, 10-year, Annual, http://www.federalreserve.gov/releases/h15/data/Annual/H15_TCMNOM_Y10.txt.

other Asian workers, who have recently been entering the world's skilled labor force in large numbers. But as their prosperity increases over time, that factor will be less able to hold product prices down. Moreover, in the past, U.S. local resistance to new developments has evaporated when any economic hardships have appeared on the scene. In recessions or even just economic slowdowns, local governments and citizens typically knock themselves out to attract new enterprises and projects to their communities.

Regarding interest rates, in nominal terms, uncorrected for inflation, U.S. long-term rates for ten-year U.S. Treasuries are shown in Figure 9-2. In earlier periods, those rates had varied between 4 and 6 percent in the first half of the 19th century, rose above 6 percent briefly during the Civil War, gradually declined to between 3 and 4 percent between 1880 and 1910, spiked over 5 percent in 1920, and plunged in the Great Depression in the 1930s to below 3 percent and to 2 percent in 1941. After World War

II, interest rates began steadily increasing as inflation escalated until the period covered by Figure 9-2. This period climaxed in another rate spike in 1981 when the Federal Reserve established a record interest rate of 13.92 percent as a means of stopping inflation. Then rates began a long and steady descent to a low point of 4.01 percent in 2003.

Thus, long-term rates below 4 percent have prevailed only during the extended deflationary periods in the late 19th century, in the Great Depression, and in the federally controlled interest rate period right after World War II. In short, very low interest rates have coincided with some type of adversity, crisis, or otherwise unusual period in our history. Long-term interest rates for Treasury securities do not seem likely to remain in the low vicinity of 4 to 5 percent—where they have been from 2002 through 2006—for an extended period into the near future. That is especially unlikely if recently rising inflationary pressures further intensify or if the Federal Reserve must raise rates to limit further depreciation of the U.S. dollar in international trade. That is an important reason why I do not believe American commercial property markets have permanently transformed themselves into the low-cap-rate, high-price form prevailing in much of Western Europe.

A Paradigm Shift in the Attitudes of Investors toward Real Estate

Probably the most important effect of the Niagara of capital in commercial property markets worldwide is a paradigm shift in the attitudes of many financial institutions, individual investors, hedge funds, and other investors toward investing in commercial real estate. Before the Niagara of capital, most such investors were highly skeptical of investing in real property, especially over the long run. Therefore, they held only very small fractions of their total wealth in commercial real estate, even though commercial real estate accounted for a large percentage of the total value of all the assets in the world. Pension funds typically had less than 5 percent of their total assets in commercial properties. But then the collapse of stock prices in 2000 wiped out many of the gains such investors had made in the last part of the booming 1990s (after 1997). Not only did real estate prices—including share prices of real estate investment trusts (REITs)—fail to collapse, but also they rose spectacularly. This result caused investors to become more favorable to keeping a significant share of their long-term assets in real estate, not just in stocks, bonds, and gold.

Enlarging the Sources of Capital Willing to Invest in Commercial Real Estate

The paradigm shift described has immensely expanded the number, variety, and nature of the sources of financial capital willing to invest in commercial real property.

Whereas American real estate was traditionally financed primarily by commercial banks, savings and loan associations, individual investors, life insurance companies, and mortgage banking companies, it is now also importantly financed by pension funds, hedge funds, mutual funds of various types, opportunity funds, and entirely new sources of capital, such as private REITs, buyers of commercial mortgage–backed securities (CMBSs), and individuals putting money into U.S. REITs, REIT mutual funds, and foreign REITs. Many financial institutions and money managers who before 2000 never considered putting any significant share of their capital into real estate have now decided to change that behavior permanently.

An important cause of this expansion of funds available to U.S. commercial real estate has been the globalization of capital flows. Capital sources all over the world have been investing in U.S. real estate with greater frequency and volume than ever before. One reason is the greater ease of moving money from one nation to another through globalized communications systems based on computers, satellites, and the Internet. A second reason is greater transparency and better sources of information about U.S. real estate. Even more significant is the worldwide perception that the United States, though in recent years often despised for its foreign policy, is still one of the world's safest and most secure places in which to invest compared to all other alternatives. As a result, the expansion of capital sources available to U.S. real estate has included a spatial enlargement across the entire world, as well as an enlargement over many different types of fund sources within each nation. In the past few years, however, an increasing share of world capital flows—including those originating in the United States—has gone into investments outside of the United States, mainly because of investor fears that the U.S. dollar will further devalue in the future. That is also true of capital flows going into real estate.

Another crucial factor contributing to this result was an explosion of securitization of all forms of financial instruments since 1990. As explained earlier, securitization both reduces the actual risks of lending money in financial real estate transactions and reduces even more the perceived risks of doing so. Widespread acceptance of the belief that securitized real estate loans are much less risky than whole loans has been a key factor increasing the willingness of many nontraditional sources of funds to invest in real estate.

These changes in attitudes could themselves be changed if some financial disaster befell the commercial property world. But until that happens, the total supply of financial capital that can potentially be tapped by commercial real property markets appears to have greatly expanded compared with its size before 1990 or even 2000.

The Rise of Private Equity Investment Funds

Another effect of the Niagara of capital in commercial property markets has been the emergence of private equity investment funds. These are investment funds established by private entrepreneurs. They put up a limited amount of their own equity capital, raise more equity capital privately from other investors, and heavily leverage that total equity capital with a lot more debt capital borrowed from other private investors, banks, and a variety of other lenders. Then they use all that capital to buy up commercial real estate—and other types of assets—at high prices and quickly resell them at even higher prices to other investors looking for someplace to put their capital. Because the small equity in each private equity fund is so heavily leveraged with debt capital borrowed at low rates, operators of many such funds have been able to reap high rates of return on their own equity and the equity of their fellow investors. This profitability has enabled them to raise even more equity capital for their next venture.

In essence, private equity funds returned to the financing tactics of the real estate developers of the 1980s. Those developers had leveraged small amounts of their own equity capital with huge amounts of borrowed capital to finance the construction of millions of square feet of new properties—often borrowing more than 100 percent of the costs of building involved. When consequent overbuilding drove rents and occupancy rates down throughout commercial property markets, many such developers were unable to cover the heavy debt costs of all their borrowing and defaulted on their obligations.

As a result, when Wall Street helped finance a new round of real estate operators in the 1990s through REITs, the purchasers of stocks in those REITs insisted that REIT borrowing be kept to much lower levels (in relation to their total asset values) than were typical in the 1980s. This prudence was regarded as necessary to avoid another credit default debacle like that which occurred in 1990. Hence, REITs and many other owners of real properties in the 1990s kept their debt levels around 40 to 50 percent of their portfolios' total capitalized value (equal to the market value of public stocks plus associated debts).

This situation created an opportunity for private equity funds to take advantage of the easy availability of low-cost debt capital. Through heavy leveraging, they could outbid REITs and many other private owners of real properties who were unwilling or unable to borrow so heavily. The principal goal of most private equity funds was short-term profits; hence, they were avowedly uninterested in the long-range prospects of the properties they bought. Their game plan was almost always to load the properties they bought with more debt secured by those properties—which was possible because of the low leverage their former owners had put on them—pay themselves handsome dividends with the proceeds of that borrowing, and then sell those properties to someone else within five to seven years. That final sale at prices higher than the private equity funds had originally paid was also made possible by the plethora of low-cost debt financing available to the ultimate purchasers, some of whom were pension funds with longer-term horizons than the private equity funds.

The most famous such transaction was Blackstone's 2006 purchase of Sam Zell's Equity Office Properties REIT for a total cost of about $36 billion, including assumed debts. Whether this and other financial coups by private equity funds should be considered a long-term effect of the Niagara of capital is debatable. Private equity funds' operations in real estate were made possible by two factors resulting directly from the Niagara of capital: (a) the flood of capital looking for something in which to invest, and (b) extremely low borrowing costs generated by intense competition among lenders trying to place all the capital at their disposal. Those factors were likely to disappear whenever that Niagara stopped flowing. Although private equity funds existed before the Niagara of capital, the recent rise and prosperity of private equity funds depended heavily on continuation of the Niagara of capital. Therefore, private equity funds probably are not a long-term structural change in real estate finance, but a short-term one dependent on continued excess amounts of available financial capital. They will endure as long as the Niagara of capital or something else like it does too. That Niagara has already at least slowed down significantly in residential markets. How long it will last in commercial markets remains to be seen.

In addition, private equity funds—like any other operations that rely on highly leveraged financing—are susceptible to financial difficulties in times of economic distress when property rents and occupancy decline sharply. Most private equity funds aim at holding properties for only short periods before selling them, but if widespread economic distress were to occur when such funds are still operating real properties, they could be caught with falling revenues that might undermine their ability to carry the debts they have placed on those properties. That would make them susceptible to the same distress—and often bankruptcies—that befell the developers who used the same type of highly leveraged financing in the 1980s and earlier. This is another reason to question whether the strong role played by private equity funds from 2004 onward will remain a permanent feature of commercial real property markets.

Increasing Importance of Financial Engineers in Commercial Real Estate Markets

The emergence of private equity funds strengthened another trend more likely to remain important in commercial property markets over the long run: the increasing dominance of financial engineers in the real estate world, as compared to the influence of traditional real estate operators, especially pure developers. This shift in the relative significance of operators with varied talents was immensely accelerated by the expanding role of Wall Street in real estate markets because of the rise of new REITs and CMBSs in the 1990s. Wall Street firms focused primarily on how to make profits by changing the financial arrangements underlying specific properties, rather than on how to create properties that met the needs of their users. Before 1990, commercial real estate markets were dominated by private developers. Their skills focused on conceiving property concepts that would appeal to users, designing buildings to carry out those concepts, choosing locations appropriate for such buildings, raising the money to finance them, getting the necessary permissions through relevant government agencies, supervising the construction process, and marketing the finished products. Although raising money was an important part of this complex process, it was not traditionally the overwhelmingly dominant part compared to all the other necessary steps.

But when real estate financing increasingly went through Wall Street to gain access to public capital in the 1990s, the financing process itself became ever more significant compared to all the other steps in development. Figuring out ways of raising money more efficiently and at less cost through such complex inventions as CMBSs, collateralized debt obligations, and mezzanine financing became more and more important. Hence, designing buildings and selecting locations became relatively less important—though still crucial.

I have been struck by the shifting composition of the real estate operators who attended various real estate conferences over the years since I started in the real estate business in 1959. At first, such meetings were attended almost entirely by active private developers, with a few bankers, insurance lenders, and architects present. But gradually, the attendance became more and more dominated by financial wizards of all types, mostly from Wall Street firms. Today, financial engineers are clearly dominant over traditional real estate operators at nearly all real estate functions, including those of the Urban Land Institute, which was founded and run by developers for decades. I believe this is a significant long-range structural change in commercial property markets. It amounts to a profound paradigm shift comparable in importance to the shift among pension funds and financial institution investors to accepting more real estate properties within their portfolios. I believe financial engineers will retain their central roles as long as Wall Street financing plays as crucial a role in real estate as it has since 1990 and especially since 2000. Even if and when the Niagara of capital slows to a trickle, financial engineers will continue to play a much bigger role in commercial real estate markets than they did before 1990.

My use of the term "financial engineers" may seem to have a negative connotation. But in reality, financial engineers have made significant positive contributions to real property markets of all types. Their creation and development of securitized financing, REITs, CMBSs, and other ingenious financial instruments has been a key factor in expanding the sources of capital willing to invest money in both commercial properties and housing. The lower actual and perceived risks resulting from use of such financial instruments helped persuade nontraditional sources of real estate capital that their money could be invested in real estate just as safely as in stocks or bonds.

One implication of this structural change is that the management of commercial properties is more likely to be dominated by persons focused almost exclusively on financial profits, rather than on such other relevant factors as employee development and morale, relations with the surrounding community, and local community and regional prosperity. REITs and other more-traditional property ownership funds and firms must take those other factors into account in their daily operations because they are ongoing, long-term organizations who must live with their communities and their employees over the long haul. But private equity firms and other operations dominated by Wall Street's financial engineers have to a great extent abandoned the concept of real estate as a long-term investment. Most want to get in and get out as profitably—and as fast—as possible. This emphasis would please the recently deceased Nobel-economist Milton Friedman and others who argued that the sole purpose of public corporations was to make profits for their stockholders—not to improve society otherwise.

LONG-TERM REDUCTION IN THE FEDERAL RESERVE'S ABILITY TO INFLUENCE THE ECONOMY

The huge growth in the pool of potential financial resources available to real estate during the past two decades has made commercial property markets less susceptible to strong cyclical movements caused by Federal Reserve limitations on real estate finance. In much of the period after World War II, the Federal Reserve Board relied on its ability to influence housing market financing as a major weapon in its attempts to check excessive inflation or recurring recessions. During an economic expansion, if rising inflation rates indicated that the U.S. economy was showing signs of overheating, the Federal Reserve deliberately raised interest rates. Its goal was to choke off the supply of funding for housing construction, which then came almost entirely from banks, savings and loans, and insurance companies. That strategy would soon slow down the entire economy. Then if the economy faltered further, the Fed would cut interest rates and turn the financing taps for housing back on to help start a new expansion.

But today the direct linkage between the Fed's short-term interest rates and the financing available for real estate activities has been greatly weakened by the ability of homebuilders and other property developers to raise money from many other sources harder for the Fed to influence. This fact means the housing industry can no longer be considered an easily controlled tap for the Fed to turn on and off to influence the course of the entire American economy. This change is reflected in the fact that, beginning in 2004, the Fed tried to raise housing interest rates for two years with little success. The Fed's efforts did not greatly escalate the long-term rate and shut down housing in 2004 or 2005 or even well into 2006, although that has finally begun to happen in 2007. Commercial property markets remained flooded with financial capital in spite of the Fed's attempts to cool real estate by slowing housing production. The broadening of the potential sources of capital accessible to commercial real property markets has definitely weakened the Fed's ability to influence the entire economy through housing markets.

ALTERNATIVE FUTURE SCENARIOS CONCERNING LONG-TERM FINANCIAL CONDITIONS

As this book was being written in 2007, global financial conditions were still dominated by an important long-term imbalance among nations that had prevailed for over a decade. The United States was running very large trade deficits because its citizens and firms were importing far more goods and services than they were exporting. To pay for thus living beyond their current productivity, they were issuing debts to foreign firms and governments, mainly in the form of U.S. Treasury securities sold to those net exporters. Balancing the excessive consumption in the United States was a lot of excessive savings out of current incomes by firms and governments in other nations, especially Asian nations. They included developing nations, such as China and India, and fully developed ones, such as Japan. Those nations were running large export surpluses to the United States in part because their citizens and governments were saving large fractions of the proceeds of their current production, rather than using those profits to increase their own domestic consumption or investment.

They were willing to accept Treasury securities in return for their export surpluses and savings for different motives. As noted earlier, Chinese households were motivated to save heavily because their government did not offer them any social safety-net programs like Social Security, Medicare, Medicaid, and others found in the United States and European nations. Japanese households were saving heavily because of the aging of their population, which relieved households from the many obligations of raising children, and because Japan had traditionally relied on export surpluses to keep its workers fully employed. The Chinese government was motivated to accept U.S. Treasury securities because it needed to keep expanding its industrial production through exports to provide more and more jobs for the millions of agricultural workers migrating into China's cities each year looking for a better life. Chinese leaders viewed this policy as a key to maintaining peace and security in their country in spite of immense differences in living standards among its manufacturing and agricultural regions. China's communist leaders were even willing to buy a slice of that ultra-free-enterprise and capitalistic firm, Blackstone, as a better way to use the funds they had earned through export surpluses to the United States than risking future value declines in U.S. Treasury securities.

The magnitude of American trade deficits, however, made this unbalanced arrangement between excess consumption in America, on the one hand, and excess production and savings in the rest of the world, on the other hand, unlikely to continue indefinitely. Yet this imbalance was probably the basic structure from which the entire Niagara of capital had originated and continued to operate, at least through early 2007. The excess of funds generated in the rest of the world by people and firms producing more than they consumed was not converted into either domestic consumption or expanded investment within their nations because most of the participants in those nations—households, firms, and governments—had various motives for saving rather than either consuming or investing more, as discussed in Chapter 2. The result was an enormous amount of financial capital looking for something from which it could get an attractive return. This source of capital was added to the surplus savings from oil exports generated by the major oil-exporting nations. All that capital became the Niagara of capital described in this book.

But how can the fundamental imbalance in this situation be remedied? In its 2007 edition of *The World Economic Outlook*, the International Monetary Fund has described two basic scenarios that this imbalance might lead to: one good and one bad.[1]

The good outlook would involve a gradual increase in domestic consumption and investment by many of the nations that are now running export surpluses with the United States and experiencing high rates of domestic saving, especially China, Japan, and some of Western Europe. Their consumption and domestic investment would increase—and thus their savings would fall. This scenario would occur because their economies are now growing faster than they were in the 1990s, in the case of Japan and Europe, and because Chinese households would raise their spending as their incomes increased. Presumably, the Chinese government would begin providing some safety-net programs for its own people to encourage them to spend more and save less. As middle classes grow larger in China, India, and other developing nations, they will naturally tend to seek higher personal living standards if they can. Their enrichment would not harm Americans because their greater spending would lead to more imports of our goods and services.

This shift would be accompanied by a gradual depreciation in the international trading value of the U.S. dollar. From January 2000 to May 2007, the U.S. dollar has already declined in value by about 24 percent against the euro, 18 percent against the British pound, and 24 percent against the Canadian dollar.[2] Savings in the United States would increase (or net borrowing decrease), mainly through lower federal budget deficits. That would have the dual effect of reducing America's trade deficit by raising its exports because of a depreciated dollar and also not causing any panic of disinvestment in U.S. Treasury securities by overseas nations. If these gradual trends persisted for two decades or so, a more-balanced relationship between the U.S. economy and the rest of the world would slowly emerge without any upsetting economic catastrophes. This scenario would also gradually reduce the size of the Niagara of capital seeking investment outlets as both consumption and domestic investment replaced excessive savings in the rest of the world. The United States would come to rely more on its own savings to meet its investment and consumption needs.

The second scenario assumes that the adjustments described in the first scenario do not take place. America continues to run large trade deficits and low rates of saving, but other nations do not expand their domestic consumption and investment. Instead, they continue high-level savings from their trade surpluses. Consequently, the trading value of the U.S. dollar declines rapidly—so rapidly that foreign holders of large amounts of U.S. Treasury debt eventually become alarmed. Many try to dump their large dollar holdings on the market to avoid further capital losses. This action produces an even more precipitous fall in the value of the dollar and an international trading crisis. The Federal Reserve is forced to raise U.S. interest rates very rapidly to slow the sell-off of U.S. dollar holdings by foreigners. Those high-level interest rates choke off economic activity in the United States—especially in real estate—and cause a serious American recession, in spite of greater exports from the United States generated by cheap dollars. Falling consumption and investment in the United States spread this recession to other nations, and it becomes worldwide. The global growth rate drops from its current high levels that raise living standards around much of the world to low levels that worsen poverty all over. World trade is disrupted by the inability of other nations to rely on the dollar as a means of exchange, but no other single currency emerges as its replacement. Protectionism spreads rapidly as each nation tries to defend its own economy from spreading recession and job losses.

Under both scenarios, the Niagara of capital is brought to a close by ending the current imbalance between America's excess imports and the rest of the world's excess savings. The manner in which this imbalance ends, however, has diametrically opposed implications for the economic welfare of the entire world.

The more-favorable alternative of a gradual decline in the value of the U.S. dollar and a large decline in U.S. federal deficits requires major changes in U.S. fiscal policy and in the domestic consumption and investment behavior of many foreign nations. Whether those changes can be achieved and sustained for a long enough period to greatly reduce the current imbalance between the U.S. balance-of-trade deficit and excess savings elsewhere is by no means clear. Wrestling with how to carry out such changes will form a major part of future political struggles within the United States after the presidential election of 2008. What is clear, however, is that which—if either—of these two major alternatives actually happens will affect U.S. real estate markets immensely. The gradual movement toward a smaller basic imbalance will slow down the Niagara of capital worldwide but at a pace that does not produce a worldwide economic crisis. In contrast, the sudden plunge of the U.S. dollar's value, followed by a major recession, would also reduce the Niagara of capital, but much faster and with far worse consequences for U.S. real estate markets and the entire world economy.

Thus, the best interests of the real estate industry, and the rest of the American economy and society, clearly lie in adopting policies that would maximize chances for the gradual reduction of the basic imbalance in the world's economic systems. Those policies include much smaller U.S. federal deficits, a gradual but significant depreciation in the value of the U.S. dollar, and continued emphasis upon relatively open international trade so that the United States could increase its exports and reduce its imports as the dollar declined in value.

Even if all those policies were adopted, the U.S. economy might possibly experience a major slowdown or even a recession along the way. Real gross domestic product in the United States last declined on a year-to-year basis in 1991, but only by 0.2 percent. The last significant recession in the United States was from 1980 to 1982, 25 years before the writing of this book in 2007. During the 24 years from 1983 to 2006, the average annual increase in real gross domestic product was 3.3 percent, and in only seven years was it below 3.0 percent. Thus, the United States has enjoyed relatively steady prosperity for almost a quarter of a century, with two slowdowns in 1990–1991 and 2001–2002.

Because gradual recovery from the current world imbalance will probably take at least two decades, the U.S. economy likely will have at least one slowdown during that period, under the best of circumstances. Even so, that scenario would be greatly preferable to a sudden drastic plunge in the value of the dollar followed by a major worldwide recession. In either case, the Niagara of capital that has dominated U.S. real estate markets for much of the past decade is quite likely to end when the basic world economic imbalance ends. Until that time, or until some unpredictable event suddenly changes the world economic scene, the phenomena described in this book are likely to continue, and some will continue even after that, as described earlier in this chapter.

CONCLUSION

Although the Niagara of capital into U.S. and other real estate markets will not continue indefinitely, many of its major effects on American real property markets will last a long time. On the positive side, it has bestowed huge long-term increases in wealth on many people—most American homeowners, many Realtors, financial engineers, developers, lenders, investors, and private equity operators. It also helped many former renter households, including many with relatively low incomes, gain ownership of their own homes by pressuring lenders to make credit terms much easier on borrowers. But on the negative side, the Niagara of capital has economically squeezed many other people—mainly low-income renter households and low-wage workers whose incomes seem frozen. It did so by raising housing prices beyond their reach and creating global competition in many low-income wage markets. Owning their own housing has probably been permanently made less affordable to millions of persons in the second of these groups. In addition, the Niagara of capital has increased the relative importance of financial engineers in the real estate industry compared to that of traditional developers and investors.

These dual and opposing effects make it impossible to determine whether the Niagara of capital into real estate markets has been a net gain or a net loss to America as a whole, or even to U.S. real estate markets as a whole. The number of gainer households has almost certainly been larger than the number of losers, but the losers are mainly among the lowest-income households in America who need economic help much more than most of the gainers did.

Regardless of whether the Niagara of capital was good or bad for the nation as a whole, it certainly affected almost every household in America in one way or another. Moreover, many of its effects are likely to persist for decades, even if the massive in-flows of money into real estate markets slow down or disappear—and they have already slowed notably in residential markets. Therefore, the most important thing for every reader of this book about the Niagara of capital is to better understand what it did to America and Americans, why it did so, and what its most likely aftermaths will be. I hope this volume contributes to such a broader understanding of this probably once-in-a-lifetime experience in the American economy and its real estate markets.

Notes

1. International Monetary Fund, World Economic Outlook: Spillovers and Cycles in the Global Economy (Washington, D.C.: International Monetary Fund, 2007), chapters 3 and 4.

2. Data on currency exchange rates from the Federal Reserve Board for 2003 to 2007, and from x-rates.com, http://www.xrates.com/cgibin/hlookup.cgi for periods prior to 2003 (accessed June 23, 2007).